The Incredible Expanding Mountain of Hope

VOLUME 1
The Mere Foundation Stone

By Joshua Herald MDiv

TEACH Services, Inc.
PUBLISHING
www.TEACHServices.com • (800) 367-1844

World rights reserved. This book or any portion thereof may not be copied or reproduced in any form or manner whatsoever, except as provided by law, without the written permission of the publisher, except by a reviewer who may quote brief passages in a review.

The author assumes full responsibility for the accuracy of all facts and quotations as cited in this book. The opinions expressed in this book are the author's personal views and interpretations, and do not necessarily reflect those of the publisher.

This book is provided with the understanding that the publisher is not engaged in giving spiritual, legal, medical, or other professional advice. If authoritative advice is needed, the reader should seek the counsel of a competent professional.

Copyright © 2023 Joshua Herald MDiv
Copyright © 2023 TEACH Services, Inc.
ISBN-13: 978-1-4796-1398-4 (Paperback)
ISBN-13: 978-1-4796-1399-1 (ePub)
Library of Congress Control Number: 2023902058

HAVE YOURSELF A MERRY LITTLE CHRISTMAS
Words and Music by HUGH MARTIN and RALPH BLANE
© 1943 (Renewed) METRO-GOLDWYN-MAYER INC.
© 1944 (Renewed) EMI FEIST CATALOG INC.
All Rights Reserved
Used by Permission of ALFRED MUSIC

All Scripture quotations, unless otherwise indicated, are taken from the New Revised Standard Version Bible, copyright © 1989, the Division of Christian Education of the National Council of the Churches of Christ in the United States of America. Used by permission. All rights reserved. Emphasis supplied by the author.

All Scripture references marked (KJV) are taken from the King James Version of the Bible. Public domain. Emphasis supplied by the author.

All Scripture references marked (NLT) are taken from the *Holy Bible,* New Living Translation, copyright © 1996, by Tyndale House Foundation. Used by permission of Tyndale House Publishers, Inc., Carol Stream, Illinois 60188. All rights reserved. Emphasis supplied by the author.

All Scripture references marked (YLT) are taken from Young's Literal Translation®. Public domain. Emphasis supplied by the author.

All Scripture references marked (NIV) are taken from the Holy Bible, New International Version®, NIV®, copyright © 1973, 1978, 1984 by Biblica, Inc.®. Used by permission. All rights reserved worldwide.

All Scripture references marked (NKJV) are taken from the New King James Version® of the Bible, copyright © 1982 by Thomas Nelson. Used by permission. All rights reserved.

Interior artwork © Alan Wolfard.

Front cover artwork: "The Crucifixion" © Lars Justinen;
"A Lamb Is Sacrificed" © Lars Justinen;
"Mary and Baby Jesus" © Review & Herald Publishing;
"Tan Feet" © Alan Wolfard.

Published by

www.TEACHServices.com • (800) 367-1844

I give special thanks:

To and for JESUS.

To Ron Price for kindly providing feedback,
tactful questions, and suggestions.
To Erica Herra for proofreading the manuscript.
To my "literary" daughter for helping with research.
To my wife and family for putting up with me,
and with my endless hours off writing.
And to my mother for making me feel
I had written something worthwhile.

Matthew 6:33:

But strive first for the kingdom of God and his righteousness ....

Table of Contents

Preface	vii
Chapter 1— Worlds Collide	9
Chapter 2— The One Thing We Cannot Live Without	15
Chapter 3— The Gods Are Communicating!	21
Chapter 4— The King's Lie Detector Test	25
Chapter 5— Troubled about the Future	35
Chapter 6— The Dreadful Colossus …	39
Chapter 7— … And the Growing Stone	49
Chapter 8— What Daniel Didn't Tell the King	61
Chapter 9— The Unhewn Altar Stone	71
Chapter 10— The Mountain of God	75
Chapter 11— "The *Kingdom* of God"	85
Chapter 12— Ancient Hints of Hope	99
Chapter 13— In Pursuit of Prophetic Ground Zero (Part 1)	103
Chapter 14— In Pursuit of Prophetic Ground Zero (Part 2)	115
Chapter 15— A Deepwater Detour	127
Chapter 16— In Pursuit of Prophetic Ground Zero (Part 3)	135
Chapter 17— A Primer Lesson in Christianity 101 (or 201)	139
Chapter 18— Ground Zero and the Great Controversy	151
Chapter 19— The Fracturing Birth	169
Afterword	197
Endnote A	203
Bibliography	205

Preface

Regardless of what spirit my insights and writing may invoke (I know not yet)—whether a spirit of Berean interest,[1] of indifference, of controversy, or even of mockery that I thought I could write or that I imagined I had something worth sharing—this book started out, I believe, with a very personal prodding from the Holy Spirit.[2] The gentle but insistent prodding was also accompanied by precious affirming experiences with God as I began, and as I kept on going in the process. It told me that I needed to start writing down some of the insights God had helped me to see through many years of profound personal experiences—and sometimes painful struggles—with Him in prayer, study, and Bible research. It told me that I should start writing regardless of the outcome, and regardless of my obvious imperfections—even if just to pass on the insights to my children, family, and friends. The prodding told me that, despite a difficult life choice I had recently made—with God's unmistakable direction—to step away from my career as a pastor, I needed to "[g]ather up the fragments that remain, that nothing be lost" (John 6:12, KJV).

However, my ambitious intention at the beginning to contain this all inside of one volume suddenly began to make the end product loom gigantic in my mind after God and I had made it through a good many chapters, and yet I had still only touched on the opening subject matter—the mere Foundation Stone—of the whole body of perspective I felt called to write down! It seemed almost as if when I began to gather up the fragments as commanded, Jesus somehow performed the miracle of multiplication once again on my *own* loaves and fishes[3] which suddenly seemed bigger than I had ever remembered. Indeed, they did grow and further develop in the process of prayerfully writing them down in the guise of a real book.

I decided at last that instead of swallowing the whole animal at once, I would try to take elephant-sized bites. This refers to the well-worn children's joke where the question gets asked: how do you eat an elephant?

1　See Acts 17:10–11.
2　See Endnote A (located at the end of this book).
3　See Matthew 14:13–21 and John 6:1–14.

To which the answer is given: one bite at a time. So, I decided to divide my elephant "bites" into volumes (volume 1 being the *irreplaceably important* foundation stone for everything that comes after it). I pray that each volume will be able to stand on its own pachyderm feet, even though all will be directly related through the Foundation Stone. I actually began by frequently referring in my writing to subject matter I would deal with in some future *chapter,* but I am now changing some references to say something like "in a future *volume.*"

May God Himself direct or desist the effort I believe *He* began as He sees fit. Whether these insights go to print, remain an unfulfilled intent, or get written only to gather dust on a shelf or vanish into oblivion is God's business, not mine. But inasmuch as I may have been given any *genuine* insights from God, I don't believe He would have given them for me to keep to myself. So, I feel impelled to share.

P.S. Although I strive to write as simply—and plainly—as possible, I have never felt called to write pablum, but rather to stretch a reader's mind, even as I try to reach out to his or her heart. If you don't know what *"pablum"* means, please look it up, as well as any *other* words of uncommon use I might have slipped into the text occasionally. Such a practice stretches the mind, the perspective, and the vocabulary just as a true higher education does.[4] We don't all have the same spiritual gifts,[5] and I doubt that writing toddler books will ever be mine. However, by—or rather, *because* of—God's grace, I love God, I love people, I love thinking, I love words. And when I mix all of these God-derived loves together by sharing the love and truth of God with others in a book, I have to be natural; I must be *myself.* I feel confident that my own spiritual gifts will connect with the very people God intended them to connect with when He gave these to me. At the very least, I hope this book will challenge a few readers to think beyond the bounds of what they have thought before, and to strengthen their faith in, their heartfelt love for, and their thinking about Jesus.

Iron sharpens iron, and one person sharpens the wits of another. (Prov. 27:17)

---

[4] See Hebrews 5:13–14.
[5] See 1 Corinthians 12:17–8.

Chapter 1

Worlds Collide

One night when I was still a boy, I experienced a nightmare so frightening that it has remained vivid in my memory bank ever since. It happened when I was living at my grandmother's house. I was living there for a short period since I was a somewhat troubled kid, with many glaring character flaws, who had not yet been found[6] by God. It was in that same house, and in that very room where I'd experienced the nightmare, that I *was* later found by my Savior Jesus, and snatched up like "a brand plucked from the fire" (Zech. 3:2). My early conversion[7] was an event so world-changing to me that it radically altered the course of my childhood, even though at the time I still unfortunately understood little about God's amazing grace, and I had a long, *long* way to go in character development too (I should mention that I *still* have a long way to go).

In the nightmare, I had dreamed I was walking outside in the street in front of my grandmother's house. As I walked, I looked up at a twilight sky and noticed that either a planet or moon loomed unnaturally massive above me, many times bigger than the moon had ever appeared to me before. Not only did it appear massive, it was also eerily rotating, as if it had been somehow thrown out of its natural order by some catastrophic cosmic event, and it was growing larger and larger in the sky with every minute that passed. *Panic* hit me. It seemed there was nowhere to escape!

My nightmare resembled a science fiction movie I had once seen called "When Worlds Collide."[8] It was a thriller about the impending collision of a rogue star with planet earth. In that movie there had been images of a strange star looming larger and larger in the earth's sky, that

---

6   A figure of speech used frequently in the Bible. Example: *"But we had to celebrate and rejoice, because this brother of yours was dead and has come to life;* **he was lost and has been found**" (Luke 15:32).

7   I've experienced several additional levels of conversion since (on various aspects of faith, understanding, and practice).

8   Rudolph Maté, director, *When Worlds Collide*, Paramount Pictures, 1951.

was on the verge of gobbling up the whole wide world in its flames. But in my dream the looming object in the sky was clearly a *solid* body, and it got clearer as it seemed to edge closer. I vividly remember being able to observe detailed craters and mountains and valleys slowly spinning past me on the titanic celestial ball as it grew—objects that someone would ordinarily need a telescope or field glasses to observe in such detail on the moon. This told my dreaming mind that those objects were getting far too close for comfort. The rogue planet (or moon) seemed to be on an inevitable collision course with the earth, and there was nothing that I, or any of earth's other inhabitants, could do to stop it!

What the dream meant, if anything, is any psychoanalyst's or seer's guess. Maybe, just maybe, the dream happened because I was subconsciously feeling a similar sense of inevitable destruction, helplessness, and hopelessness in my own life at the time. It is hard to say. Maybe God had something to do with my having the dream. I don't know. But while I was trapped inside the horrible dream, it spoke of inevitable doom to me, so that I cannot tell you how extremely relieved I felt when suddenly I woke up sweating and realized to my ecstatic relief that the whole terrifying scenario had all been just a bad dream! *Whew!* Or *had* it? A possessing doubt suddenly began harassing my mind. The menacing dream had seemed so *very* real to me that for a long time even after I woke up, I still had the hardest time convincing myself that the dream *was* only a *dream* after all! I could still palpably taste that wretched experience!

"Oh, *no!* Maybe it *was* real?!" I thought.

Pinching myself was not enough to dispel the bewitching spell the apparent demon had malevolently cast over me in the blackness of my bedroom. I actually had to get up out of my bed, quietly put some clothes on so as not to wake up my grandmother, tiptoe through a dark house without bumping into furniture or causing the floor or a door to creak loudly, walk outside into the twilight of the early morning, and gaze upward at the lightening sky from the same perspective I had seen it in my dream (the middle of the street), before I finally convinced myself—beyond every horrid shadow of a doubt—that I had only been dreaming.

One fact I *do* know is that not long after that dreadful dream occurred, a titanic *spiritual* world of *God's* making *actually* collided with my own world, though it brought to me the total *opposite* of the dreadful consequences I had imagined in my nightmare. The explosive impact of *its* collision began to reform itself into a brand-new swirling world of thought inside of me, and to completely transform the world of my life as I had known it. Even though the life journey it initiated has included untold tears, trials, personal failures, and setbacks almost beyond believing, it nevertheless led me, in spite of everything, to fall deeply in love with the Savior who took a hold of me in love[9] at that time: the One whose triumph in His own cosmic collision with our world thousands of years ago had enabled the happy collision of His world with my doomed life. I didn't know much yet, but I suddenly knew that **Someone** (with a capital S) *loved* me! Despite everything ugly and bad in my young life, despite my bad character and habits, despite *everything,* God saw something worth saving in me! (By the way, this also meant that God actually *liked* my very *essence* as well,[10] that **He actually liked** *the kernel of me,* which at the time was lying largely buried from the view of surface-seeing[11] humans, beneath my various obvious unlikable traits of character.[12])

If I read my Bible right, it was the very same Savior whose world collided with my own so many years ago, the same One who has so often been so merciful to me—who has counted unworthy me as the treasured "apple of his eye"[13]—who also Himself once gave a perplexing dream of a colossal character to an ancient despot, who like me possessed something of a bad character, though in different ways than I. It was a dream that could only be described as a nightmare to the person who had dreamed it, though its ancient contents, when understood rightly, contain the greatest of *good* news for all the inhabitants of planet earth even today. *Amazing* good news of *"Amazing Grace."*[14]

The ancient despot was Nebuchadnezzar, the king of ancient Babylon during its short-lived glory days. But when Nebuchadnezzar had his famous dream that you can find in Daniel chapter 2, he wasn't feeling

---

9 See Jeremiah 31:3.
10 Which *He* is responsible for having created!
11 See 1 Samuel 16:7.
12 I have mentioned this because I've noticed that some Christians can get so hung up on the difference between *liking* and *loving* people whose characters pose a challenge to their emotions that they (we) can end up actually *loathing* many of the very same people they (we) claim to love as Christ commands them (us) to do (see Matthew 22:39; John 13:34, and Luke 6:27). I am no exception to this internal struggle and Christian conundrum, and I truly know that *"Humanly speaking, it is impossible. But with God everything is possible."* (Matt. 19:26, NLT)
13 See Deuteronomy 32:10.
14 The title of arguably the most internationally famous Christian hymn in the English language—perhaps even the most famous and universally known in *any* language. Jonathan Aitken, John Newton: From Disgrace to Amazing Grace (Wheaton, IL: Crossway, 2007), pp. 223–224. Amazing Grace (the song) was written late 1772 for Newton's New Year's sermon of Friday, January 1, 1773. " 'Amazing Grace' … is the most sung, most recorded, and most loved hymn in the world. No other song, spiritual or secular, comes close to it in terms of numbers of recordings … frequency of performances … international popularity … or cultural longevity" (p. 24).

particularly helpless or hopeless in his private life at all! No! Unlike me at the time of *my* nightmare, everything had been going quite well for him because God had given the world into his hands![15] And, *indeed,* God *loved* the man! Despite his pagan practices and beliefs, despite his personal arrogance, despite even his *brutality,* God saw something worth saving in him. Amazing love!

It is no wonder the king was a bit arrogant though. Babylon's conquests under his father, Nabopolassar, and then under him (not to mention his unprecedented building projects already in progress) had been opening up a great golden era in which, like King Midas, everything this man touched was turning to gold. It must have felt *so* good! It must have given the king a godlike feeling, even at that early stage of his reign. He was himself an imposing colossal character, at least from all human perspectives. Almost everyone in his world feared him as if he *were* a god, even if he and they all knew better deep down. No, he wasn't feeling helpless at the time *at all*, that is, until he had the terrifying dream; terrifying to him only because it seemed somehow to forebode some catastrophic intrusion that would one day threaten this great pride and glory belonging to the object of his greatest affections, of his chief god (besides himself). That god was not Marduk[16] or Nabu[17] either (chief gods in the Babylonian pantheon), as we will see in evidence later, but it was the mighty kingdom, the new Babylonian *Empire* that had been earned through tremendous bloodshed and through the crushing pain and grief of many subjugated peoples. His chief god at that time was the empire he adored so very much since it brought to him so much happiness and pride and satisfaction, not to mention a sense of meaning in the flow of history. All of history seemed to Nebuchadnezzar to have led up to his great and glorious kingdom which would now last forever as a sort of ancient *new world order.* Perhaps he had even imagined upon occasion that his and his father Nabopolassar's costly and brutally tragic conquests were to be *the wars to end all wars,* and to bring on the earth an eternal *Pax Babylonia!* Perhaps he imagined himself becoming known as *Nebuchadnezzar the Great,* the bringer of the Utopian Babylonian peace which eternal generations would certainly feel gratitude for, and so always honor his memory.

---

15 See Jeremiah 27:5–11.
16 Also known as Bel.
17 Also known as Nebo.

With such possible grandiose thoughts in his mind, it would be quite understandable if the contents of the dream God gave to Nebuchadnezzar should trouble him, and even unsettle his confidence a bit in his own megalomaniacal historical world view, especially after the king was given a *partial* understanding of them (for as we shall see, that was *all* he was given of the dream's contents)!

Chapter 2

The One Thing We Cannot Live Without

Before I move on to that ancient king's dream, however, it occurs to me that sometimes we can all feel at least a little like I felt in my nightmare by just reading headlines or by listening to news reports. There is nothing quite as frustrating as feeling out of control in a frightening situation, but we now live in a world that technology has shrunk to a virtual neighborhood, so it can sometimes be difficult to escape the constant barrage of frightening situations technology throws up at us. We can hear about news happening at distant points of our planet just moments after it happens, or even play-by-play coverage. But what kind of news is most of what we hear? *Bad* news! And it makes me wonder sometimes if this doesn't do something *bad* to our modern psyches. There is also very little any one of us can do to *remedy* the bad news we hear about either (in most cases). Today, if we wanted to, we could listen to, or read about, bad news happening at the moment, 24/7, around the clock, nonstop. And unlike newspapers of old, through technology available today we can easily interact *with* many dangerous and sometimes bizarre news stories we hear (a real temptation to some), as a few intrepid, though foolish, souls have frighteningly learned out of curiosity.

Crisis after crisis, and scandal after scandal, parade across our multiplying gadgets. And it certainly doesn't help that it is even hard these days to distinguish true stories from the myriads of *false* stories—fake news stories or else half-true, slanted, misleading, or grossly exaggerated stories with less than honest intentions behind their creation, proliferating almost unchecked in the name of truth. We sometimes don't even know *what* to believe anymore, especially when spying search engines now specifically target us with only the stories (and ads) that they *think* we want to see and hear! We see so much information, and far too much of it (in the age of tabloids, twenty-four-hour news channels, infomercials, and the Internet) has been designed to inflame, deceive, control, tempt, advertise, spy on, trip up, or even to con and entrap those who feed upon it! This sounds a bit like the devil, doesn't it? Even worse, is that it isn't just blatant crooks disseminating deception, but also misguided fanatics and vigilantes with various ideological intentions: people who feel very self-righteous about the whole thing. I speak of smug people who, like the violent zealots in Christ's day, or like Saul (Paul) persecuting the ancient church, or like the self-righteous religious authorities who once paraded a shamed and humiliated woman (who had been caught in adultery) in front of a crowd Jesus was teaching,[18] also love to imagine that their unloving actions are doing some great good (especially if those unloving actions can bring them personal gain at the same time). But the worst news of all is that even respected governments, corporations, and organizations people once trusted are in the deception and demonizing game too! God forbid! At least that's the news *I* have heard. Who *can you* believe any longer?

I wonder if you've ever wished you might just wake up one morning, as if from a terrible nightmare, and discover to your great relief that all the bad news you've been hearing was just a bad dream. It makes me think of the heavy toll Jesus once predicted that the added intensity of normal troubles and chaos near the end of time would take upon human hearts. He predicted:

> *[deceptions].... wars and rumors of wars .... nation[s rising] against nation[s] ... kingdom[s] against kingdom[s]... famines and earthquakes in various places .... [torture,] [murder] and [hatred of believers]. [Believers] fall[ing] away ... [people] betray[ing] one another and hat[ing] one another .... [M]any false prophets ... lead[ing] many astray .... [T]he increase of lawlessness ... love [growing] cold.* (Matt. 24:4, 6–7, 9–12)

He also said:

> *There will be signs in the sun, the moon, and the stars, and on the earth distress among nations confused by the roaring of the sea and*

---

18   See John 8:1–11. This story apparently became so controversial during an early self-righteous era of Christianity that there is historical and textual evidence suggesting scribes and authorities of the time attempted to eradicate it from the gospel record. It is my studied opinion that a much *higher* Authority preserved the account!

the waves.[19] *People will faint from fear and foreboding of what is coming upon the world, for the powers of the [skies] will be shaken.* (Luke 21:25–26)

The King James Version puts it: "Men's heart's failing them for fear." Today we call that anxiety and mental illness. Distressing news takes its toll on the human psyche. What is coming upon the world is not always in physical ways only! Emotional distress and mental illness are also a prediction of Jesus. But the emotional toll is never as hard as when it affects us personally, when the headlines come home. Don't headlines come home sometimes? When someone we love is wounded or killed or dies; when we get in a wreck, get accused, get threatened or mistreated, receive a pink slip, a ticket, an injury, a diagnosis, a lawsuit, a conviction, an eviction notice. Or here is one that more and more people relate to at times when economic headlines dominate: it's when we just can't seem to "make ends meet"! Sometimes we just can't seem to get it all together in *other* ways. We get tired, make mistakes, struggle against weight gain, health conditions, depression, addictions, marital discord. Or more acutely, we have a heart attack, a stroke, a personal disaster; we get rejected, attacked, *misunderstood!* Do distressing things ever happen to you? How do they make you feel? Sometimes we don't wake *up* from nightmares because we can't wake up from real life!

The same awful sensations I had in my dream may be produced from life experiences that make us feel helpless. We don't know what to do, and we feel our own destinies are painfully out of our control. Many readers may not relate to such troubles just now. If that's true for you at this time, then please just treat these few paragraphs like a bone for the time being (as we should also do with portions of Scripture we don't immediately relate to), and move on to parts of the fish you *can* eat.[20] Some day you may well develop a hunger for what you now consider inedible bones (and even some fish bones can actually be eaten, at least after undergoing certain pressure-cooking methods, as is evidenced by canned varieties). However, I do know that there *are* some people reading these words who are experiencing, right now, the same awful feelings I once felt in my dream and in my life at the time that I had it. I don't know *what* difficulties you are facing, but if your life has you feeling out of control, I truly believe

---

19 Tsunamis?
20 Sorry, lifelong vegetarians, for this illustration you will have to just *imagine* what eating a bony fish might be like.

you'll find encouragement from unlocking the symbols of help and *hope* found in Nebuchadnezzar's famous ancient nightmare.

I love that word: *hope!* People can endure living without almost anything for a long time, but the one thing we cannot long bear to live without is hope.

Believe it or not, as dastardly as it sounds, some of the same sorts of unscrupulous people who have made it hard to trust news have also historically used (and still use) this well-known psychological principle in their efforts to control societies. They have, in many cases, mercilessly harassed outspoken champions of controverted causes *anonymously* (sometimes to the point of suicide), with plausible deniability cloaking them as the devious[21] source of the harassment. However, in other well-documented cases, such as a case involving Dr. Martin Luther King, Jr. during the civil rights clashes of the sixties, their identities are known. These same sorts of controlling individuals (even at times occupying high positions of power in widely respected organizations) have attempted to make great champions of controverted causes lose *hope* through a systematic personal harassment.[22] They do this in the hopes that the prophetically critical voices they despise might be silenced through desperation that leads to suicide.[23] May the tribes (and organizations) of those who do such evil decrease!

In just the last few years of my life there have been half a dozen people who were either related to me, or who were connected to my life by some thread, who have succeeded in taking their own lives. Each time it happens, it is a shock, hard to believe, and hard to digest. Suicide's wake always leaves the living speculating about what could have driven a human being created in God's image[24] to such a drastic humanly irreversible act of self-destruction. But regardless of the varied—and sometimes secret— circumstances in each life tragically lost, there is but one ultimate answer to our grief-stricken speculation. If we want to know the single answer to what it is leading very many men, women, and children to attempt and complete suicide every year, this *hope principle* also provides the answer. The cause in nearly every *real* case[25] is none other than a persistent feeling of *hopelessness!* There is a sense inside every soul facing perplexing

---

21 "Devil-ous."
22 Often using the threat of scandal, as they did in Dr. King's case.
23 In Dr. King's case, suicide was brazenly suggested by his tormentors as his only solution to save face.
24 See Genesis 1:27.
25 Some suicide attempts are made merely to gain attention.

realities that, though we can bear to live a long time without many, *many* things, *hope* is not one of them!

But I am here to tell you—even as one who has struggled with profound bouts of clinical depression, anxiety, and feelings of hopelessness in my lifetime (as well as some harrowing experiences that I *will not* share)—that there *is* hope!

If by any chance there is someone reading these words who feels there is no hope, I encourage you to hope right now, at least for a *reason* to hope, to consider that maybe it was Hope itself that brought you to reading this book: the Hope that is sparked and planted by the mysterious moving of God's Holy Spirit because of His amazing love for you! I urge you to consider that maybe, just maybe, it was no accident that you picked up this very book. I encourage you, I plead with you, to read on, at the *very* least, to hear the hope contained in the ancient dream, and how that hope has been unfolding for you in God's eternal plan of redemption!

> **If by any chance there is someone reading these words who feels there is no hope, I encourage you to hope right now, at least for a reason to hope, to consider that maybe it was Hope itself that brought you to reading this book: the Hope that is sparked and planted by the mysterious moving of God's Holy Spirit because of His amazing love for you!**

Chapter 3

The Gods Are Communicating!

The gods were communicating with mortals! This was the almost universal assumption made by pious people in the world of ancient pagan religions (especially in the region of Mesopotamia) whenever a particularly vivid or strikingly unusual dream occurred, especially if that dream happened to be dreamed by a ruler. Rulers were considered, after all, to possess special favor from the gods to whom they often gave credit for bringing them to power. In many cases I believe the assumption that the gods were communicating (allowing for pagan misinterpretation) *was* a fact, because the God I know has always loved *all* people. He continually strives to reach all hearts, to direct all to better things, and to bless those who will respond *at all* to His invisible efforts, regardless of our faulty world views. Yes, I say "our" worldviews (despite the bad grammar) because it is my observation that none of us (and I mean *none,* not even the prophets of old) have a perfect worldview in every respect, even if we are privileged with improved knowledge as were the ancient called-out people of God. In this case, for certain, I am convinced the gods *were* communicating with pagan mortals! Or, as *we* understand it (assuming a monotheistic readership of this book), the *only true God* was *indeed* on that night shining a special light of gracious revelation into the murky world of pagan confusion.

What an unspeakable privilege—whether you are a pagan or of the families entrusted with the oracles of God—to be communicated with directly by the deity! I am convinced that several times in my life I was privileged with similar communications directly from God or through His messengers whom we call angels. Especially since my experiences all came as messages of comfort, mercy, or direction during times of very great distress or uncertainty, my response to these rare and surprising experiences with God was something of unspeakable gratitude. These were instances that led me to weep tears of joy! One dark night I even woke up singing the chorus to a song that I'm still convinced I had been listening to an angel in my room sing to me: "Only trust Him, only trust Him, Only trust Him now. He will save you, He will save you, He will save you now[!]"[26] "Only trust Him," three times and, "He will save you," three times! If you recognize what song I woke up singing the chorus of, on a night I'd begged God not to let me wake up, you will know that the song begins, "Come, every soul by sin oppressed, There's mercy with the Lord; And He will surely give you rest By trusting in His word."[27] Even writing these words down just now has brought the tears back once again (though many years have gone by) by just remembering the precious experience! Words fail me!

But to the ancient pagan monarch (also totally convinced that the gods had just tried to communicate something of importance to him) the gracious gift brought only a foreboding and worry. Perhaps it had something to do with his view of the gods as well. Nebuchadnezzar awoke from his famous nightmare feeling profoundly vulnerable. Daniel chapter 2 begins:

In the second year of Nebuchadnezzar's reign, Nebuchadnezzar dreamed such dreams that his spirit was troubled and his sleep left him. (Dan. 2:1)

The dream he had dreamed could only be described as apocalyptic in its nature, but by that I don't mean that it was devastating, but rather that it falls into the category of symbolic Bible prophecy. In fact, I have come to believe that the symbols found in this particular dream became the Foundation Stone[28] upon which later Bible prophecy was built. This is why it is paramount to understand its symbols correctly in order to understand certain important themes throughout the New Testament, especially the "apocalyptic" book of Revelation (a redundancy, as you will shortly see). Indeed, it opens to our mortal eyes the *one* theme which gives all proper context to *any* Bible prophecy!

The word apocalyptic is usually used today to describe a scene of utter devastation, and this comes from its association with the end of the world.

---

26 John H. Stockton, "Only Trust Him," *Hymns of Faith* (Wheaton, IL: Tabernacle Publishing Company, 1980).
27 Ibid.
28 It will become clear later why I decided to capitalize these words.

But the word is only associated with the end of the world because when transliterated from the ancient Greek it was written in, *The Apocalypse* is the true and long-used title of the prophetic Bible book we (in English) now call *Revelation*. And although there are scenes of devastation portrayed in Revelation (as there are in the king's dream), and although the book does deal with the end of the world as we know it (also like the king's dream), the true message of Revelation and of all symbolic Bible prophecy, is anything but devastating, nor is devastation the end of the story at all! The word itself has nothing to do with devastation, but simply indicates a communication of the eternal God with mortals! It indicates a revealing of divine secrets: a *revelation!* We should consider it a tremendous privilege to have in our possession such revealed secrets written down in ancient times for us to read and study and ponder. These divine secrets, however, in Bible prophecy, are usually couched in symbols which require careful interpretation to understand (for reasons we will explore later). This is part of the reason many of us avoid the symbolic prophecies of Scripture, and it is also why so many ridiculous things are said about them by those who interpret the prophecies recklessly. This mysterious nature of such prophecy, and the fact that he could not understand his dream's meaning, was also part of what troubled King Nebuchadnezzar!

Nebuchadnezzar was a powerful king who was used to being in control of things, so it is understandable that he was troubled since the dream made him feel very much out of control. The "gods"—or rather, the one *true* God—will do that to us sometimes, but those who have really come to *know* God in history, have all found that the experience of God, His truth, His purpose, and His amazing love, is ultimately worth the humbling price we must pay for it. As one author likes to put it, heaven will be cheap enough![29] Those who truly love God, though they have seen His form only faintly in His revelations, yet they have seen *enough* to have an unshakable faith that there is so much more they will one day see—when someday our

---
29 Paraphrased from E.G. White, *Life Sketches* (Mountain View, CA: Pacific Press Publishing Association, 1915), p. 67.

now cloudy vision will be replaced with perfect sight. So much more that it will constrain us, along with the four mystical creatures described in Revelation 4:6–11—the ones with *absolute vision* of God, who are said to be "full of *eyes* in front and behind"[30]—to cry out, "Holy, holy, holy" and to cast our crowns of pride before His throne, singing that He *is* worthy "to receive glory and honor and power," and our worship: our *worth*-ship!

---

30 Emphasis is mine.

Chapter 4

The King's Lie Detector Test

Before giving us any details *about* the king's dream, Daniel 2 first elaborates about a human drama which unfolded immediately on account of the king's disturbing dream, and of his determination to take control of his situation at any cost, even at the cost of torture and destruction of human beings. Little did the king's closest advisers (or wise men, as they are commonly called) dream, as they slept pleasantly on their soft pillows that night, that they were about to be rudely awakened and caught up in a hard and cruel snare of impossible circumstance, that their lives were even then in mortal jeopardy! And oh, what a death they would die! Because in order to seek out an understanding of his troublesome dream, we are told that the king called for these important men of his court to bring him answers in the middle of the night! The trouble is none of the men whose counsel Nebuchadnezzar first sought out, could possibly know the real answers he was seeking. As we move through the text you will be able to palpably sense their great and growing desperation even filtered through English translations of the ancient Aramaic text! The text of Daniel switches here from Hebrew to Aramaic—the language once spoken by many Babylonians, and also later by Jesus—right in the middle of verse 4, where these doomed wise men first speak, and it continues through chapter 7.

> In the second year of Nebuchadnezzar's reign, Nebuchadnezzar dreamed such dreams that his spirit was troubled and his sleep left him. So the king commanded that the magicians, the enchanters, the sorcerers, and the [astrologers[31]] be summoned to tell the king his dreams. When they came in and stood before the king, he said to them,

---
31 Chaldeans.

> *"I have had such a dream that my spirit is troubled by the desire to understand it."* The [astrologers] said to the king (in Aramaic), *"O king, live forever! Tell your servants the dream, and we will reveal the interpretation."* (Dan. 2:1–4)

Though we may not put much stock in magicians, enchanters, sorcerers, and astrologers, the king had actually sought answers from the logical place in his own world and worldview. He sought out the important people, the VIPs, the wise men of his kingdom who made claims to have a special knowledge of and connection with the gods! Though it may seem like a stretch, in some ways it would be like us going to a preacher, a rabbi, or some other religious leader today to find out answers about God. Surely if anyone could help him understand his dream *they* could, he must have thought. In Nebuchadnezzar's day these were also the highly educated people, the PhDs, if you will, the "people who ought to know." But at the same time the wise king also harbored some healthy suspicion about their claims of divine connection and superior knowledge, and so he devised a plan to test those claims. He wanted to know for sure if they spoke the truth when they gave their interpretation of his dream. It was a sort of lie detector test that he had cunningly devised in his mind, though a very cruel one to be sure. Any person who cares about people ought to feel a significant sense of pity for the plight of the poor wise men, even if they were in reality a bunch of fortune-telling blowhards!

Instead of telling the wise men his dream, as they had requested, the king, with more than a hint of irritation in his reply, offered his wise men a type of worldly heaven or hell, depending on whether they could tell him both the dream *and* its meaning:

> *The king answered the [astrologers[32]],* **"This is a public decree:** *if you do not tell me both the dream and its interpretation, you shall be torn limb from limb, and your houses shall be laid in ruins [literally, made into a dunghill: a place to dump sewage, or an outhouse]. But if you do tell me the dream and its interpretation, you shall receive from me gifts and rewards and great honor. Therefore tell me the dream and its interpretation."* (Dan. 2:5–6)

Any common, conniving fortuneteller from the streets, with even a smattering of intelligence, should be able to hear a dream described in

---
32 Chaldeans.

detail, and then come up with some plausible sounding interpretation. So, if the wisest and best educated men in all of Babylon couldn't come up with an explanation for a simple dream, then they ought to be in another profession! But the king threw an impossible monkey wrench into his request, and this is where I believe a lot of people misunderstand the text today (although they are in good company). Very many interpreters of Daniel 2 throughout centuries and millennia have assumed, because of a textual ambiguity in the original language, that the king had actually *forgotten* his dream. However, textual evidence as well as contextual evidence in the story itself both support a very different interpretation.

The reason that many assume the king had forgotten his dream has to do with an ancient phrase used in the text which would have been well understood in its original context of the Babylonian court, but which had lost its original connotation in minds of later readers unfamiliar with the old Babylonian jargon. The phrase is the one translated above (correctly, I believe) as "**[t]his is a public decree**" (Dan. 2:5). The actual phrase literally translates as "**the *word* has gone from me**," and only secondarily as "the thing [or matter] has gone out from me." The word *"word"* is actually what is used. Later interpreters, unfamiliar with the fact that this was a common phrase used to describe a command, or an irreversible decision[33] of the king, made the understandable assumption that the dream was what the king was referring to. Thus the translators of the widely used King James Version translated it: "**The thing is gone from me**" (Dan. 2:5, KJV), leaving most English readers to naturally assume, for centuries (through no fault of their own), that "the thing" referred to the dream. A very understandable misunderstanding.

However, both the fact that the key word (literally "word") of this phrase is used later in Daniel 2 in a context that can *only* refer to the king's decree, and also the immediate context of the story itself, both tell us that something quite different was most likely going on.

The text goes on to say the wise men asked the king a second time, pleading with him to be reasonable:

They answered a second time, "Let the king first tell his servants the dream, then we can give its interpretation." (Dan. 2:7)

Now, let me ask you: **if the wise men themselves had understood the phrase Nebuchadnezzar used, to mean that he had actually forgotten his**

---

33 Or "stubborn word."

dream, would they then have once again pleaded with the king to please tell them the dream that they now knew he had no possibility of telling them? Not likely! No, something else is clearly going on here. They understood that the king was *refusing* (in anger, and in skepticism about their abilities) to tell them the dream, not that he *couldn't!* From *their* perspective, it probably seemed as if he was picking a fight with them, but it was a fight they would be the certain, and fatal, losers of. The king's wrath had come down upon them, and the only possibility of escape was an impossibility in their minds, though I'm sure they began hoping against the faintest hope!

> *The king answered, "I know with certainty that you are trying to gain time, because you see I have firmly decreed* **[the same phrase used in verse 5]**: *if you do not tell me the dream, there is but one verdict for you. You have agreed to speak lying and misleading words to me until things take a turn. Therefore, tell me the dream, and* **I shall know** *that you can give me its interpretation."* (Dan. 2:8–9)

That phrase, "and I shall *know*," is the key, I think, to understanding what was actually going on in the king's mind. He wanted to *know*, not *what* he had dreamed, but that the wise men could really interpret it! What was evidently[34] going on is that the king knew all too well the plausible answers devious wise men might come up with to appease or flatter him. This cruel decree was the conniving king's trump card up his sleeve to test the wise men's pretentious claims of connection with the gods! "You have agreed," he said, "to speak lying and misleading words to me" (Dan. 2:9). He suddenly felt fed up with their phony baloney. To try and understand why, let us consider for a moment the plight of any ancient monarch who might find himself wanting to hear, for once, unvarnished *truth*. It may not happen often, and it may even take an act of God to get them there, but every once in a while, even people in power come to that rare place in their journeys where they actually wish to hear unvarnished truth even about themselves!

As alluring as the job of an ancient king may sound, to be an ancient despot holding unquestioned power of life or death over all of his subjects was not entirely positive, just as being a billionaire, a powerful politician, a famous movie star, or a public heartthrob, today, is not all a bed of roses. To be king was also to be surrounded by many whose chief aim was to tell

---

34 Derived from *evidence* in the text itself.

the king only what they thought he *wanted* to hear, and never what might awaken his wrath, if it could be at all helped. I can almost guarantee that these wise men surrounding the king did not rise to their high positions in government by telling him the whole truth about himself! To truly succeed under an authoritarian regime (even today), your top virtues must become blind loyalty and flattery; truth must often be sacrificed on the altar of expediency. In other words, to be king was to be surrounded by *yes-men*, men who would invariably flatter the king and his ego, and who would "toe the party line" (as we would say today) rather than tell the king what he might *need* to hear, at the risk of their lives and limbs. Nebuchadnezzar must have known this all too well, even if it usually suited him. He was a very intelligent man. He had his blind spots and faults, to be sure, such as his infamously ferocious temper, but being susceptible to confidence schemes was not one of them; he was nobody's fool. Under normal circumstances he no doubt tolerated, philosophically, the day-to-day tomfoolery of the myriads of religious leaders who existed in his pagan realm of multiple gods, and the often dubious claims made by its cult leaders. It all came with the polytheistic territory he existed in. However, this time was *different* somehow. Somehow, he knew instinctively that *this* time it really counted, and he wanted to know truth! *Real* truth!

Have you ever faced a time in your life when you instinctively knew that "*this* time" it really counted? Perhaps you're facing such a time right now. There comes a time when we need something beyond just what gives us a flattering verdict about ourselves, and about our pet ideologies and worldviews. There comes a time in every life when people get the sudden urge to begin a search for real answers, for real meaning, for real *truth*. And I hope that time doesn't come for you just before you die! *Then* is a time when it really counts!

It's been nearly eighteen years[35] already at the time of my writing this, but surely some of you are old enough to still remember what New Yorkers did immediately following the 9/11 attacks on America. I could almost not believe it when I witnessed it! In the secular unbelieving bastion of the world, in a city containing so many agnostics and atheists, where did the masses suddenly flock to? They flocked to places of worship! Why? Because there is no other consolation when it really counts! There is a deficit of hope today, and King Nebuchadnezzar's experience shows us that even the most powerful, even the most successful, can become fed up with the

---

35 Going on two decades already …. *Wow!* How very fast our brief lives fly by!

"fluff of life" for no apparent reason, suddenly seeking "what is the point of it all?" And the pagan world the king lived in was a lot like *our* world, by the way. There was a deficit of hope back then just as there is today.

> **There is a deficit of hope today, and King Nebuchadnezzar's experience shows us that even the most powerful, even the most successful, can become fed up with the "fluff of life" for no apparent reason, suddenly seeking "what is the point of it all?"**

I am convinced that humans today are more insecure spiritually than they have been for a very, *very* long time. Some people have just given up on the whole idea of a God or gods for a lot of reasons. I think this helps explain a lot of trends in our world, like marked increases in violence, addictions, depression, suicides, kids killing kids, to name a few. The problem is, I believe, **we weren't made to live without hope, without meaning, without some all-consuming purpose for life beyond hedonism, without a sense of some control over our destiny**! And wherever there is a deficit of real hope our solution seems to be, as humans, to fill the void with *any* old hope, even a *false* hope.

Now, is a false hope better than *no* hope? I would say yes, I believe it is. *Anything* that gives our lives some paltry sense of purpose and security, is better than living purposelessly and feeling exposed to unfriendly fate![36] And I think that is why people worshiped all kinds of things in Nebuchadnezzar's day, and why they still do all around the world. We all worship *something!* I don't care if someone says, "I don't believe in a god." That person still *worships* something. We are all made (shall I say *created?*) in such a way that we attempt to gain ultimate meaning from something in our lives, whether true or false. We get some sense of security out of it: maybe it's money, maybe it's success, maybe it's science, maybe it's nature, maybe it's politics and power;[37] maybe it's an ideology, an organization, a government or some form of activism; maybe it's pleasure, maybe it's other people, maybe it's romance, maybe it's popularity and fame. But every one of us worships *something.*

---

36 Ironically, even that word, *fate,* refers to another ancient false god.
37 Perhaps, for some, it is even *military* might and *policing* power.

The ancient pagan beliefs actually served a purpose for people: to provide a sense of meaning and security in otherwise empty lives. But there's only one problem. When it *really* counts, in a time of real crisis, that false security just won't hold up! This is why people went flocking to the churches after 9/11 because the futility of their worldly, godless ideologies came flooding into their minds at such a time! There *was* no other answer. It became starkly apparent that their philosophies had "feet of clay." Have you ever heard that expression used about someone or something? The expression actually alludes to the very dream we are about to study! It means someone or something cannot stand up to a crisis. And that is the problem with *all* of our modern idols as well as the ancient ones. When I was actively pastoring, I always warned every new church district I entered that I too have feet of clay (I think some didn't believe me, until they *saw* my feet break)! But I also told them, at the same time, that if God could speak out of a donkey's mouth,[38] then I'm pretty sure He can speak through even me. I can't even share a few of the colorful King-James-flavored responses I got from *that* biblical reference.

We ultimately find that none of the idols we have satisfies our longing for something (or Some*one?*) we were made for. They all fit my personal definition of paganism—the worship of gods that are not gods! Even one of our greatest modern gods, the god of hedonism (living for pleasure), of saying, "eat, drink, and be merry, for tomorrow we die," fails to fill the void we feel. The expression "happy hedonist" is really an oxymoron since hedonism is actually evidence of the opposite of happiness. Hedonism is escapism. It is a vain attempt to escape our essential unhappiness, to forget all of the nagging questions and troubles we harbor inside, the persistent sense of meaninglessness and hopelessness that always surrounds and infuses a godless outlook on life! When it really counts, we become starkly aware of our need to know in *Whom* we have believed! We need a God who is *real!* And Nebuchadnezzar was at just that point. He needed someone he could trust. He was spiritually hungry and thirsty in a barren desert of pagan philosophy.

Not just anyone could tell a person what they had dreamed! So if any of these wise men could actually tell the king his very dream, Nebuchadnezzar must have reasoned, then surely that would make him certain their claims of connection with the gods were no phony baloney! Their pretentious pagan claims had proven far too often to him to be something like a bowl

---
38 See Numbers 22:21–33.

of wax fruit, merely an object for decoration, which may be aesthetically pleasing to look upon—alluring, even, in its deliciously elaborate forms—but if you ever got actually hungry, a bite from that fruit would prove quite unsatisfying! I remember once taking a bite out of a bunch of good looking rubber grapes that fooled me, and I promise you the experience inside my mouth was not what their appearance had promised! Incidentally, my taste of Jesus, on the other hand, has been so much *more* than His appearance had first suggested, or than I had ever expected. As suspicious as the king was, he also longed, at the same time, to know if someone out there might have an *actual* connection with the gods!

Listen to the ironic statement made by the pagan sages, when claims of godly connection became suddenly inconvenient to them. Hear what astounding claim the greatest minds of ancient paganism made about "the gods":

> *The [astrologers[39]] answered the king, "There is no one on earth who can reveal what the king demands! In fact no king, however great and powerful, has ever asked such a thing of any magician or enchanter or [astrologer]. The thing that the king is asking is too difficult, and no one can reveal it to the king except the gods, **whose dwelling is not with mortals**."* (Dan. 2:10–11)

They made the ironic claim—in light of their reputations for connection with the gods—that the gods are far away and distant from our humanity—*untouchable*.

There is a "Christian" version of this same notion that is called deism, and in practical reality it is only a hop, skip, and a jump from atheism. It was one of the main driving philosophies leading eighteenth century France into the atheism responsible for the worst elements (and atrocities) of the French Revolution. And the atheistic philosophy of the French Revolution later led to communism, as well as indirectly to other godless movements, which have, like communism, also been responsible for untold atrocities and inhumanity in relatively recent world history. Those same terrifying results of French atheism actually helped inspire Hitler and his National Socialists (although Adolf Hitler was *not* an atheist): the Nazi's famous "Heil Hitler" salute being borrowed directly or indirectly from a famous French Revolution painting which depicts the purposeful

---

39 Chaldeans.

putting away of human pity, love, and compassion in the name of revolution *(another* false god of history).[40]

However, despite the wise men's protests that the gods do not dwell with mortals, I'm sure most of them immediately went home, or to some of their many temples after the fateful meeting, and began a desperate attempt to get in touch with their gods! However, it would be to no avail because their gods *were* no gods! They may have been inventions of impersonating demons, at best, but the true God at this time did not permit the demons to step in, apparently. Even if they *could* have, there would still be a question in my own mind as to how much of the king's dream these fallen angels, who often masquerade as gods,[41] would have been able to know anyhow!

The wise men's hopeless claim had been that "There is no one on earth who can reveal what the king demands" (Dan. 2:10). So how fascinating it is that in the story there *was* one on earth found—a different sort of "wise" man from the king's collection of wartime captives, taken in chains out of a tiny vanquished kingdom called Judah—who not only was able to reveal what the king demanded, but who also ended up saving the lives and limbs and houses of all the foolish wise men[42] in the process of doing it! The king had flown into a rage after those wise men before him claimed the gods are too distant to reveal anything.

> *Because of this the king flew into a violent rage and commanded that all the wise men of Babylon be destroyed. The decree was issued, and the wise men were about to be executed; and they looked for Daniel and his companions, to execute them. Then Daniel ... asked Arioch, the royal official, "Why is the decree of the king so urgent?" Arioch then explained the matter to Daniel. So Daniel went in and requested that the king give him time and he would tell the king the interpretation. Then Daniel went to his home and informed his companions, Hananiah, Mishael, and Azariah, and told them to seek mercy from the God of heaven [the sky]... so that Daniel and his companions with the rest of the wise men of Babylon might not perish. Then the mystery was revealed to Daniel in a vision of the night, and Daniel blessed the God of heaven [the sky] .... Therefore Daniel went to Arioch, whom*

---

40 Simon Schama, *Citizens: A Chronicle of the French Revolution* (New York, NY: Alfred A. Knopf, 1989), pp. 172–174 and 359–361.
41 That's an entirely different Bible study.
42 As well as many who had not been in the original meeting of the king.

the king had appointed to destroy the wise men of Babylon, and said to him, "Do not destroy the wise men of Babylon; bring me in before the king, and I will give the king the interpretation." (Dan. 2:12–19, 24)

The ironic reputation Daniel also earned for revealing what the king demanded is found recorded in the words of the king regarding a later incident in Daniel chapter 4:

At last Daniel came in before me—he who was named Belteshazzar after the name of my god, and **who is endowed with a spirit of the holy gods**. (Dan. 4:8)

So one *was* found with whom a god *did* dwell, and this very element of the story itself hearkens forward to one of the greatest truths revealed in the king's dream, when rightly understood from *our* vantage point: the good news of a coming God *with* us! A God so different from the pagan deities! Not a god *far distant* in the stars, or *against* us, or one who does not see, or take pity, or hear our prayers, or care, or forgive, or walk with us, or talk with us, or intervene to save us from the desperate situation we find ourselves in! But I am getting ahead of myself.

Chapter 5

Troubled about the Future

We know from something Daniel the prophet later told the king that it wasn't only the dream which had been troubling King Nebuchadnezzar. No! He had been brooding over something even before God gave him the dream.

> *To you, O king, as you lay in bed, came thoughts of what would be hereafter.* (Dan. 2:29)

What was Nebuchadnezzar brooding about that night as he drifted off to sleep? It seems as if he was wondering, "What's going to happen *after me?!*" And the dream was a divine response to the king's troubling thoughts about future events. Perhaps he was even wondering about the gods, and about eternity? Or perhaps even about the possibility of eternal life, or the next best thing, of an eternal *kingdom?* Such pondering (any heartfelt pondering, I think) is very important. It's at the very *heart* of spirituality through which we seek to find out if there is a real purpose and *meaning* to our existence. Among all animals on our planet only humans, apparently, seem to sit (or lie) around and brood over such things. Although I think it would be fascinating to have a philosophical discussion with my cat, it's not likely to happen, even if she could talk.

"Just give me some more of that tasty food, please," she'd likely say, while sniffing the air to see if I might be holding anything of value to offer her (the cat I'm thinking about especially likes corn and green beans, as strange as that may seem) or, "Shut up, and rub my fat belly!" she'd quip as she would roll her soft fluffy mass onto her back, motioning up at me with beckoning paws, in her most seductive cuddle-cat manner. "I've got way more important matters to attend to than all your silly questions; such as napping, for instance, or lunging at the sliding glass door when birds come twittering around, or working on this confounded hairball in my tummy that I've been trying to cough up for three days now! Merroowww! We cats may be curious, but you humans *think* too much!"

Such thinking, however, is a *godlike* element in our natures, and without it we are diminished in our essential humanity. According to Genesis 1:27, humans, alone among earth's creatures, were created with a likeness that is somehow similar to God, and I have never personally believed we should take that likeness to be primarily *physical.*

I think these were the sorts of things the king was probably wondering about. "Is this all there is?" "After me, what happens?" "Is there any real *meaning* to my life, to my empire, and everything I've accomplished?" It was the brooding Spirit of God, whom I believe had already stirred up Nebuchadnezzar's heart with such godlike ponderings about life. So, if you start pondering and thinking philosophically sometime, maybe it's God trying to speak to *you!* If you start wondering why you exist, or thinking about the fact that you're getting old, and you wonder "How much life do I have left?" and "What am I going to do with it that matters?" then maybe it's the Spirit of God talking to you! Please don't try to fill up your aching emptiness with destructive or empty stuff that cannot meet your deepest hunger or answer the cry of the soul, such as illicit affairs or buying a new sports car. Get on your knees! And stay there, even if your knees start looking like camel knees! You would be in grand company, for ancient historians report that James, the stepbrother of Jesus and author of the book of James, developed knees as hard as a camel's in his old age because he prayed so much.[43] Stay on your knees

> **"Please don't try to fill up your aching emptiness with destructive or empty stuff that cannot meet your deepest hunger or answer the cry of the soul, such as illicit affairs or buying a new sports car. Get on your knees! And stay there, even if your knees start looking like camel knees!"**

---

43 Eusebius, Bishop of Caesarea, and Christian Frederic Crusé, *The Ecclesiastical History of Eusebius Pamphilus: Bishop of Caesarea, in Palestine*, Translated by C. F. Cruse (Watchmaker Publishing, 2011), p. 64.

until the many illusions and delusions presented to us in false flattering lights by an invisible enemy,[44] are shown up for what they really are: gods that are no gods, gods that can only disappoint and utterly destroy us in the end!

The same God who stirred up Nebuchadnezzar's philosophical questions, then took his brooding over the future that fateful night as if it was a prayer, and He answered it in a dream filled with mysterious symbolic images and events. But symbolic images in Bible prophecy, as important as they are, don't mean literally what you see; they mean *something else*. Taking prophetic symbols literally is the single biggest error readers of prophecy make, and sometimes even very learned interpreters fall into this pitfall. So the codified dream left the dumbfounded king more than brooding, but now extremely anxious to know the dream's real meaning since it seemed to carry profound import, though he couldn't quite put his finger on what that import *was* for certain! The mystery must be solved!

The dream *was* a message from a god, just like the king would have expected, but not just *any* god. It was from the one *true* God, who had sent to the king a troubling mystery which he could not possibly solve on his own, and then He graciously *revealed* Himself to the anxious king as the "Revealer of mysteries," as the One who *can* solve the troubles that we mere mortals cannot, the One who is *Himself* the answer to what it is our hearts are seeking after:

> *To you, O king, as you lay in bed, came thoughts of what would be hereafter, and the revealer of mysteries disclosed to you what is to be.* (Dan. 2:29)

---

44 We'll get to that subject more directly in a later volume.

Chapter 6

The Dreadful Colossus ...

When Daniel sought mercy from *his* God in prayer, along with his three closest companions, he was not only seeking mercy from the God who dwells with mortals; he was seeking help from a personal Friend. The revelation in this story doesn't end with this God only *dwelling* with Daniel. No! This God was also a *friend* of Daniel! This God—the only *true* God (with a capital G)—several times describes Daniel, through His messenger,[45] as one "greatly beloved."[46] That's *friendship!* And the Friend and Father,[47] who longs to dwell with all of His fallen mortal children, heard Daniel's humble prayer so that Daniel was enabled to go in and stand before the intimidating king with confidence. In the eyes of the Babylonians, Daniel then performed a feat of divination so amazing to them that it forever after drew striking contrasts between Nebuchadnezzar's man-made gods, and the one true God whom Daniel worshiped, "the revealer of mysteries" (Dan. 2:29). This was a God who was not a distant, helpless, *unfriendly* God, but a real God with real answers, who dwells *with* and *loves* His people. Let us take a look now at what Daniel told the king about the dream which earned him the enviable reputation as one "endowed with a spirit of the holy gods" (Dan. 4:8).

First of all, Daniel demonstrates to the haughty king the priceless quality of humility. He gives credit to God alone for *His* mercy, and then, though he has just been honored by God above all his peers, he minimizes his own importance in the important matter at hand. Perhaps this quality in Daniel is one reason God was able to entrust him with such an honor. Humility is such a rare quality, even in some of God's truest followers.

---
45 An angel.
46 See Daniel 9:23, 10:11, and 10:19.
47 We'll come to that element later, in another chapter, and, more completely, in another volume.

Even the great apostle Paul was shown that his ego could not be held in check under the influence of the great revelations he was being entrusted with without those revelations being accompanied by some hurtful "thorn in the flesh" (a "messenger of Satan") to keep him humble.[48] Daniel begins:

> *No wise men, enchanters, magicians, or diviners can show to the king the mystery that the king is asking, but there is a God in heaven [the sky] who reveals mysteries, and he has disclosed to [you] what will happen at the end of days. Your dream and the visions of your head ... were these: To you ... came thoughts of what would be hereafter, and the revealer of mysteries disclosed to you what is to be. But as for me, this mystery has not been revealed to me because of any wisdom that I have more than any other living being, but in order that the interpretation may be known to the king and that you may understand the thoughts of your mind.* (Dan. 2:27–30)

> **First of all, Daniel demonstrates to the haughty king the priceless quality of humility. He gives credit to God alone for His mercy, and then, though he has just been honored by God above all his peers, he minimizes his own importance in the important matter at hand.**

Here was *Yahweh*[49] showing up to help Nebuchadnezzar, a pagan dictator, understand the thoughts of his mortal mind which He, the Eternal Existent One *Himself,* had implanted there.

After this, Daniel describes to the king the very details of the visionary dream which the king had held the other wise men in such panicked anguish over (although I strongly suspect he secretly doubted all along that anyone could tell its contents to him). I can see the king's jaw suddenly drop, and the dumbfounded look in his eyes as Daniel began to describe what only a real God, who really *exists,* just as His name attests, could possibly have revealed. And then I can feel

---

48 See 2 Corinthians 12:7–9.
49 The true name of our God given to His ancient followers which is most likely a variant of the phrase meaning simply, "I am," or "I exist."

the chills suddenly run up his spine, and down again, then fly upward once more to his brain, as the realization finally hits home! I can run my mental fingers over his taut goosebumps and even touch the warm humbling feeling (in memory nerves of my own mind) that must have all of a sudden overwhelmed the haughty king only a moment later, after he had digested this too-fantastic-to-be-true revelation long enough to start reveling in a startling new thought. I know the thought myself! It is the thought that at least one of the gods is *real*—all *too* real, that "I exist"[50] *exists!* I know it because I have been in that same place in my own walk with the same God, in various contexts, more than a time or two. To find yourself graced with that mentally prostrate position, which is the natural consequence of a meeting with your Creator, creates a humbling sensation. But the sensation is not *humiliating* since there is a deep joy involved in it, especially if you have suddenly realized at the same time that the God who is now yanking back on the rope you had only pulled at halfheartedly is actually *on your side!* There is deep joy in the humbling encounter if you realize God is not there to communicate *anger* at your many sins at all (as you might have expected), or to "upbraid" [51] (even though you know you deserve it and much worse) but rather to give you a hand up somehow.

> **There is deep joy in the humbling encounter if you realize God is not there to communicate anger at your many sins at all (as you might have expected), or to "upbraid"(even though you know you deserve it and much worse) but rather to give you a hand up somehow.**

Daniel's description of the pivotal dream often brings to my mind a kind of worldly dream of my own (perhaps just a daydream?). The scene of Daniel 2 is among the many prophetic scenes in Scripture I would love to see professionals in Hollywood try to literally and meticulously reproduce someday—along with the visions seen on Patmos by John the Revelator—using all of their best possible special effects. I would love to see them paying scrupulous and well-researched attention to every minute detail since

---
50   See the previous footnote on the meaning of the name *Yahweh*.
51   Scold—see James 1:5 in the King James, and then in *other* versions for comparison.

even tiny details matter in Bible prophecy, instead of making up their own invented fantasies out of the material, or slanting elements toward some pet cause, ideology, or theology. Sticking to God's script would truly take humility in Hollywood.

> *You were looking, O king, and lo! there was a great statue. This statue was huge, its brilliance extraordinary; it was standing before you, and its appearance was frightening.* (Dan. 2:31)

What we have at the beginning of the description is a massive statue, or what later ancients in the time of Rome would have called a *colossus!* It was excessively bright and dazzling, and it was standing imposingly, or threateningly, in front of the king. It glittered and shone to be sure. That is part of the description. However, one other detail stands out to me above and beyond the glitter, which apparently has not stood out to most biblical artists over the years. It is the fact that the colossus was said to be *frightening* in its appearance. Please allow that fact to simmer on a back burner of your mind as we move onward. Out of all the artists' depictions I have ever seen of this prophetic statue, I can honestly say that none of them have ever appeared to me as very *frightening* in their appearance, and I wonder "Why?" Maybe it's just not in the nature of a biblical artist to try and capture evil. Or maybe they think there is not a market or a stomach among their biblically-minded audience for the gruesome. But the meaning of the word used in the original text literally indicates something that causes *fear*; something terrible! Which makes me wonder whether we have a true conception in our minds of what Nebuchadnezzar really saw in his dream, whether we like to think about such things or not. Whatever it was being described about the statue, that fearful element Daniel mentions had intimidated and disturbed, even scared, the king at first by its very appearance!

Perhaps it would help us to better understand the meaning of that dream from God, if we could imagine something more evil in the appearance and features of this monolith than the placid, almost fatherly, kingly face that most paintings depict! Perhaps imagining a face rather wholly lacking in any tender mercies or humanity or compassion might help us out tremendously. Or maybe borrowing from our own photographic age, historical images of Hitler's heartless storm troopers shooting men, women, and children in cold blood up against their own village wall while ignoring their pitiful pleas for mercy, might aid us. Or maybe we should borrow from mental images that have been burned (by documentaries and movies) into our modern psyches, of rigorous Gestapo goons intent on getting their harassed and hunted man at any human cost?

I dare not insert just here any more recent or close-to-us examples of what I see as pernicious evils[52] since I know that most of us have a hard time admitting, or even *seeing*, contemporary evil when it is still gaining ground; unless, of course, we have been jolted into super-sight through a painful personal encounter *with* that evil. It is human nature to merely shrug off the "normal," when just-as-true evil is still being promoted under a guise of noble names, of unquestioned societal causes and practices which people would look like fools (or even endanger themselves) to oppose. I speak of "good" evils that are still gradually being adopted, and being widely called good by "good" people, by people who, sometimes even because of self-righteous zeal, never bother to question the ultimate destination of the dangerous paths our society ventures down, or of the unintended consequences awaiting us at the paths' ends (not to mention along the way). The situation is very similar to how most German citizens in Hitler's era failed to see the "good" things in their own society and government as *evil* until it became too late. I fear I would surely be labeled a crank or *worse*. I wonder out loud (on paper or screen) though whether this reality isn't also part of the meaning contained in the gargantuan statue's shiny glitter? Was it a clever cover of apparent light, perhaps, over the lurking undercurrent of dark elements, which God momentarily caused to frighten an intelligent king before he had even had a chance to understand *what* was frightening him or what the statue actually stood for? Perhaps God was trying to put a subtle realization about his own culture into the back of Nebuchadnezzar's mind. Perhaps God was trying to tell even this ancient king that he too had profound blind spots to contemporary evils of *his* society, so much so that left to his own understanding he would have always labeled the evils a great good.

Perhaps imagining a look of demonic possession is another method that might help the frightening appearance of that colossal face to grow stronger in our minds. I once witnessed a massive demonic evil eye staring me down in the darkness of my bedroom, right at the foot of my bed, during a frightful nightmare long, long ago—a vision which still gives me

---

52 Which I, *personally*, might imagine in the statue's face as a fear factor.

the heebie-jeebies when I think of it! I'm sure many of us have had at least one similar sort of fright in our lives. So why can't we be more imaginative and creative about the fear created by that face on Nebuchadnezzar's statue?

Can artists capture such imaginary elements in sculpture or paintings or other mediums? You *bet* they can! Have you never perused the video game section of your local Wal-mart store, and observed how well someone somewhere has been able to capture such gruesome elements on packages of games marketed to children? Arrogance, coldness, hate, vengeance, murderous intent, merciless harassment, demonic control, even living decomposition—it is all there! And what I see lacking, more often than not, are all the signs of vibrant, healthy, joyous life, and the godly love qualities such as gentleness, consideration, forgiveness, and tender mercies. Not that the pictures don't intrigue even me, though, in some macabre sort of way, because they are quite stimulating, and they all seem to promise "action, excitement, and adventure." But rather than merely celebrating our instinctual need to toy with evil, and with things that scare us,[53] that same stimulation could be put to a far better effect in describing a prophetic scene that carries redeeming value in its interpretation! The teaser trailer for my own dreamed up prophetic scene movie might begin: "Get ready for some *redeeming* action, excitement, and adventure—written by God!" And the central theme of human redemption purchased through a nearly inconceivable gruesome act of grace (the cross) by a God of unexpected love for, and defense of, totally undeserving and indefensible sinners, should be easily detected throughout by the keen viewer since that essentially is what the symbols of Bible prophecy ultimately center around, despite prophecy's many fantastic (that is, fantasy-like) visual elements.

Prophecy's colossal clashes between good and evil, and even its judgments, are so unlike the pat and cliche black-and-white of comic book superhero stories, which are stocked with *stock* "good guys" and "bad guys." No, the plot of prophecy is so much more uplifting and surprising, so much more subtle, so much richer when understanding gets applied since the colossal conflict (which is the reality behind *our* reality) is actually all ultimately about the vindication of our God's maligned character. On a purely human level it is also about the vindication of Yahweh's accused and harassed children who have no actual defense for themselves

---

53 Which most people, *thankfully,* are only brave enough to do vicariously through entertainment mediums.

beyond the blood of Jesus, and their testimony about what He has done in them.[54] It is also that testimony which helps vindicate God (and His giving of grace to sinners) in the whole ordeal. Those who study prophecy long and prayerfully, more often than not discover that it is God who is really on trial in the big picture. It speaks also of a battle to expose well-disguised *evils* which on the surface look to be only *good*, and which have everything to do with an enemy deliberately distorting God's character of love until God looks like the villain who is out to get us. And the totally *un*-comic book aim of the villainized superhero in prophecy is not even to "*get*" the "bad guys" who have helped villainize Him, nor is it to give them "what's coming to them." Scripture actually calls that much misunderstood[55] and hated[56] aspect of His story His "strange act" and "alien task"![57] The destructive element, which we too often wrongly assume to be an arbitrary act of God done in anger, and which I'll get to in a future volume (God willing), is an "alien task," because it is alien to the Hero's character! The Hero is surprisingly not actually out to *get* even the so-called "bad guys."[58] He who was nailed to a criminal's cross takes pleasure in nailing no one! On the cross He cried out, "Father, forgive them" (Luke 23:34), referring to the very men who had nailed *Him!* His aim is rather to conquer the hearts and minds of "bad" guys *and gals,* if at all possible, and to transform them into gracified *good* guys and gals, after *shielding* them, and after taking the rap for all their bad acts *Himself!*

> **He who was nailed to a criminal's cross takes pleasure in nailing no one! On the cross He cried out, "Father, forgive them" (Luke 23:34), referring to the very men who had nailed Him!**

---

54 See Revelation 12:11. And on a related note, I propose that no matter how many theologians assert we are "saved by grace, but judged by our works," we are *not* judged by our "works" *per se,* but rather by the *change* (the *difference*) Christ has brought about in us (as it was *evidenced* by good works when given time). *If* we were judged simply by a perusal of all our life works (even *after* our acceptance of Christ), *none of us* would have hope, and what Paul attests in Romans 8:1 could *never* be true, that:
>   There is therefore now **no condemnation** for those who are in Christ Jesus.

55 By us.
56 By God.
57 See Isaiah 28:21.
58 See God's solemn oath in Ezekiel 33:11.

From a limited human perspective, it may be the greatest apparent injustice of all time. Perhaps this is another reason why God may be on trial, and why the end results in our lives (at least part of the "word of [our] testimony"[59]) will matter so much. And if such cases as ours (because we are the onetime "bad guys" He came to save) were being tried in an earthly court, you might even call another thing He does the greatest apparent *cover-up* in history: when He covers our shameful nakedness *(our* true record) with His own perfect robe[60] of righteousness *(His* true record) instead of leaving us exposed. And the greatest *concealment of evidence* may seem to be happening when He covers up the evidence of our guilt with His shed blood![61] I guess it's a good thing He is also the judge![62] This amazing true story, which is hard to do human justice to, is what Nebuchadnezzar's dream is all about, too, when rightly understood. But, again, I get ahead of myself.

---

59 See, again, Revelation 12:11.
60 See Revelation 3:18.
61 See Revelation 1:5.
62 See John 5:22.

Chapter 7
... And the Growing Stone

What was more frightening to Nebuchadnezzar at first, before he finally understood his dream—whether the statue's appearance, or what came next to undermine and then to finally destroy the statue—is hard to say. But as you will soon see, the power of the interpretation would naturally tend to shift the king's anxieties, due to prejudice, from the former fear to the latter fear, as long as he was still thinking from a self-absorbed, fallen human perspective. Daniel continues his description:

> *The head of that statue was of fine gold, its chest and arms of silver, its middle and thighs of bronze, its legs of iron, its feet partly of iron and partly of clay.* (Dan. 2:32–33)

This frightful colossus is composed mostly of precious metals, with gold—the most precious known to the ancient world—composing the head. Then as each new segment going down the body gets mentioned, we find that it is composed of a different precious metal, and each one being both progressively stronger, and at the same time inferior in value, to the metal that came before it, until finally the feet are described as being mixed with a substance so very inferior to everything preceding it that it isn't even a metal! What is more, as we will soon see, this clay (or rather what we would call terra-cotta or pottery) that became mixed into the feet somehow, becomes the Achilles heel of the whole colossus since earthenware is fragile.

Pay special attention to the feet because the feet become the linchpin of the entire prophecy. They are the part that really excites me since it is at the feet that the statue experiences a severe collision which undermines, and then eventually destroys, all of the statue's imposing bulk.

> *As you looked on, a stone was cut out, not by human hands, and it struck the statue on its feet of iron and clay and broke them in pieces [a first fracture].* (Dan. 2:34)

Notice, I put in brackets here that this is a *first fracture,* or we might call it break number one. I gave you this heads up because I've studied the text very carefully and have found that there are actually two breaks mentioned in the original text using two distinct verb forms. It says in this verse that the mysterious stone, cut out of something as yet undefined, by supernatural hands, broke the statue once, and the first verbal form of the ancient word used (properly translated) gives the idea of a *fracturing* break, or of a cracking up. It doesn't mean that the statue was destroyed at the very moment of impact. Right here is a vital point of interpretation where I believe a profound misunderstanding has made a lot of sincere translators and interpreters miss the most beautiful elements of this Christ-centered prophecy. But we will get to that soon enough. After a *first* mention of breakage, in the next verse comes the *second* mention of breakage using a *different* form of the same ancient verb which I am confident was no mere textual accident.

> **If the great God of the universe is the author of a vision or a dream, should we not also pay close attention to His every detail? Details matter especially when symbols are being used!**

In prophecy, by the way, do details *really* matter? What do you think? All great authors pay close attention to their details which is why their words are often later picked apart by whole classrooms full of students in an effort to understand deeper meanings in their texts. If the great God of the universe is the author of a vision or a dream, should we not also pay close attention to *His* every detail? Details *matter* especially when symbols are being used! That conviction in my heart is why many years ago, when I was still young and fresh in mind, I prayerfully studied this prophecy very closely and carefully almost as if with a magnifying glass and microscope. I ended up discovering some refreshing new insights in it that I would never have noticed had I comfortably breezed over the familiar story with all of my old inherited assumptions about it left unquestioned and untested.

Notice the first word of the next verse: *then*. That means later, or *after*, the initial fracture break had already taken place:

> *Then the iron, the clay, the bronze, the silver, and the gold, were all broken in pieces [a final collapse—they became disintegrated] and became like the chaff of the summer threshing floors; and the wind carried them away, so that not a trace of them could be found. But the stone that struck the statue became a great mountain and filled the whole earth.* (Dan. 2:35)

The second breaking (or break number two) in the ancient text uses a different form of the verb, indicating that all the elements of the statue were finally totally *disintegrated,* that there was a final collapse that happened afterward, an inevitable result of the initial impact, but happening in sequence later on. So they were all broken in pieces and they became like chaff on the summer threshing floor, and the wind (remember that symbolic detail) carried them away until eventually all traces of the ancient statue would be swept away, not the *memory* or *influence* of it, mind you, but the active *presence* of it.

The first break was the critical undermining of the colossal structure and the start of an ensuing crisis (however long that may have lasted), while the second break describes the final collapse that the crisis led up to. So I ask you, readers, who might remember the year 2001, does this sequence of destruction sound familiar to you at all? The destruction of the colossal Twin Towers in New York City is, I think, a perfect example of what I actually discovered going on in this text not long *after* 9/11 had happened. It is a perfect example of a two-part process[63] that often takes place in the destruction of a colossal structure (a process that can also be found in nature). On 9/11 those imposing towers remained standing for quite some time after being hit by the jet airplanes filled with fuel that then burned for a long time on their insides. I remember sitting in our apartment watching it all unfold on television. Even though the buildings still stood for a long time, their superstructures had been irreparably damaged (their doom had been struck) and they became even

---

63   *Three*-part, if you consider the intermediary crisis.

more undermined as the jet fuel continued to melt their insides down.[64] Eventually, there was a sudden catastrophic collapse! First one tower went, then the next, coming down in what seems in my memory bank like slow motion, but which impression might have been at least partly due to their massive size, and the time it takes for such mighty structures to fall! They were suddenly disintegrating—just like the second verb form in our text indicates about the ancient statue—into massive clouds of dust and rubble along with many people who searchers never recovered even a trace of! I couldn't believe my eyes! The whole scene was far too much like imaginary paintings depicting the end of the world that I had seen since my childhood. But those paintings hadn't even come close to doing justice to the reality of what skyscrapers falling can *actually* look like! The heart-sickening vision of these colossal buildings I had meditated and prayed beside earlier that same year, roaring to the ground, caused me to weep like I've seldom wept in my life, as I sat there in our living room/kitchen[65] thinking of all the precious *people* involved, and of the doomed rescuers I had just witnessed running *toward* the burning buildings. A great many *more* people are involved in the meaning of this ancient prophecy, however, which is why it is so important that we strive to interpret its symbols correctly since I believe it is a key prophecy of the *everlasting* gospel message to the entire world—the word gospel meaning "good news"—which good news is all about *Jesus!*

> **" Let me now insert a prophetic heads-up: winds in symbolic Bible prophecy usually signify the bloody conquests of armies by which history in our fallen world advances, civilizations are upset, kingdoms change hands, and societies are forever changed over time. "**

> [A]nd [they] became like the chaff of the summer threshing floors; **and the wind carried them away.** (Dan. 2:35)

---

64 At least that's the official explanation, as I understand it.
65 Our apartment at the time was *extremely* small.

Let me now insert a prophetic heads-up: *winds* in symbolic Bible prophecy usually signify the bloody conquests of armies[66] by which history in our fallen world advances, civilizations are upset, kingdoms change hands, and societies are forever changed over time. And I believe that Bible prophecy is generally consistent in its symbols (not to mention the book of Daniel being consistent within itself). Let's keep that thought in the back of our minds as we move forward in interpretation. And what does it say would be happening to that mysterious stone that struck the image at the same time?

> *But the stone that struck the statue **became a great mountain** and filled the whole earth.* (Dan. 2:35)

Does the text say that the stone which struck the statue already *was* a mountain when it struck, or rather that it *became* a mountain *after* it struck the statue? As elementary as this question sounds, it is pertinent since many interpreters glide right past this detail that seems at least slightly important to me, and they talk of the stone almost as if it had smashed into the statue already a full-grown mountain, as if *only* one event was being symbolized by the dream, and as if all of the event's train of consequences happened almost *instantly!* They too often leave out symbolic elements of the text that in literal life would necessarily require *time* to accomplish, one of them being the action of wind, but, even more importantly, they leave out the time-consuming element of *growth*. This is significantly a *growing* stone! Whether that growth happens quickly or slowly doesn't really matter at this point of interpretation because growth still requires *time* to happen regardless. This was a huge *aha!* realization for me the very first time I started paying precise attention to the minute details of this time prophecy.[67] A specifically *Christian* light bulb switched on inside my mind which suddenly illuminated everything else about this prophecy! The mysterious stone's growth, while the winds of history would be sweeping away the last vestiges of the crumbled colossus, would finally lead whatever the stone symbol stands for to fill the whole earth! This is at least a very *significant* stone, isn't it, even if we are not reading the prophecy in light of Christianity? The stone's meaning must be more colossal than even that of the colossus! But let me put

---

66   Compare Daniel 7:2–3 (and the symbolic conquest imagery that follows it), 11:4; Jeremiah 49:36–37, and Ezekiel 17:21.
67   We will soon see how the statue stands for a virtual timeline in history.

what I'm hinting at another way to help you see the specifically *Christian* light that suddenly lit up *my* understanding. It is a stone that will grow until it finally fills the whole earth! So, in other words, the stone spreads itself "... into all the world, as a witness to all nations ..."![68] A worldwide movement of this stone takes place until it has reached "... every nation, and kindred, and tongue, and people ..."![69] These are famous words of *Jesus* and about the everlasting gospel (good news) I have just purposely quoted!

Daniel then goes on to interpret the details of the dream that he has already described. Now remember, what was it, *specifically,* that the king had been wondering about as he lay in his bed that night? He had been wondering what would happen in the *future*. And here is God's answer to his wondering!

I like to imagine that the very moment the king heard the first part of the interpretation, his earlier foreboding, palpably felt ever since he had witnessed the frightening colossus, suddenly vaporized, and a new foreboding took its place, attaching itself to the vivid cinematic scene of that mysterious stone smashing into the feet of his great colossus. Yes, *his* colossus by then, for he had just been told by Daniel that he *himself* was included in the symbolism of the great colossus! It couldn't possibly have remained quite as frightening to King Nebuchadnezzar after *that* revelation. And his part in the colossus was no mean element, either (even if it was a *mean-looking* element[70])!

> *You, O king, the king of kings—to whom the God of heaven has given the kingdom, the power, the might, and the glory, into whose hand he has given human beings, wherever they live, the wild animals of the field, and the birds of the air, and whom he has established as ruler over them all—you are the head of gold.* (Dan. 2:37–38)

Nebuchadnezzar was the *head of gold!* How flattered he must have felt—for a moment, at least! And what a panegyrist[71] Daniel must have seemed—at *first!* But there was more, which the king would probably rather never have heard. It involved the eventual conquest and overthrow of his golden empire (here called a *kingdom)* which he loved so

---
68 See Matthew 24:14.
69 See Revelation 14:6.
70 Pun intended.
71 A eulogist: i.e., one who makes up flattering words about people, especially about rulers. *Webster's Deluxe Dictionary, 10ᵗʰ Collegiate Ed.* (Pleasantville, NY: Reader's Digest, 1998).

much, and which he hoped would last forever! Archaeologists have dug up a cuneiform tablet among the ruins of ancient Babylon actually containing an inscription on it by the very Nebuchadnezzar spoken of in Daniel, saying: "Babylon, the delight of my eyes! May you last forever!"[72] But Daniel's interpretation to the king spotlights a future changing of the hands of power over the territory that composed Nebuchadnezzar's one-time realm, not once, but *several* times! So much for our human *forevers!*

> *After you shall arise **another kingdom** [of silver] inferior to yours, and yet **a third kingdom** of bronze, which shall rule over the whole earth. 40 And there shall be **a fourth kingdom**, strong as iron; just as iron crushes and smashes everything, it shall crush and shatter all these.* (Dan. 2:39–40)

By the way, there are *only four kingdoms* actually mentioned in the original language that this portion of Daniel 2 was composed in. It is easy to confuse the number of *actual* "kingdoms," but there are only *four* in the numbered list, and there is no way, grammatically, to get around that fact without wresting the text. Inserting numbers into a translation doesn't count either (as some paraphrases do) because they just don't exist in the original text. This is important to pay close attention to. The misconception arises out of distinctions made in verses 41-43:

> *As you saw the feet and toes partly of potter's clay and partly of iron, it shall be a divided kingdom; but some of the strength of iron shall be in it, as you saw the iron mixed with the clay. As the toes of the feet were part iron and part clay, so the kingdom shall be partly strong and partly brittle. As you saw the iron mixed with clay, so will they mix with one another in marriage, but they will not hold together, just as iron does not mix with clay.* (Dan. 2:41–43)

The feet are so very unique in Daniel's interpretation of the dream. Although they are also iron, like the legs, their iron becomes mixed up with the inferior element of clay. As I briefly suggested earlier, the clay is not to be taken as raw clay (it would not stay that way long anyway, even if someone *did* construct an image out of it, since natural clay dries rapidly),

---

72 See Mark Finley, *Solid Ground* (Hagerstown, MD: Review and Herald, 2003), p. 157.

but most likely what we would call terra-cotta or baked pottery. The most literal translation of the Aramaic words describing the substance is clay potsherd, i.e., earthenware, most likely of a baked variety. There are some instances in the ancient Near Eastern world, as well as in the Americas, where relatively small articles of clay were simply allowed to dry, and there was also a wide use of sun-dried bricks, but this does not seem likely for the colossal and elaborate statue seen in a dream dreamed by the sophisticated builder king Nebuchadnezzar.

This mixture of a fragile earthenware into two additional divisions of the fourth iron "kingdom" may easily create the false impression that the feet constitute a fifth kingdom, and then that the toes constitute yet a sixth. However, even a casual reread of the text can demonstrate the error of this thinking, since in verse 41 both the feet *and* the toes are mentioned as a single unit without the mention of a kingdom number, and referring simply to "the kingdom," or to "it," depending on the translation. Then, in verse 42 *only the toes* are mentioned in an almost identical formula once again.

It should be obvious that if the feet *and* toes first constituted a *single* kingdom in the narrative, then the toes, by themselves, could not possibly constitute an *additional* separate kingdom one verse later. Something else *must* be going on with this formula, rather than identifying new "kingdoms." Probably the best hyper-literal translation of verse 41 is, "a kingdom divided **it** will become," similar in construction to the version I quoted above. But what we miss in the English is that the pronoun "it," which in the original language is supplied, or implied by the verb form, would tie directly back to the substantive in the previous verse, "the fourth kingdom," and cannot possibly stand in place for the feet and toes, which are not even singular. However, even using the form of other translations, which say "the kingdom will be divided," the question, *"which* kingdom?" naturally points us back to the substantive, "the fourth kingdom," in the previous verse, since no new number has been introduced to distinguish this portion as a distinct kingdom in what was clearly a numerical list—not to mention the continuance of the fourth kingdom's symbolic iron. Where the word "it" is found in the English translation I used above, in verse 41, we should insert "the fourth kingdom." The way we really should read verse 41 (which speaks of both feet and toes, collectively), therefore, is: "As you saw the feet and toes partly of potter's clay and partly of iron, **[the fourth kingdom]** shall be **[or shall** *become***]** a divided kingdom." It is worth noting here that the "be" verb used in this passage may be translated "become" as well as "be" depending upon contextual clues.

The modifications, first to the feet, and then to the toes of the statue, don't refer to *different* "kingdoms," but to **historical changes** that would take place within the *same* "kingdom" at different points along its timeline, which is kingdom number four: the *iron* kingdom. And the inclusion of both the toes *and* the feet in verse 41, and then later, the *exclusion* of the feet in verse 42, tell us first (in verse 41) of a characteristic that would be shared by both the feet *and* the toes, and then (in verse 42) of a characteristic that would be *exclusive* to the toes' division alone. But since in the English both descriptions seem to be only a variation on (and an elaboration of) the same theme,[73] this doesn't seem to distinguish the toes at all!

Let me propose that verse 42 is usually translated incorrectly because of an assumption on the translator's part that the two different descriptions *are* simply a variation rather than a *distinction*. Most translations have Daniel's interpretation in verse 42 saying that the toes' portion in history would be "partly strong and partly brittle." However, I think that a more *literal* translation is that the toes portion would be partly strong *also* (that there would still be some iron continued in it) **but that its strength would at some point be** *broken,* in other words that the strength of the toes would become finally *disintegrated* and cause everything that the statue stood for to finally collapse in a grand catastrophe! Significantly, to me,[74] the verb form indicating this breakage in verse 42 is the *second form* that I mentioned earlier, first found in verse 35, which indicates a final collapse and *disintegration* of something! So, *very* significantly, the two-part description of the feet and toes, I believe, corresponds *directly* to the two-part destruction process I have already discussed! We are told first that the stone struck the statue, significantly (again), **"on its feet"** (Dan. 2:34) *(not* on the toes portion), indicating that the impact would first cause (in history) a *fracturing* break. And now we are told that *later on,* **at the period in time that *just the toes* stand for** (in the statue's timeline), a final *collapse and disintegration* of whatever the whole statue stands for would take place![75]

The clay and iron narrative ends with one additional comment reiterating that this odd mixture of elements in the feet and toes would *not*

---

73 That the kingdom would become divided into partly strong and partly brittle.
74 I must overuse the word *significantly* in these next few sentences, since I can think of no better word to describe the astounding connections I discovered in the text.
75 I had to overuse the exclamation mark as well! Please excuse me, editors!

ultimately adhere to each other no matter what people might do to try and make them adhere, even though they would for two periods be mixed together. This spells a prophecy of gradually increasing *internal* political trouble during the latter two historical periods of the fourth "kingdom" which it indicates rulers involved would try to ameliorate, possibly[76] through the contracting of mixed marriages between power players of factions at odds, but to no ultimate avail. Such political unions, contracted for the sole purpose of making an alliance, have been used as a Band-Aid® to cover up political wounds since the most ancient of times. But although they are sometimes successful in the short-term, they have seldom succeeded in their purpose for the long haul of history. However, this symbolism of marriage may possibly indicate, just as well (in addition to literal marriages), many other political attempts which are made to mingle races and factions, militarily and otherwise, which rhetorically are also called marriages.[77] Indeed, this rhetorical type of marriage (or simply *genetic* mixing) possibly has the stronger textual support, since in the original language, a word for *marriage* is not actually used, the narrative simply saying, as Young's Literal Translation puts it, that they would be "mixing themselves with the seed of men" (Dan. 2:43). The New International Version, which probably abbreviates too far the *other* direction, simply translates: "the people will be a mixture and will not remain united" (Ibid.).

> *And in [during] the days of **those kings [i.e., the kings of the feet and toes]** the God of heaven [the sky] will set up a kingdom that shall never be destroyed, nor shall this kingdom be left to another people [i.e., it will not be overturned and conquered like all earthly empires]. It shall crush all these kingdoms and bring them to an end, and it shall stand forever.* (Dan. 2:44)

And it shall stand for *how* long? Forever! ***This**,* the **kingdom of God** is what the mysterious stone symbolized!

> *But the stone that struck the statue **became** a great mountain and filled the whole earth.* (Dan. 2:35)

So, God's answer to Nebuchadnezzar's brooding and troubled mind was this mysterious stone, symbolizing a great "kingdom" that

---

76 See the final sentences of this paragraph.
77 And lead to many literal marriages, or at least to the inevitable mingling of human "seed."

someday Daniel's God would set up. It would eventually wipe away Nebuchadnezzar's own realm, and ultimately all those kingdoms following his because it would inherit *how much* of the earth? It would eventually inherit *all* of the earth!

Chapter 8

What Daniel Didn't Tell the King

But where does this mysterious stone come from?
It is on *this* question I was personally surprised during the brutally honest study of Daniel 2 that I made many years ago. The whole study started out by an apparent accident during a private worship time one morning as I was spending quiet time alone with my Creator, flipping through my Bible for something to read and to meditate on. I had never intended my devotional reading to turn into such an in-depth study, a study which I would continue delving into for years to come. As I read my Bible that morning something seemed to jump out at me, almost as if it had been newly inserted into the old narrative, and I thought to myself: "Wait a minute! There is something here that I never *noticed* before!"

We all have biases, don't we? You are probably not alive if you don't have any bias. But we must prayerfully try to minimize biases whenever we come seeking for truth in God's Word. If I was preaching right now, I would ask, "Can I hear an *'amen'?*" Because it's obvious this prophecy is all-encompassing, for a long time I had just assumed, with other intelligent and sincere interpreters, that the mysterious stone in Daniel 2 must simply refer to **the end of the world**, and that that was all the dream meant, that *way* down at the end of time, this stone would smash into the image, everything would be immediately gone, and suddenly—*presto chango!*—the stone would be a mountain covering the whole earth, having destroyed all of the earth's kingdoms forever. And this notion relating to the end of the world couldn't have been *all* wrong either since the stone itself becomes a kingdom that will last for how long? *Forever!* So, I couldn't have been *very* wrong, at least about *the ultimate results* of the stone's impact.

> *[T]he God of heaven [the sky] will set up a kingdom that shall never be destroyed .... and it shall stand forever.* (Dan. 2:44)

This would be an *everlasting* kingdom! Therefore, whatever the stone stands for must at least *include* the end of the world. But my biased mind had wrongly led me to assume that the end of the world was the *only* thing that the stone could possibly symbolize. And because of this conclusion I had always jumped to (along with many other interpreters), I also assumed the stone had just appeared out of nowhere in the dream, maybe out of the sky just like the second coming of Jesus will appear at the end of time.[78] But due to this assumption, many times I had passed right over several important details in the text without giving them a second thought. This is the danger of biased Bible study. We can pass over important details, and we can end up looking truth in the eye and still not be able to see it! As they say, if it was a snake it would bite us. And one early morning the snake *bit* me!

Verse 45 suddenly virtually *jumped* off of the page at me, almost as if I had never read it before!

> *[J]ust as you saw that a stone was cut **from the mountain** not by hands.* (Dan. 2:45)

"*Wait* a minute!" I said to myself. There wasn't any *mountain* mentioned in the *first* telling of the dream—*was* there?

> *As you looked on, a stone was cut out, not by human hands, and it struck the statue on its feet of iron and clay and broke them in pieces [a first fracture].* (Dan. 2:34)

The mountain was not even *mentioned* in verse 34! It simply said that a stone had been cut out from something. It had not indicated from *what* the stone had been cut. Later, I discovered that this seems to be a common practice in the book of Daniel. Important clues are several times left out in a first description, which clues are finally given to the reader in a *second* telling of a dream or vision. I personally think

---

78 See Acts 1:11.

God allowed this to happen on purpose, and here is why. I believe it is because God wants those who discover His truth to be those who *care enough* to search for it!

> *And you will seek Me and find Me, when you search for Me with all your heart.* (Jer. 29:13, NKJV)

This means careless readers will seldom *get* those important clues that happen to be found in the description of a prophetic scene only the second time around. They are like some small towns. If you blink while traveling through them, you miss them. Since a first impression of a thing is always strong, that impression may trick the mind into missing new details later on. It is good psychology. I believe this is also true because Daniel was intended to be a "sealed" book:

> *But you, Daniel, keep the words secret and the book sealed until the time of the end.* (Dan. 12:4)

Even though the actual book (a scroll) was probably never secret (to my knowledge), God wanted to conceal the *meaning* of certain things in it until a certain time in history. I believe He wanted only certain kinds of *believers* to discover the hidden meanings when the time had come for them to be understood. The difference in interpretive results, between those readers who *care enough* to search and those who jump to biased conclusions, will invariably be like that between the fictional bungling detectives of Scotland Yard, and Sherlock Holmes.

> *[J]ust as you saw that a stone was cut **from the mountain** not by hands, and that it crushed the iron, the bronze, the clay, the silver, and the gold. The great God has informed the king what shall be hereafter. The dream is certain, and its interpretation trustworthy.* (Dan. 2:45)

Verse 45 enlarges on the original telling, mentioning for the first time that there was also a *mountain* in this dream. And how was this stone cut out of that mountain? It was cut *without human hands* (verse 34). It is a stone *of godly origins,* rather than merely human, cut out from an earthbound mountain (not from the sky), presumably also of godly origins. It's on this point I believe Daniel knew something very important about the dream which he never told King Nebuchadnezzar! For some reason

Daniel never explained *the mountain* to Nebuchadnezzar. He explained everything else, but why not the mountain? Think about that. I think you'll soon see why telling the king what the mountain meant might not have been a good idea for Daniel at that time. But first we need to understand the mountain's significance.

What do *you* think this mountain symbolizes? It must have some purpose since there are few accidental details in symbolic prophecy. Every detail is there on purpose! So what is it about? I'm convinced that God, in His meticulous care, also does not leave us without *keys* to unlock what the *meaning* of a prophecy is. Proper interpretation of symbolic Bible prophecy is not a guessing game, though many have unfortunately made it seem to be. God always provides a key somewhere for anything He desires us to learn the meaning of. But where should the first place we look in our Bibles be in searching for a key to the mountain in Daniel? Maybe Revelation? Isaiah? Where do you think? How about *Daniel!* A most basic principle of Bible interpretation is to look first in the immediate context of what you are reading for clues to understanding before moving outward in your search. To truly understand *any* writing—ancient or modern—*context* is king! That is why statements from *any* author, taken out of their proper context, can be severely misleading. We should look first in the immediate sentence, then the paragraph, then the section or chapter, then the whole book before finally going elsewhere for answers. And we must consider the *time period* of writing and its contextual history as well. Before we leave *this* author, *Daniel,* we want to see: *is there a mountain in Daniel's book* that can help explain this symbol?

Daniel is the best interpreter of Daniel. And an important historical fact to remember about the book is that it is an *ethnocentric* book from beginning to end. This simply means that everything Daniel thought and wrote was with the beloved kingdom he had been taken captive from in

> *Proper interpretation of symbolic Bible prophecy is not a guessing game, though many have unfortunately made it seem to be. God always provides a key somewhere for anything He desires us to learn the meaning of.*

the back of his mind. As a good Jew,[79] Daniel naturally possessed a kind of national narcissism, if you will. But his Jewish narcissism actually rested on a good foundation, even if it sometimes distorted even the prophet's understanding; you might even say it rested on a *Stone-solid* foundation. Daniel was, in fact, most likely a member of the royal family of Judah.[80] He would therefore possibly be a prince[81] by birth, even though he had been made a eunuch in a foreign court; and *if* so, he would then be of the genetic line of the famous kings David and Solomon. And the kingdom he was possibly a prince of had once been established directly by his God Yahweh! The kingdom of Judah itself had been formed, if you will, "not by human hands!" And God had once promised King David that his throne would be eternal![82] Judah had only recently been conquered by the armies of Babylon, in an age when warfare still had few of the nice restrictions we now take for granted[83] since the Geneva Convention laid down a few international boundaries (not geographical, but behavioral) to what we consider decency in killing! In Daniel's mind, also, the very *purposes* of his God, the God who made both heaven (the skies) and earth, and the only *real* God that exists, were tied up with the fate of the then small kingdom He had established at the crossroads of the ancient world.[84] However, because of His people's ancient and persistent disobedience, Daniel's God had finally allowed Babylon to invade. Daniel was hoping, praying, and believing throughout the book that this traumatic invasion and his people's captivity were only a temporary setback in the progress of God's kingdom, which Daniel believed with all his heart had to still involve Judah somehow, as well as the eternal throne of David! And he was not wrong either, despite his inability to wrap his mind around just how God might keep His ancient promises under the current circumstances. Daniel's ethnocentrism (and possibly the trauma he had already experienced along with other captive Jews) so distorted his perspective

---

79 Simply meaning a patriotic person from the kingdom of Judah at that time period—the general time period when the word "Jew" was apparently coined.
80 See 2 Kings 20:18 and Daniel 1:3.
81 Or at least, a "noble," although the word in Daniel 1:3 that gets translated as "noble" is itself sometimes translated "prince."
82 See 2 Samuel 7, 1 Chronicles 17, and Psalm 89:27–37.
83 See Psalm 137:8–9, although it is possible this description may refer to a later, more brutal, reaction to Judah's persistent revolts.
84 A region that the Romans, in later times, cynically decided to call "Palestine"—as in the land of the *Philistines* (the ancient sworn enemies of the Israelites)—in their effort to distance the sacred land from the by-then-hated Jews, who they (the Romans) had expelled from its once-Jewish capital.

during at least one incident in his book, that I think a revelation about some still far future persecutions of "the holy people" (whom he couldn't conceive being anyone but *his* people) nearly killed Daniel![85] Even the directions of north and south, found later on in the book of Daniel, must be understood by the reader through ethnocentric eyes (in relationship to the land of Judah) in order to make real sense.

When I first noticed the mountain, I had no immediate idea what it might mean, so I became curious. Is there any other place mentioning a *mountain* in Daniel? And after a prayerful search, I was not disappointed! This most sacred mountain that Daniel refers to, in fact, as "[God's] holy mountain" (Dan. 9:16), is mentioned in a prayer of great beauty in chapter 9 which was all about Daniel's people the Jews. It is a prayer of Daniel for mercy; a model prayer of repentance and sorrow for sin, since the reason Daniel's people were in captivity in the first place was that they had been so long unfaithful to God. In it, Daniel passionately pleads with God:

> [L]et your anger and wrath ... turn away from **your city** Jerusalem, **your holy mountain**; because of our sins and the iniquities of our ancestors, Jerusalem and your people have become a disgrace among all our neighbors .... for your own sake ... look at our desolation and **the city that bears your name.** (Dan. 9:16–18)

The mountain, the city of God, was **Jerusalem!** This city, the capital of the kingdom of Judah, mattered **because it bore God's name**—His *reputation!* And what was the reason for Daniel's prayer? He was saying, "God, we bear your name! Have *mercy* on us!" *For your own sake*, help us, because **Your reputation is at stake!**" And notice next, on what *other* basis Daniel asks for God's help and forgiveness:

> We do not present our supplication before you on the ground of our righteousness, but **on the ground of your great mercies**. O Lord, hear; O Lord, forgive; O Lord, listen and act and do not delay! For your own sake, O my God, because your city and your people bear your name! ... I ... was praying... on behalf of **the holy mountain of my God.** (Dan. 9:18–20)

By the way, if you want real success in your prayers, here is a little secret! Don't go to God with the attitude: "I'm so good, God, You've *got* to

---
85 See Daniel 8:27.

listen! I've been performing so *well* today. I've only *eaten* the right things, only *done* the right things, only *gone* the right places, only *said* the right things, and I'm *so much better* than those other hypocrites in church (and I'm *humble* too!), not to mention all the open sinners who don't even go![86] I'm being such a good boy, such a good girl; so You've *got* to listen to me!"

Even the seemingly perfect Daniel doesn't pray on the basis of any righteousness belonging to *him,* but *only* on the basis of God's "great mercies"! And, by the way, I don't believe Daniel actually *was* perfect—a heresy in some minds, I know—though I'm certain he aimed to *perfectly* follow the God he dearly loved! He was *good,* by God's grace, and *mature* in his walk with God, but not *perfect* in the sense that our modern language far too often implies—whether authors utilizing the language intended the implication or not.

Ancient biblical words that get translated as "perfect,"[87] actually are meant to indicate the very different concept of **wholeness, completeness,** or **maturity,** as in a person being "full-grown." To be "perfect," with the problematic *modern* implication, on the other hand, suggests not only that a person never thinks even one bad thought, but also that he or she never, never, *never* makes a mistake! I pity the person who is arrogant enough to make such a presumptuous claim about him or herself, or who thinks he or she must pretend to live up to such a concept, because in my own one-time ignorance of God's saving grace (when I was a new Christian), I once upon a time used to *be* just such a *pretending* person (the *actual* meaning of the word hypocrite, a word used in the Greco-Roman world for play-actors in the theaters). This perfection concept in our culture comes down to us from a lofty notion in Greek philosophy of an absolute ideal that may be conceived of in the human mind, but which, nevertheless, can never be reached in the reality we presently inhabit, and which notion of perfection made ancient Greek philosophers despise the "imperfect" physical world around them. It is the same concept which later on made Christian converts, who began mixing Greek philosophy into their doctrines, start imagining that God, being utterly perfect in this way, must also be unapproachable. This idea, which turned into doctrines, carried with it unpleasant unintended consequences that we will talk more about in a later volume (God willing, and the creek don't rise).

---

86 See Luke 18:11–14.
87 See Matthew 5:48 for example and notice that the context is about loving even those who don't love us.

The prayer of Daniel is evidence that He knew even the *best* of us (i.e., the most complete and *mature*) are still undeserving sinners and are saved *only* by an act of God's kindness, otherwise known as *mercy!* Daniel even uses the pronoun *we* repeatedly throughout his prayer, instead of *they* when he is confessing sin! He humbly identifies *himself* with his people's sin! And on whose behalf was Daniel praying? It was **on behalf of "the holy mountain of [his] God"** (Dan. 9:20). Daniel knew *exactly* what the mountain in the dream had symbolized. It was no mystery to *him!*

The mountain on which Jerusalem was founded is the mountain Daniel was talking about! If you know Bible history, you know that this very city that Daniel had been taken captive from had made itself obnoxious to the Babylonians by rebelling many times, in spite of the fact that the prophet Jeremiah had warned them repeatedly to submit.[88] This history was still happening, and far from being resolved, at the time that Nebuchadnezzar had his first prophetic dream, and future continued rebellious actions of Jerusalem's leaders were yet to make the Babylonians even angrier. The Holy City was yet to be destroyed more completely in the future! But at the time of the dream in Daniel 2, the city had not yet been utterly destroyed. So, you see why it might not have been wise for Daniel to reveal this incendiary detail to the king: that a kingdom which would someday take its origin from the tiny little kingdom which Jerusalem, the symbolic and literal mountain, was capital of, would one day undermine Nebuchadnezzar's and all succeeding empires! Daniel could have lost his head if he had revealed this fact! Not to mention, it may have inspired further destruction of another most important and sacred landmark that still stood upon that mountain at the time of Daniel's interpretation!

I've already mentioned something of Nebuchadnezzar's fanatical patriotism for Babylon, not to mention his temper. And the very next chapter in Daniel serves as a perfect illustration of just how stupid it would have been for Daniel to say to the king: "By the way, *that mountain you saw* in the dream: that's *our* mountain! That's *Jerusalem!* And some day a stone cut out of *our* system is going to undermine everything you and *your* kingdom are about!" Chapter 3, following right on the heels of Daniel's interpretation from God, tells us how at some point following his disturbing dream, King Nebuchadnezzar erected a huge statue which was almost certainly an idea borrowed directly from his dream. But what sort of material do you suppose the king made *his* entire statue out of? It was

---

88 Jeremiah 21:8–10, 27:8–22, 28:11–29:7, 37:7–10, 38:1–3.

made *all* of gold! What was he trying to say? He was saying: *my* kingdom, that head of gold, will never end! The gold will continue not *only* in the head, but all the way throughout history, even down to the toenails, and right into whatever comes after *them!* It sounds very much like the inscription that the same historical king had stamped onto a cuneiform tablet: "Babylon, the delight of my eyes: may you last forever!"[89] "If I can help it, or my *gods,*" he seemed to be saying in rebellion, "I'm not going to let that stone come and undermine what *my* empire is all about, nor destroy our everlasting glory—*ever!*"

This real man Nebuchadnezzar (known to historians as Nebuchadnezzar II) was in a way a lot like all of us. We may at times be genuinely grateful to God for many things, but a battle with other gods still rages (a battle with the god of selfishness) in our proud hearts, and we need the great God to continually change us from the inside out. Nebuchadnezzar's god turned out to be his great city (and empire), the mighty Babylon which he prided himself in, which he thought he could control. He loved mighty Babylon, and it was a splendid city by all ancient accounts. Historians have been right in calling the Neo-Babylonian era that he, the great builder king, helped to usher in, the "golden age" of Babylon. But there was a serious problem with Nebuchadnezzar's great Babylon which the spiritual meaning of the mysterious stone can illustrate.

---

89 See Mark Finley, *Solid Ground* (Hagerstown, MD: Review and Herald, 2003), p. 157.

Chapter 9

The Unhewn Altar Stone

Remember, the stone was to be the seed of a "kingdom" cut out of the mountain that Daniel knew to symbolize Jerusalem, the ancient capital of Judah. What does this tell us about it? The stone had something symbolically to do with the ancient Jews, or more precisely, the ancient representative people of Yahweh, the *Israelites*,[90] of whom the Jews were, by the time of Nebuchadnezzar, the only known remaining political representatives.[91] Elsewhere in Scripture this mountain is called "Mount Zion."[92] It was, since the time of King David, the location of Jerusalem—at first the national capital of the nation of Israel, then of the subdivided southern kingdom of the Israelites called Judah. But there was something else significant about Mount Zion besides the fact that it was the location of the Jewish capital and the governmental seat of their kingdom. This other significant thing can be found hinted at by the description given to the mysterious stone. How was the stone described?

> *As you looked on, a stone was cut out, **not by human hands**.* (Dan. 2:34)

The stone was cut out *how?* And remember, how many details matter in prophecy? It is fascinating to me that there is only one other thing in the whole Old Testament that God declared must *never* be cut

---

90 See Daniel 1:3.
91 For a history of the ancient monarchy once united in Jerusalem, but which split soon after the death of King Solomon, see 2 Samuel through 2 Chronicles.
92 2 Kings 19:31; Psalm 48:2, 48:11, 74:2, 78:68, 125:1; Isaiah 4:5, 8:18, 10:12, 18:7, 24:23, 29:8, 31:4, 37:32; Joel 2:32; Obadiah 1:17, 1:21; Micah 4:7.

using human hands. What do you suppose that was? He said to the ancient Israelites:

> *[I]f you make for me **an altar of stone**, do not build it of **hewn stones**; for if you use a chisel upon it you profane it.* (Exod. 20:25)

An altar of what? Of *stone!* God's system of worship was not to be man-made! The symbolism of a chisel (a tool for human creations) would speak of human wisdom, of human origins, of human ideas, and of merely fallen human opinion.[93] We weak humans see things weakly, selfishly, and imperfectly, but God sees as we cannot see. That is why He said through His prophet Isaiah "[M]y thoughts are not your thoughts, nor are your ways my ways, says [Yahweh]" (Isa. 55:8). This apparently human origin was the serious problem with great Babylon and with its extended empire, as well as with *all* of paganism, which was (and still is), in reality, influenced by other behind-the-scenes spirits who may subtly take possession of, and influence, fallen human spirits if they are not protected by, and in subjection to *God's* Spirit.[94] This is a serious theme relating even to modern religion and government, and we will explore it further in the future. So, the only true God told His children to take only stones from nature as they are found (i.e., cut out by God). Otherwise they would symbolically profane any altar of stone dedicated to Yahweh.

Is it *possible* that the stone in Daniel contains symbolism from an ancient altar of sacrifice? I think it is not only possible, but *probable*, considering what else was also found on Mount Zion! And what *structure* am I speaking about? There was a *temple* upon Mount Zion that was especially sacred to the Jews! It was the especial burden of Daniel's prayer:

> *O Lord … let your anger and wrath … turn away from your city Jerusalem, **your holy mountain** …. let your face shine upon **your desolated sanctuary**.* (Dan. 9:16–17)

So, you see, by the time of Daniel's prayer, Nebuchadnezzar had long before put down repeated rebellions of the Jews, and in that process he had

---

93 It is entirely possible there might be a connection between this concept and the fact that ancient Nazarites (those who consecrated themselves to Yahweh by a vow—see Numbers 6:1–21) were not to use a razor upon their hair. Although the ancient word for Nazarite can also mean "prince" (as in one consecrated and set aside for a special purpose), its root meaning is actually "untrimmed vine," i.e., a vine in its natural state and still unchanged by human innovations.

94 Consider the spiritual battle portrayed in Daniel 10:11–14, 20–21.

finally sent Nebuzaradan, the captain of his bodyguard, to demolish the magnificent temple of God built by King Solomon, along with every other structure of great value yet remaining in Jerusalem, including its walls. This destruction happened during the 19th year of Nebuchadnezzar's reign.[95] Daniel's impassioned prayer had come much *later* in his life than the time of the dream of Daniel 2. His prayer of Daniel 9 came even after the Medo-Persian Empire had already conquered the Babylonians! Nebuchadnezzar and his head of gold had both already been laid to rest by that date, and by then Daniel was an old man filled with a load of grief over the long-continued desolations of his cherished childhood city of Jerusalem, especially of the temple upon Mount Zion which had by then already been destroyed long before! But it had not been so at the time of the story in Daniel 2 which took place during only the second year of Nebuchadnezzar's reign.[96] Just keepin' track of history, I am.

King Solomon's temple[97] that Nebuchadnezzar had destroyed was a structure so magnificent in its time that it was once considered one of the wonders of the ancient world. The special sanctuary services that took place in that bedazzling structure on a daily, seasonal, and yearly basis, all revolved around, and depended upon, one profoundly significant central event which modern people might consider gruesome. What *was* that event—gruesome as it necessarily was *from God's perspective*—without which nothing else could be accomplished in that ancient temple? It was **a bloody sacrifice!** The same kind that for ages had been made upon natural **altars of stone** before an earthly sanctuary had finally been constructed according to plans given to Moses by the great "I Am." It was the repeated literal death of a symbolic (though real) innocent animal on behalf of Yahweh's guilty people, *and*—if prophets of Yahweh mean anything at all—also *on behalf of the whole world.*[98]

---

95 See Jeremiah 52:12–16.
96 See Daniel 2:1.
97 See 2 Chronicles 1–7 and 1 Kings 5–6 for descriptions of its construction and dedication.
98 See Isaiah 56:6–8 and John 1:29, and I *could* give a long list of other references.

Chapter 10

The Mountain of God

To me, the mysterious stone is clearly symbolic of an altar of blood sacrifice as well as of a sanctuary (a temple), and yet it turns out to become a great mountain in the end, symbolic of a great *kingdom*. But *a religious sanctuary*—our modern political minds might subconsciously object—at the center of a political state? Yes, there was a *religious sanctuary* at the center of the ancient Jewish kingdom! And such a concept was universally accepted in the ancient world—the world in which the Jewish kingdom then existed—although even then, clearer-thinking people *always had realized* a practical need for some degree of religious tolerance. Even the Israelites were warned by Yahweh to treat strangers and foreigners in their midst (who would certainly often have different beliefs than the Israelites) with special kindness and hospitality, remembering that they had once been foreigners in a strange land themselves.[99] And even in pagan countries, those who failed to give some measure of religious tolerance inevitably got labeled, in the stream of history, as tyrannical! In my mind, almost certainly some portion at least of the frightful appearance of that monolithic statue in Nebuchadnezzar's dream must relate to such tyrannical persecutions (among *other* governmental abuses) as they happened to Yahweh's own people at one time or another by every single pagan empire that ever came on the ancient scene, and that had any contact with the Israelites or Jews.

In the ancient world every kingdom and city-state had its patron god or gods. To the ancient mind the Jewish religious state was only unusual because their *God,* and some of His requirements, seemed so very unusual from a secular or pagan perspective, as they still often do today. The reason modern politics has providentially (I believe) broken away from those ancient attempts to make religion the basis of secular government has more to do with the unalterable limitations of the imperfect

---

[99] See Exodus 22:21, 23:9; Leviticus 19:34; Deuteronomy 10:19, 24:14.

world we inhabit than with any mistaken notion that God has no claim on human society. Even in America (where I live) **we should be careful about confusing the separation of *church* and state with a deeper separation of *God* and society** which would make our official philosophy akin to the French Revolution's brief and disastrous experiment with official atheism—a precursor, by the way, to the official atheism and atrocities of Communism (has the world learned its lesson yet?). The modern advent of church and state separation was also based upon the conviction (especially in the hearts of often-persecuted Christian reformers whose history helped bring about this separation) that God does not coerce the individual conscience, but wants only freely-given worship based on love and a personal conviction of conscience.[100] The modern history of religion's separation from state policy was born out of the many and great persecutions religious people have endured throughout history (rife with human rights abuses) that will always follow whenever a human government attempts to enforce *any* religion using the power of "the sword," the power of force backed up by the threat of violence. Only if there were a kingdom "not *of* this world,"[101] and not spread or enforced by the power of "the sword,"[102] would the limitations of this world lose their great concern in the equation. Oh! If only there *were* a kingdom that was *in* this world and powerfully influencing it on every level, though not *of* it,[103] not compromising with the coercive methods of human government in a misguided effort to give it power!

The fact is that Yahweh, the God of the ancient Israelites, loves liberty[104] a lot more than some of His ancient (and modern) people realized, and that if His ancient people had trusted *Him,* instead of their *own* understanding,[105] their own government in ancient times would have been politically thousands of years ahead of its time! Even the "kingdoms" of Israel, and then of Judah, as we now know their history, were actually *a concession* to human frailty, mistrust, and failure![106] God's original plan for His representative ambassadorial people had never been to be ruled and judged by a fallen and fallible *human* king. God *Himself* was always intended to be His people's perfect, fair, and *merciful* king, a king who

---

100 See Romans 14:4–5.
101 See John 18:35–37.
102 See Matthew 26:52.
103 See John 17:15–18.
104 Consider Genesis 2:16–17.
105 See Proverbs 3:5–6.
106 See 1 Samuel 8:6–7 and the whole chapter.

would not make the same terrible mistakes in judgment and behavior seen far too often throughout the sad histories we read of human sovereigns! It would have made each citizen a freeman (to use a medieval term) to a degree unheard of in the ancient world, and it would have allowed a great deal of responsible latitude for every individual conscience. Even the practice (still currently followed in many Christian denominations) of paying tithes to God was in ancient times a very tangible acknowledgment that God was the *rightful* king over His people since tithing itself originated from ancient taxation requirements of kings whose subjects owed them the universally understood and accepted obligation of **10 percent** of their increase, for the oversight and protection a king then afforded a population.

King Nebuchadnezzar would have also known that, although the rock grew into a mountain to represent a political "kingdom," **a mountain symbolically represented *more* than a kingdom to ancient people**. Have you ever heard how ancient pagans would build altars on "high places"? This is why Yahweh's ancient prophets condemned the practice of worshiping at the "high places" in the kingdoms of Israel and Judah. It was because these were the locations of a multitude of detestable pagan shrines, and of even more detestable practices (everything from sacrificing and eating forbidden meats and vermin, to self-mutilation, to ritual fertility-cult prostitution, to human sacrifice) that took place at those shrines! It wasn't because elevated places were in and of themselves somehow evil. Yahweh's own temple happened to be located on a prominent high place *itself!* Mountains, hills, and high places represented *worship* to ancient people! Just think about Mount Sinai and of the many *other* mountains even Yahweh used in Old Testament history in His interaction with His people.

The ancient pagan government itself was an extension of religion, as was the kingdom of Judah. So a symbolic mountain representing both a kingdom and a religion at the same time would have made total sense to any ancient king. In fact, when people didn't live *in* mountains in ancient times, they created their *own* mountains—for worship, for burial, or for religious symbolism. **Mountains were seen as a tangible link between earth, the realm of humanity, and the sky, the realm of the gods.** Thus, we have in the *old* world, the many mighty Ziggurats of Mesopotamia (the region of Babylon. The word "Mesopotamia" meaning the land "between the rivers," referring to the Tigris and the Euphrates Rivers) in one valley land, and the great burial pyramids of the Pharaohs in another (the

Nile River Valley). Even later, in the Americas, we find the same religious mountain building instinct in the mound builders of North America as well as in the temple pyramid builders of Central and South America—not to mention the many *other* evidences of mountain symbolism, such as religious communities and human sacrifice burials located on inaccessible and inhospitable peaks in the forbidding Andes mountains.

The fascinating reality we are witnessing is that the entire Jewish religious system, which was the basis of their government, was based upon *a sanctuary system,* a system which had become permanently located on *their mountain*—also a high place. The whole system—as adapted to our fallen circumstance—revolved around the repeated ritual blood sacrifice of an animal that symbolically brought about a thing we call (in English) *atonement.* If we break down that English word used to describe the ancient concept, it fascinatingly captures the beauty of what atonement really brings about between a once-alienated sinner and his or her sinless, and sin-consuming, Creator—a state of ***at-one-ment.***

This atonement—this at-one-ment—was required to forgive violations of Yahweh's most holy law because through violations of that sacred law, oneness with the only true God was deeply broken. An actual state of broken oneness has permeated the atmosphere of our entire world ever since the time of the first fallen humans (our proto-parents[107]) when they first *feared* their loving Father. Yahweh and His alienated and condemned children at that time became no longer *naturally* at-one. Our parents were now in the new and ever-strange state of being outlaws[108] to an unalterable law which, from a purely legal and sterile perspective,[109] demands the sinner's destruction—the breaking off of the breaker of that law:

> *[B]ut God said, "You shall not eat of the fruit of the tree that is in the middle of the garden, nor shall you touch it, **or you shall die.**"* (Gen. 3:3)

By disobedience to God, our first parents had—without fully understanding it all (they were, as yet, children *in experience)*—become sudden outlaws to a law intrinsic to God and to His universe, that was, and is, actually a beautiful law of liberty and love,[110] but that nevertheless—or

---

107 See the early chapters of Genesis.
108 See Romans 8:7.
109 A completely valid, though elementary—oversimplified or *incomplete*—and therefore a somewhat *misleading* way to look at the sin predicament.
110 See James 1:25 and Matthew 22:35–40.

all the more so—became a source of profound grief to our first human parents when they suddenly found themselves condemned by it. Like immature children having been warned not to touch a hot stove lest it burn them, our first parents had been similarly warned not to venture onto God's forbidden ground, or else the result would be certain death! Although death did not complete its promised process instantly, immediately following their disobedience, a death sentence had surely come down upon their heads. And the inevitable dying process (the sidekick of Sin) was already evidenced by a wilting fear that the puzzled pair suddenly felt upon the evening approach of their beloved Friend and Father[111] in whose presence they had previously taken their greatest delight. They must also have been perplexed by the inexplicable feeling of *shame* which made them fear Him, a brand-new emotion that erupted at the point in the story where they suddenly discovered that they were *naked*—exposed to God's now *unwanted* gaze[112]—a subject I will go into more depth on in the next volume!

But lest we imagine this law that demands our destruction to be an arbitrary or *unnecessary* contrivance of God (one of the many subtle lies of Lucifer, no doubt), let me restate what I said earlier, only in a slightly different manner: our parents were now in the new and ever-strange state of being outlaws[113] to an **unalterable law of God's character and universe**—the law of love is a *transcript* of God's character—which demands *sin's* eradication, **because He knows** sin[114] to be the cankerous cancer that it is! It would ultimately undermine all of the "very good" life in His universe (wherever it might be found) if the demand were not so! And this unalterable demand (I think it not a stretch to call it a natural *consequence*) would then mean the natural and inevitable breaking off of any *breaker* of that law of everlasting life, unless a remedy should be made **to separate sin from the sinner**! It would even mean *instant destruction* (if no temporary shielding should be provided for the sinner) from God's sin-consuming presence! God's very unshielded presence would mean *(naturally,* if you will) instant death—both to sin and to any sinners still attached *to* sin. It cannot be any other way:

> *For the LORD [Yahweh] your God is **a devouring fire**.* (Deut. 4:24)

---

111 See Genesis 3:8.
112 See Genesis 3:9–11.
113 See again Romans 8:7.
114 Genesis 2:9 calls the tree Adam and Eve partook of the tree of "the *knowledge* of good and evil."

Here is a tantalizing truth God has revealed about His presence which tells us that sin cannot even remain in existence in the unshielded reality of His glory! But there is nothing arbitrary about this. Nor is this merely the result of an out-of-control emotion on God's part, a bad temper, or anything similar to capricious human anger, though God (the author of emotion) clearly *does* also have and expresses profound emotions regarding evil (if you don't believe this, read the prophets!). God's "wrath,"[115] however, is much more intrinsic and profound a concept and reality, separate and distinct from mere emotion as *we* often experience emotion. The above statement from Deuteronomy, though it is a dire warning, was not a *threat,* so much as it was (like God's warning to Adam and Eve) simply **a factual description about God's profound nature.** Even Moses (one of God's favorites, if you will, though also a fallen human) was told in a friendly manner by Yahweh:

> [Y]ou cannot see my face; for **no one shall see me and live.** (Exod. 33:20)

This verse clearly demonstrates that there is nothing arbitrary about the sin-consuming fire of God! If this sin-consuming portrayal is the reality of God's profound presence, then we may view the very separation from God, which the human race experienced upon the entrance of sin—and even the new emotion of fear that had entered Adam and Eve's hearts upon the approach of God's presence—as actual **measures of** *mercy* **that God had long before built into nature to shield our first parents and to shield us** from inevitable destruction! Even the negative experiences we now routinely experience, such as harsh defense mechanisms, emotional walls, and pain may also be seen as providential elements of nature meant for coping, which God foresaw would be necessary in our new sin-infested environment, an environment that is now rife with danger in every direction we turn. And despite the deep sadness such a separation has brought into the heart of God our *Father,* it was (and it still *is*) a necessary consequence if we are to be protected from the "devouring fire" long enough to experience the deep plan of salvation that He had from eternity already prepared in order to deal with such an overwhelming expediency.[116] But the separating shield and the concealing clouds He now communicates with us from are the polar opposite of the at-one-ment He has always

---

115 A subject I hope to deal with more completely in another volume.
116 I will speak more about this plan in chapter 17.

longed for, and for which we still (in spite of sin) also long for at a subconscious level without our always realizing what our unspeakable longings deep down are actually all about (the ones we often vainly try to fill up with drivel). When the source of all life turned His face away from us that fateful day in order to shield us (and our environment), nature itself wilted with horror as the curse of natural consequences—like an onrushing train that cannot be stopped—cast its vaporous pall over Eden. That great and almost inexpressible intervention God had long before planned, would now be required to intercede on behalf of the impossibly (from *our* perspective) fallen race and planet.

A copy of that sacred law of Yahweh—which expresses the very heart of our God which is love[117]—was located inside of the Holy of Holies, the inner sanctum of the ancient sanctuary on Mount Zion. It was in the very spot where a manifestation of God's sin-consuming presence had also once dwelt (consuming only to what is unloving and destructive to the principles of everlasting life); a presence Jews call the Shekinah glory. How would *you* like to be around God's very presence once again, I wonder? What if you could do it without any fear or without any lingering feelings of guilt and shame?! Today we call that law, once found in the Holy of Holies, the Ten Commandments. Those commandments, originally contained on two tablets of stone, were deposited in the sacred golden ark of the covenant underneath its ornate symbolic lid that served as God's throne.[118] In some English versions of the Bible, this cover is called the *"mercy* seat," but in ancient Hebrew the name for it meant literally a "place of ransom for life."[119] We sometimes think of the Ten Commandments as merely a list of rules, but they may be better understood as the ten principles of everlasting life, or of love to God and to humanity.[120]

The symbolic location of ransom, or of *atonement,* directly over that spot where Yahweh's law was anciently contained speaks silently, but profoundly, of the intrinsic connection between our God's law and His grace. The person who has violated the principles of everlasting life becomes subject to the deep natural consequence of death (which necessary consequence is beyond our ability to *fully* comprehend), and a ransom becomes required to restore that person back to everlasting *life.* That person then needs *mercy;* she or he needs a *cover* over sin (a "mercy seat," if you will)

---

117 See 1 John 4:8.
118 Exodus 25:16, 21–22, 30:6, 32:15–16 (this one refers to the two tables (tablets) of the "testimony."
119 It comes from the root כפר (kopher), which means "ransom for life."
120 See Matthew 19:17 and Matthew 22:36–40.

as his or her shield between the demands of that unchangeable law of Yahweh's character (a law every bit as real as gravity) and Yahweh's sin-consuming presence. But that desperately needed mercy has always had a profound price tag attached to it, and that price tag was symbolized in the ancient sanctuary services by the lifeblood of an innocent sacrificed animal. On a yearly occasion called the Day of Atonement that blood was brought by a symbolically sanctified priest into the sacred first compartment of the sanctuary to symbolically cleanse away all traces of symbolic guilt from everything that was contained inside of it. Finally, after all else had been cleansed, that blood of cleansing was then taken into the innermost sanctum, the Holy of Holies, and was solemnly sprinkled upon that sacred spot (situated above the law and below God's presence) to symbolize the completion of a long-prophesied costly ransom for human life.

But what was the deeper purpose of the ransom, or of the at-one-ment, that was symbolically completed at this spot? What was the deeper purpose of all the sacred symbols involved in Yahweh's sanctuary (which we will explore in more detail in a later volume)? The answer goes to the heart of the original purpose of the sanctuary, to the heart of Yahweh and of His unchangeable law, and to the purpose of the mountain on which the temple stood. God gave the reason for the sanctuary's construction when He originally instructed the Israelites to build it. *Here* is His stated purpose:

> *And have them make me a sanctuary,* **so that I may dwell among them**. (Exod. 25:8)

The heart of God that constitutes His glory,[121] is not *just* love in a general sense or merely a love for the lovely and the deserving. It is love specifically for *us* who have fallen from the *principles* of love! It is *personal!* And in this beautiful symbolic picture, His love for lost *sinners* even triumphs over the demands of His justice (which is, ironically, also an outgrowth of His deep love)! This says that even though we have fallen, God desperately wants you and me to be together with Him as we were always *meant* to be, in His powerful presence once more without any lingering feelings of fear and shame concerning our pardoned pasts! He wants this wonderful reality far more than even *we* might long for it! The mountain was important because it was God dwelling *with* His fallen people again! It represented a promise that ought to be spelled with a capital P! *The*

---

121 See Exodus 33:18–23.

Promise of the ages! A whole system symbolizing untold oodles of potential made possible only by God with us: Emmanuel![122] It meant the reverse of the curse! But because God's people had sinned, and because we all exist in a fallen world, this was only possible—in our *present* existence—through a great sacrifice that the slaying of innocent animals had symbolized for thousands of years before Christ (BC), sacrifices that pointed forward to an *actual* sacrifice for sin. They were collectively the antitype that merely reflected a future type, a reality still to come. "God with us" was the desire of Daniel's prayer in Daniel 9! The great pain in Daniel's heart had been the ruin of his city where the temple of "God with Us" had once stood!

> *The heart of God that constitutes His glory, is not just love in a general sense or merely a love for the lovely and the deserving. It is love specifically for us who have fallen from the principles of love! It is personal!*

It has always been thus: that the greatest loss from sin is not that we are lost *merely*, but (whether we can recognize it or not) it is the experience of being cut off from our God, our Creator, our ultimate *Source*, our *Father*. It is being *separated* from God! So the wise men of Nebuchadnezzar had actually been telling a partial truth when they said, "The gods don't dwell with mortals!" (Dan. 2:11, paraphrase). They were telling a partial truth because we have been *separated;* we have been cut off from Yahweh's direct presence! Even God's own temple was filled with unfortunate, but necessary, barriers, cutting people off from God for their own protection. Even though God dwelt among His people, there still had to be barriers and walls through which average humans dared not go, and even the most devoted and sanctified priests dared not go beyond them unless they were properly cleansed symbolically (standing in for a greater reality) by that sacrificial blood.

---

122 See Matthew 1:22–24.

Chapter 11

"The *Kingdom* of God"

Yahweh's earthly sanctuary was an imperfect dwelling, but its symbols, which filled Solomon's temple, held the promise of a much greater reality that it all foreshadowed—and what was that reality? It was:

> *Behold! The Lamb of God who takes away the sin of the world!* (John 1:29, NKJV)

In the New Testament we see everything that has to do with cleansing by blood in the Old Testament represents *whom*? It represents *Jesus*[123] and His sacrifice on the cross of Calvary! But if that's true, then my mind is racing wildly since I remember words that were once obscure to me! The stone from *this* mountain was to grow into *what*? It was to grow into *God's kingdom!* But on reflection, I realize the symbols of this kingdom were all about *whom*? They were all about *Jesus*! And I truly believe He was the "Lamb," the great sacrifice of Yahweh, who takes away the sin of the whole world! What was it I've read so many times about "the kingdom of God" in the New Testament but that I never quite understood? I think that if many other Christians would honestly think about it, they too would admit they've never quite fully[124] understood that phrase "the kingdom of God" either.

Notice what phrase we find Jesus using at the very opening of His earthly ministry:

> *Now after John was arrested, Jesus came to Galilee, proclaiming the good news [gospel] of God, and saying,* **"The time is fulfilled**, *and* **the kingdom of God has come near;** *repent, and believe in the good news [gospel]."* (Mark 1:14–15)

---

123 See Hebrews 9 and 10.
124 I think *quitefully* would be a most unique, new compound English word, don't *you*?

What specifically did Jesus say the good news—or gospel—was? The gospel message—the good news—was, *and still is,* that "the time is fulfilled, and the kingdom of God has come near"! Of course, we have to understand what that *means* to us. He says, "repent, and believe in the good news," but good news about *what?* It is good news about the "kingdom of God"! Jesus comes to the earth and claims that the prophetic kingdom spoken about in Daniel 2 has, at the time of His first coming, already come near! The phrase, "the time is fulfilled," refers to a famous time prophecy in the book of Daniel, which we will examine in a later volume. It is only logical to assume Jesus is alluding to the same kingdom of God predicted in the dream of Daniel 2 as well!

> *What specifically did Jesus say the good news—or gospel—was? The gospel message—the good news—was, and still is, that "the time is fulfilled, and the kingdom of God has come near"!*

How many modern Christians connect these kingdom references together? We need to realize that the "kingdom" concept is not something Jesus just invented out of the blue, or that He had pulled out of a historical vacuum like a magician pulling a rabbit from an empty hat. No, He was referring to well-known scriptural prophecies, and especially to the time prophecies of Daniel that He was very fond of alluding to (in more ways than most people actually notice)! The coming "kingdom of God" was a deeply ingrained concept that people regularly talked about in those days,[125] and that they sort of understood too, even though gross misconceptions had grown up around the concept. In fact, reading the gospels with an eye open to the pregnant phrase, one might gain the impression that there was even a "kingdom of God" craze going on among the people of Yahweh at the time that Jesus collided with our world! It was a promised-something that every devoted Jew or "God-fearer"[126] had long been yearning for and looking forward to. And now, still newly under the galling yoke of rigorous Roman rule and its sapping policy of universal taxation, the appeal of a liberated kingdom had become stronger than ever to these expectant people. The phrase "kingdom of God" or "kingdom of heaven" (as

---

125 See Mark 15:43.
126 Any ancient Gentile who believed in the Jewish Scriptures, and who worshiped the Jewish God.

these are interchangeable phrases in the New Testament) is found all over the gospels, and throughout the New Testament. However, most Christians don't seem to connect the phrase to the prophecy in Daniel that it comes most directly from!

It is no wonder that many people don't see "good news" in prophecy—"Oh, that's just *scary* stuff!" they say—because too often there is, I believe, a disconnect between *Jesus* and **the awesome prophecies that Jesus *alone* fulfills**! Luke also quotes on this line:

> *The law and the prophets were in effect until John came;* **since then the good news of the kingdom of God is proclaimed.** (Luke 16:16)

This John (in the text) refers to John the baptizer who was the forerunner to Jesus. He proclaimed the Messiah at hand, and he is the prophet who baptized Jesus in the Jordan River after recognizing Him as the promised One through the agency of the Holy Spirit, thus initiating Jesus' earthly ministry. Jesus Himself tried with many illustrations to disabuse the people of misconceptions they held about the "kingdom of God," and at the same time He gave them more than subtle hints as to what, or *whom*, it was *really* all about:

> *Once Jesus was asked by the Pharisees when the kingdom of God was coming, and he answered, "The kingdom of God is not coming with things that can be observed; nor will they say, 'Look, here it is!' or 'There it is!' For,* **in fact, the kingdom of God is among you.**" (Luke 17:20–21)

It isn't coming with things that can be observed! In other words, it is not *earthly* armies conquering; but neither is Jesus here referring to His *second* coming—He *cannot* be—which He very clearly states will be observable to all people like lightning flashing from one end of the sky to the other![127] And when Jesus said "the kingdom of God is *among* you," *who* do you suppose He was talking about? That phrase "among you" (literally, "in your midst") is also sometimes translated *"within you,"* and I think it also *can* carry that connotation through the agency of His Holy Spirit.[128] What I mean by that, is that the "kingdom of God" is a rule of love that truly exists and grows *within* human hearts

---
127 See Matthew 24:27.
128 See Matthew 28:18–20.

and minds rather than being contained by geographical boundaries of the earth. When the human subjects of Christ's kingdom move from one geographical location to another, so does His *kingdom* because His kingdom—His *rule*—exists *inside of them*. However, other statements Jesus makes about "the kingdom" also indicate that by that phrase He was clearly referring to *His own presence* that was in their very midst 2,000 years ago, not (at that time) *through* the Holy Spirit merely, but *physically*. When Jesus commissioned seventy missionaries to go ahead of Him to announce Him in towns and places He intended to visit, part of the instructions He gave them were:

> [C]ure the sick who are there, and say to them, "**The kingdom of God has come near to you.**" But whenever you enter a town and they do not welcome you, go out into its streets and say, "Even the dust of your town that clings to our feet, we wipe off in protest against you. **Yet know this: the kingdom of God has come near.**" (Luke 10:9–11)

Those who assume (as I once did) that the stone's collision with the image in Daniel 2 was to happen way down at the end of earthly time (I used to think of it as the toenails of time) will inevitably ask themselves the same bewildering question I once asked myself, if they allow themselves to pay *too* close attention[129] to the actual words of Jesus! How could the "kingdom of God" have already come near—as Jesus emphatically stated—nearly 2,000 years ago? "But-but-but-" — changing minds will inevitably stutter — "doesn't the stone *have to* represent the end of the world and all earthly kingdoms since no earthly kingdom follows (overthrows) it?" I would answer here, as I mentioned earlier, that yes, in fact, it must *include* the end of the world, but I will also add this: **the stone symbol can*not* represent *only* the end of the world** if it represents not only

> **"**
> **The stone symbol cannot represent only the end of the world if it represents not only a single event, but a Person! That person is Jesus, the promised Messiah, the long-promised deliverer God-king!**
> **"**

---

129 *Too* close for *comfort*.

a single *event*, but a *Person!* That person is *Jesus,* the promised Messiah, the long-promised deliverer God-king!

> *For a child has been born for us, a son given to us; authority rests upon his shoulders; and he is named Wonderful Counselor,* **Mighty God***, Everlasting Father, Prince of Peace.* **His authority shall grow continually,** *and there shall be endless peace for* **the throne of David and his kingdom.** *He will establish and uphold it with justice and with righteousness* **from this time onward and forevermore.** *The zeal of [Yahweh] of hosts [armies] will do this.* (Isa. 9:6–7)

Just as Nebuchadnezzar was told by Daniel that he *himself* was the head of gold, which symbol represented his "kingdom" of Babylon, so Jesus is also identified directly with *His* kingdom, which he told Pilate was not *of* this world:

> *Jesus answered,* **"My kingdom is not of this world.** *If My kingdom were of this world, My servants would fight, so that I should not be delivered to the Jews; but now* **My kingdom is not from here."** (John 18:36, NKJV)

But His kingdom was to be very much *in* this world, and profoundly influential throughout world history, to the point that the whole world—in spite of itself, and despite a demonic controversy raging against the kingdom, and despite the never-absent faults of its imperfect ingrafted[130] human subjects—**now even measures time itself in direct reference to the stone's strike upon the statue (I'm getting ahead of myself again, but this time only *just*)!**

Prophecy is not meaningless trivia, nor is it just about events of history, nor is it only about the end of time. Prophecy centers ultimately around a *Person,* and around His supreme sacrifice for the whole world, around His tireless efforts to win back battered beings who have been taken captive from birth by a deceiving, destroyer despot! Therefore, the "kingdom of God," that is the foundation stone upon which Bible prophecy is built, is not merely about politics. It too is about a *Person,* and about the prisoners[131] He came to rescue from an enemy kingdom by His unspeakable sacrifice because of His unspeakable love for them! It is about the historical

---
130 See Romans 11:17–24.
131 See John 8:34–36.

reconquest of *soul territory* through which the good news about this liberating love gets spread into all of the world (the entire realm claimed by the rival king) to usher in the fullness of its fruits (its rescued subjects) for Jesus, the rightful and worthy king, to receive[132] as the final *fullness* of His "kingdom" at His second coming! That is *more* than a mouthful.

> And this **good news of the kingdom** will be proclaimed throughout the world, as a testimony to all the nations. (Matt. 24:14)

> ***It is not good news about only the second coming event that is being proclaimed throughout the world, it is the good news about Jesus Himself!***

It is not good news about only the *second* coming event that is being proclaimed throughout the world, it is the good news about *Jesus Himself!* Therefore the kingdom *cannot* be something we experience only *after* His second coming!

Perhaps as a mere matter of interest, I might mention that I did a word study on the New Testament phrase "kingdom of God" that was used so often by Jesus, and on its origins in the Old Testament. What I discovered was that although *the concept* is clearly found throughout much of the Old Testament prophetic record, similar *wording,* using the actual word for "**kingdom**" in direct association with the generic word for "**God**," is confined exclusively to the book of Daniel. That nearly identical wording is, in fact, found throughout Daniel, and the very origin of the kingdom concept *in* Daniel happens to be the dream found in Daniel 2! The closest any of the other prophetic books comes to the exact phrasing Jesus used is the powerful Messianic prophecy found in Isaiah 9:7. That prophecy does *not* refer to the "kingdom" of "God" specifically, but to the "kingdom" of the promised Messiah prince, which ancient peoples may or may not have automatically equated with God since their understanding of the Godhead (as most Christians now understand it) was rather limited to say the least. Another interesting fact is that the "God" in Daniel, whose kingdom the stone would become, was specifically described to Nebuchadnezzar as the "god of heaven [the sky]" (Dan. 2:37, 2:44), a fact that may account for the variation of the interchangeable New Testament phrase: "kingdom of heaven

---
132 See Daniel 7:13–14.

[sky]." What this all means, unless I am mistaken, is that the very word "kingdom," which many Christians banty about as an often-nebulous reference to Christianity itself, is being used by most without even a thought of the stone in Daniel 2, which it originally referred to.

What *do* we mean when we talk about "the kingdom"? And what did Jesus intend when, even though He had stated that the kingdom was already among His hearers, He still taught His disciples and us to pray: *"Thy kingdom come. Thy will be done in earth, as it is in heaven"* (Matt. 6:10, KJV)?

As is the case with many profound truths, some ambiguity exists in the New Testament over the use of the word "kingdom," and over the "kingdom" concept. Sometimes Jesus seems to use the word one way, and at other times He seems to use it another. It is no wonder if average Christians sometimes find it hard to nail down the word's exact meaning. But Jesus' use is very purposeful, and the ambiguity itself reveals a deeper truth about the "kingdom of God."

Real truth about God is often complex (such as the Trinity doctrine, for instance), and this should not surprise us at all since trying to understand God, His existence, and His purposes, might be akin to our trying to describe *our* existence and purposes to an ant. Even if an ant *could* talk with us, it might have a very hard time conceiving of things from our comparatively massive perspective. Ease of oversimplification, and of conceiving, is usually a hallmark of human error, not of deep truths about God. There are exceptions, of course (especially in the case of ancient Gnosticism), and this obviously does not mean complexity equals truth. But it is why I've always felt that "Keep it simple, stupid!" is a *stupid* motto for the genuine study of God. The real challenge is to gain a glimpse of God in all the complexity His revelation will allow, and to do it for the sake of our love for *Him!* Only *then* should we try to share that vision of truth with others in the simplest possible way, but without dumbing it down to utter insignificance.[133] I think if this process was followed more often, then those speaking to others about God, even to children, would have something much more profound to say *about* Him than is often said. There are souls of all ages hungering for just such a communication. Please don't sell short anyone who can communicate.

Many times, when Jesus talks about the "kingdom of God," He is clearly talking about things that are coming in our world right now, such

---

133 The especial fault, in my opinion, of a certain class of animated children's "Bible" videos—I use the term "Bible" quite loosely here—on the Christian market in the last several decades.

as when He compared the kingdom's influence to yeast that has been mixed into a lump of bread dough (our world), which from small beginnings eventually leavens the whole lump.[134] But sometimes it seems to be clearly referring to an altogether *otherworldly* experience. One of the clearest examples I can think of (unless I am seriously misinterpreting) is when Jesus, at His last supper, pointed His ancient disciples (and us) forward to the "blessed hope"[135] of His second coming, with His promise:

> *Truly I tell you, I will never again drink of the fruit of the vine until that day when I drink it new in the kingdom of God.* (Mark 14:25)

If we pay closer attention to *all* of his "kingdom" references, we will see that all together they paint a picture of a process and progress toward an end goal which requires time to fully achieve. No parable is perfect in all its parts because a parable is a simile, not an exact description. It is a comparison with limited points of similarity (often just one) such as when a mother says, "My son is growing like a weed." That mother would not be suggesting that her son was in every way like a weed, or that his growth had the ability to produce flowers and thorns on his head, for instance, but only that her son is growing rapidly just as weeds grow rapidly. Therefore, Jesus used many different imperfect similes to try to describe various important aspects of His kingdom. The kingdom is like a sower sowing seed, for instance, but on that account, a farmer's crop necessarily takes *time* to grow before a harvest can be fully reaped, just as the stone in Daniel 2 necessarily had to grow in order to become a mighty mountain. Or how about this one:

> Therefore He said: *"A certain nobleman went into a far country to receive for himself a kingdom and to return."* (Luke 19:12, NKJV)

Jesus is clearly the person the symbolic nobleman is supposed to represent—though in the imperfect manner of a parable (a simile, not an exactness)—and the message in this sentence says something His expectant hearers badly needed to hear (see verse 11), that even though Jesus was a rightful king already, and even though His kingdom had come near

---

134 See Luke 13:20–21.
135 See Titus 2:13.

through His presence and incarnation,[136] it would still require *time* for Jesus to "receive" the fullness of His kingdom! The Jews of Christ's day would have been quite familiar with the process of a nobleman who had come into a "kingdom," having to travel to a far country before receiving his political prize, since the Jewish nation was at that time under the thumb of the Roman government which happened to be headquartered in the far country of the Italian peninsula.

However, part of the reason for the delay in Christ's receiving *His* kingdom (the point where the reality veers from the simile) has to do with the fact that *His* kingdom would not be made up of mere territory, but of *people,* and that His *true* kingdom does not wish to capture subjects by force, but rather by winning their hearts and their minds! This takes time because His true rule is to be inside of the mind and heart of each of His kingdom's human subjects.[137] In the meantime, not at all unrelated to this time-delayed receiving process, His servants were to be entrusted with His kingdom's treasure—a treasure that fascinatingly is placed by His Holy Spirit within His very servants as if **they are the true treasure chests, the receptacles of His very treasure**,[138] if Christianity has historically interpreted the parable correctly. In the version found in Matthew 25, that treasure is called *talents*. A talent was originally a monetary unit, and only *symbolic* in the parable of personal spiritual gifts, which we now label as "talents" even in secular contexts such as "talent" shows. Every time we use the word *talent,* it is a testimony to the profound effect of this parable (and *also* of the "kingdom of God") on even our language. The servants were to invest their "talents" and cause the treasure found only within *people* to increase! This is the servants' part in building up the fullness of the kingdom, part of the reason time would be required. And, of course, these investments of the nobleman's servants, which cause an increase in His "kingdom's" wealth, also correlate to the expanding work of the yeast in the previously mentioned kingdom simile. They are both really about the acquisition, not of money, nor of bread dough, but *of human beings*, of precious soul subjects being added to the growing kingdom, and who are being transformed by His amazing grace[139] into the likeness of His own goodness that is rooted in love!

---

136 See John 1:14.
137 See Hebrews 8:10–12.
138 See 2 Corinthians 4:7.
139 See Ephesians 2:8–10.

Just for a matter of demonstration, let me quote a few of the tantalizing "kingdom of God" remarks of Jesus that can be found in varying contexts throughout the gospels:

> But if it is by the Spirit of God that I cast out demons, then <u>the kingdom of God has come to you</u>. (Matt. 12:28)

> He also said, "<u>The kingdom of God</u> is as if someone would scatter seed on the ground, and would sleep and rise night and day, and the seed would sprout and grow, he does not know how. The earth produces of itself, first the stalk, then the head, then the full grain in the head. But when the grain is ripe, at once he goes in with his sickle, because the harvest has come." (Mark 4:26–29)

> He also said, "With what can we compare <u>the kingdom of God,</u> or what parable will we use for it? It is like a mustard seed, which, when sown upon the ground, is the smallest of all the seeds on earth; yet when it is sown it grows up and becomes the greatest of all shrubs, and puts forth large branches, so that the birds of the air can make nests in its shade." (Mark 4:30–32)

> But he said to them, "I must proclaim <u>the good news of the kingdom of God</u> to the other cities also; for I was sent for this purpose." (Luke 4:43)

> I tell you, among those born of women no one is greater than John [the baptizer]; yet the least in <u>the kingdom of God</u> [**i.e., those living in the greater light of Jesus, or Christianity**[140]] is greater than he. (Luke 7:28)

> Soon afterwards he went on through cities and villages, proclaiming and bringing <u>the good news of the kingdom of God</u>. (Luke 8:1)

> [A]nd he sent them out <u>to proclaim the kingdom of God</u> and to heal. (Luke 9:2)

> But Jesus said to him, "Let the dead bury their own dead; but as for you, <u>go and proclaim the kingdom of God</u>." (Luke 9:60)

> Instead, <u>strive for his kingdom,</u> and these things will be given to you as well. (Luke 12:31)

---

140 See, again, Luke 16:16.

> *People will come from east and west and north and south, and will take their places at the feast in <u>the kingdom of God</u>.* (Luke 13:29, NIV)
>
> *Jesus answered, "Very truly, I tell you, no one can enter <u>the kingdom of God</u> without being born of water and Spirit."* (John 3:5)
>
> *And he said to them, "Truly I tell you, there is no one who has left house or wife or brothers or parents or children, <u>for the sake of the kingdom of God,</u> who will not get back very much more **in this age, and in the age to come** eternal life."* (Luke 18:29–30)

OK, so that's more than a *few*, but I think the demonstration speaks for itself. Actually, I think the scriptural demonstration presents a withering argument that delegating the stone and its kingdom of God to only *after* the second coming of Jesus is a profound misunderstanding, not only of prophecy, but of the fundamental mission of Jesus, as well as of the proper identification of Christianity! Despite its tares (weeds),[141] and tears (as in the tearing of a cloth), and tears (as in weeping), true Christianity *is* the "kingdom come" in at least one sense—in the sense of its being the growing **kingdom of God's glorious grace***!* And though a joyful change will take place in it, it will not be a different kingdom of *people* from **the kingdom of God's gracious glory** that will be ushered in at the second coming! Gracious to those receiving it because they know all too well their own unworthiness, and just how profoundly naked they would appear to gazing eyes if their sins had not been covered up forever by the robe of Christ's own righteousness,[142] but not to those who will call to the rocks and to the mountains to hide them and their exposed nakedness at that time[143] because they have so long refused the King's gracious, pleading offers of healing and life.

I was making a bit of a play on words in the previous paragraph because authors and theologians who recognize this two-phase nature of the "kingdom of God" have often labeled its two phases as **the "kingdom of grace"** and **the "kingdom of glory."** However, as fitting as these imperfect labels are (labels are almost *always* imperfect representations—of people and also of God's purposes), there is glory, too, in His kingdom of grace, and there will certainly be grace in His kingdom of glory! An example of this labeling is found in a very old book called *Thoughts from the Mount of Blessing*:

---

141 See Matthew 13:27–30.
142 See Zechariah 3:1–7.
143 See Revelation 6:15–16.

> *The kingdom of God's grace is now being established, as day by day hearts that have been full of sin and rebellion yield to the sovereignty of His love. But the **full establishment** of the kingdom of His glory will not take place until the second coming of Christ to this world.*[144]

I think that misgivings about the perfection of these labels is even evident in the way this author carefully worded her *own* statement, by inserting the moderating adjective "full," instead of simply stating that the establishment of the kingdom of His glory would not take place until the second coming. But the labels do serve the important purpose of helping us to think about, and to make distinctions between, the phases of **His-story**. I added a dash and an extra "s" in history because, whether some like to admit it or not, history *is* all ultimately (my own moderating *adverb*) about *Him*. It is *His* story!

Another way to think about this division of kingdom history is that we now live in the midst of a still-occurring colossal collision (a great *controversy*, if you will) between two worlds, so that even though the new world of God's everlasting kingdom has already arrived, and has been steadily increasing in its own unobservable manner[145] for centuries, yet at the same time the old undermined world of sin and death is still spinning 'round and 'round, and is still putting up a fantastic fight in the process, against the swirling elements of the new world. The old world is putting up a literally demonic fight, the likes of which only the powers of hell can, to retain its own deceived soul subjects, and to discourage, by means of deceptive appearances, the saved subjects of the already—but not yet *visibly*—victorious new world! This puts the "kingdom" in the tension-filled reality of being **already, but not yet**. You might also think about it as overlapping ages that we are now living in. It is our place to decide inside of our hearts, and with our own God-given minds, just which one of these ages we will believe in, attach our fondest devotion and allegiance to, and throw our "talents" into supporting! And we must not let the strivings and worries of our lives consume our energies to the point that we end up neglecting the urgency of the kingdom's call! Jesus warned about this danger in a famous passage where He also gave His hearers a wonderful promise we can cling to when worries of life overwhelm us:

---

[144] E. G. White, *Thoughts From the Mount of Blessing* (Mountain View, CA: Pacific Press, 1896), p. 108, emphasis mine.
[145] See Luke 17:20–21.

> *No one can serve two masters .... Therefore do not worry, saying, "What will we eat?" or "What will we drink?" or "What will we wear?" For it is the Gentiles who strive for all these things; and indeed your heavenly Father knows that you need all these things. But strive first for the kingdom of God and his righteousness, and all these things will be given to you as well.* (Matthew 6:24, 31–33)

In a world war it is hard for anyone anywhere to remain neutral forever. So it is, and will be, for all of us, as this other kind of world war becomes more and more universally recognized. There will come a time for all when we cannot escape finally making a decision one way or another, to follow one world or the other, to live our lives for one age or for the other. Ignoring the issues will no longer be an option. I have heard that the famous evangelist Billy Graham most aptly stated our modern situation (a situation in which we are saturated with Bibles, and in which there is existing at least a secondhand knowledge of the profound claims of Christianity throughout the world) when he once told a large gathering of hippies that there is one question no person in the modern world can avoid or escape finally answering. It is the question: What will I do with this Man called Christ?! We can try harder and harder to ignore Him, we can reject Him and His message by calling Him a liar or a lunatic—because only a lunatic or a liar would make the claims He made, unless they were true. Or we can finally bow at His royal, pierced feet in gratitude for the unmerited favor (grace) He bought us through that unfathomable blood sacrifice of Himself and call Him by the very same title that got nailed in three languages to the head of His cross: [146] *king!*

> *"I have other sheep that do not belong to this fold. I must bring them also, and they will listen to my voice. So there will be one flock, one shepherd. For this reason the Father loves me, because I lay down my life in order to take it up again. No one takes it from me, but I lay it down of my own accord. I have power to lay it down, and I have power to take it up again. I have received this command from my Father." Again the Jews were divided because of these words.* **Many of them were saying, "He has a demon and is out of his mind. Why listen to him?"** *Others were saying, "These are not the words of one who has a demon. Can a demon open the eyes of the blind?"* (John 10:16–21)

---

146 See John 19:19–22.

Chapter 12

Ancient Hints of Hope

Reevaluating the symbolic meaning of the stone in Daniel 2 is not an either/or proposition. If we look deeply enough into the matter, it is not a choice between the stone's symbolizing either the *first* coming of Jesus or the *second* coming of Jesus, the kingdom of grace or the kingdom of glory. It is a *both/and* proposition because understood in its fullness, this prophecy is not merely about *events!* **The *stone* (in all its phases)—just like the sacrificial system that it was symbolically cut out of—is simply symbolic of Jesus, *period*, in *all* His fullness! End of story, *fullness of His-story!***

The stone is symbolic of Jesus, and of the good news—the *hope*—of Christianity. If there is any accuracy at all to one of the claims Jesus' accusers made concerning a statement Jesus once made—and I think there *is*[147]—then Jesus was tantalizingly not referring only to His *second* coming when He once not-so-subtly connected *Himself* with the famous prophecy of the stone/kingdom in Daniel chapter 2, which stone/kingdom had been famously prophesied to be cut out of the spiritually symbolic mountain of Nebuchadnezzar's dream "**not by human hands**"! [148]

> *We heard him say, "I will destroy this temple [the physical building*[149]*] that is made with hands, and in three days [most probably <u>prophetic</u> days, i.e., years*[150]*] I will build another, **not made with hands**." (Mark 14:58)*

---

147 I think they were most probably essentially accurate about the *words* Jesus had used; they simply failed to understand Jesus' cryptic *intentions* for those words. They were, whether deviously or ignorantly, trying to take His words hyper-literally, just as far too many Bible interpreters *still* try to take many aspects of prophetic *symbolism* hyper-literally.
148 See again Daniel 2:34.
149 Most representative, in Christ's day, of the religious system once symbolized by "the mountain" in Nebuchadnezzar's dream.
150 Referring, if so, to the approximate years of His earthly ministry. Even if Christ had been referring *only* to His literal body, as His disciples came to take a similar cryptic statement recorded in John 2:18–19, He would still have been—with the added phrase contained in the accusation quote—connecting *Himself* with the stone/kingdom of Daniel 2!

This dream, dreamed by an ancient "gentile" king, is one of the great Messianic prophecies found in the Old Testament! However, I think a great many Christians have never recognized it as such. I am convinced that the prophecy encompasses *both* advents and everything in between, and most beautifully to me—a person who, since his birth, has had *more* than his share of Satan's vicious scheming attacks that belong to *this* age—it also encompasses everything that will *not* follow since the symbolic mountain will be an everlasting kingdom of peace!

> *[H]e will destroy on this mountain the shroud that is cast over all peoples, the sheet that is spread over all nations; he will swallow up death forever.* ***Then the Lord GOD [Yahweh] will wipe away the tears from all faces, and the disgrace of his people he will take away from all the earth, for the LORD [Yahweh] has spoken.*** *It will be said on that day, Lo, this is our God; we have waited for him, so that he might save us. This is the LORD [Yahweh] for whom we have waited; let us be glad and rejoice in his salvation. For the hand of the LORD [Yahweh] will rest on this mountain.* (Isa. 25:7–10)

I also absolutely crave the reality that is described in another powerful "mountain of God" prophecy from the latter half of Isaiah that also gets itself attached to the eternity of peace in God's kingdom, as well (although there is evidence in the context of that very passage that suggests it might have been at least *symbolically* fulfilled even in *this* world had God's ancient people accepted His leading, even back then)![151]

> *The wolf and the lamb shall feed together, the lion shall eat straw like the ox; but the serpent [a prophetic symbol of Satan]—its food shall be dust [i.e., he will be <u>dead</u> in the dust]!* ***They shall not hurt or destroy on all my holy mountain, says the LORD.*** (Isa. 65:25)

And speaking of dust, there is no question about the utter beauty of the *event* of Jesus' second coming to those who are world weary, even as foundational elements of it are powerfully portrayed in the book of Daniel. When Daniel 12 flashes a light from heaven about the resurrection from the dead,[152] for instance, it gives me spiritual goosebumps!

---

151 A theme I plan to return to in another volume.
152 Another topic I plan to deal with extensively in a future volume, including shocking evidence of Christ's resurrection that would stand up in a court of law today.

> *At that time Michael [prophetic symbol of Jesus], the great prince, the protector of your people, shall arise …. at that time your people shall be delivered, everyone who is found written in the book.* **Many of those who sleep in the dust of the earth shall awake ….** *Those who are wise shall shine like the brightness of the sky, and those who lead many to righteousness, like the stars forever and ever.* (Dan. 12:1–3)

But there is another shining event that strikingly stirs (I almost said *stars*[153]) my soul as well, without which none of the glorious eventualities of the kingdom could even have been made possible. It is the enlightening astronomical event around which a Davidic slingstone struck a Goliath statue in the midnight of human history. In *this* version of David and Goliath,[154] however, the slingstone got aimed, not at Goliath's forehead, but at another specific location on his gigantic body, because the Goliath in this version—the idol in Nebuchadnezzar's dream—represented a particular chunk cut out from a timeline of human history. And when *I* finally got past my own preconceptions about certain of the timeline's segments, and when I had a sudden flashing realization of **the significance of that spot in history where the slingstone** *actually* **hit**, it blew me away! To understand exactly why, though, we first need to go back to Nebuchadnezzar's dream, and examine the details of that timeline precisely, a journey that may take a little longer than others in this book because I plan to include some sightseeing along the way.

---

153 In case you're wondering, this is a *hint* of something special to come (a sort of riddle); it is *not* a random, unintelligible comment any more than God's own sometimes mysterious Messianic prophecies in ancient times were.
154 See 1 Samuel 17 to read the *original* story.

Chapter 13

In Pursuit of Prophetic Ground Zero (Part 1)

The meaning of Nebuchadnezzar's colossus becomes even clearer when we understand the actual world history that followed the dream's predictions.

> *After you shall arise **another kingdom** inferior to yours, **and yet a third kingdom** of bronze, which shall rule over the whole earth. And there shall be a fourth kingdom, strong as iron; just as iron crushes and smashes everything, it shall crush and shatter all these.* (Dan. 2:39–40)

And I am really interested in that *fourth* kingdom because we are told in no uncertain terms that the stone collides with one of its three segments.[155] It represents, in effect, the prophetic ground zero of all Messianic prophecies. The problem is that Daniel 2 doesn't actually identify all of these kingdoms. However, we *can* see them clearly identified if we simply put up parallel prophecies—also found in the book of Daniel—side by side with the statue of Daniel 2. Let's take a look now at just how these equivalent prophecies *do* relate to each other.

Here is a chart I have developed to help you see the bigger picture in Daniel's parallel prophecies. I will more sharply hone my argument *for* the parallelism between these prophecies (since not all interpreters agree) as we progress in our pursuit.[156] It will look something like this (below) to start out.

The pieces of information we need (keys to unlock the prophecy, if you will) are all available inside of the book of Daniel (for us to compare with secular history, which we must have some knowledge of to understand most prophecy). The identity of the fourth kingdom—ground zero—is, in effect, now merely an

---

155 Refer back to chapter 7 of this book if you need to refresh your memory about those segments.
156 If you need a sneak peek, see the beginning of chapter 14.

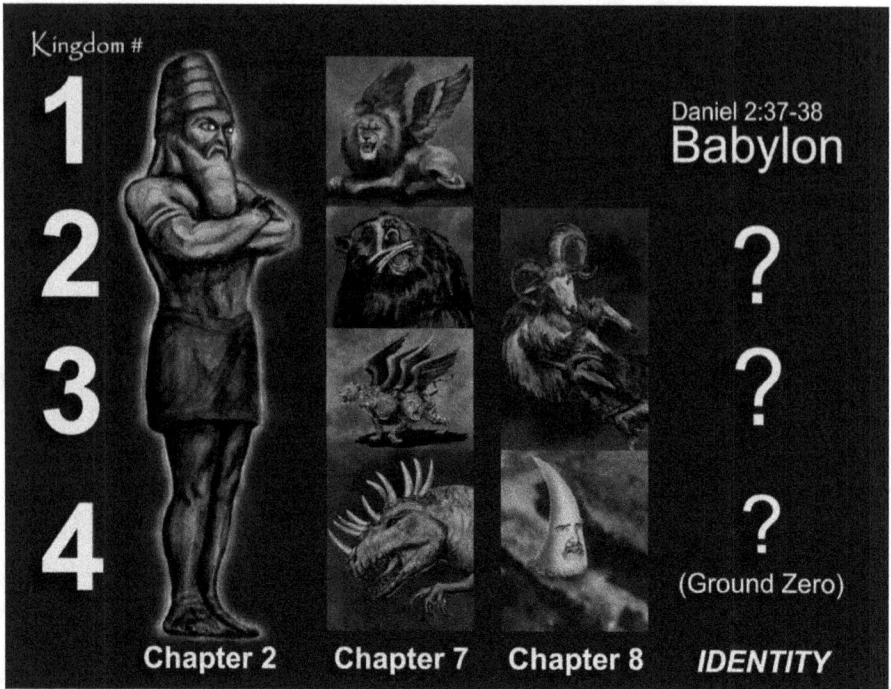

equation to be solved. To solve it, we have to simply input the known data into the proper places in the equation in order to calculate by it what-equals-what to determine the unknown values. It is as simple as that. OK, so some of us probably don't consider things like algebraic equations *simple,* but they are profoundly **logical** (perhaps the next best thing), and so is the equation to be solved in Daniel. Let me try to *make* it simple (hopefully not famous last words!).

While heading toward this destination, however, I intend to take you down a sightseeing detour or three (or *more?).* This is a calculated risk to your attention span, I know, but it is one I feel I need to take at this juncture of our journey down a few perhaps winding, bumpy back roads to help you take in a broader view of the landscape surrounding these prophecies. It will also give you a broader view of important issues that are involved in their true meaning, and in the meaning of Jesus coming to our world as a baby, and later dying on a cross. The intent is that you might start to see a bigger picture before we reach the journey's goal. If it helps you to navigate, just consider and treat each detour (which I will point out along the way) as sort of mini sub-chapters that necessarily got embedded—like padding in a walking shoe or in a vehicle's seat—at critical spots into the fabric of the main theme.

Notice that in both Daniel 2 and Daniel 7, Babylon is the starting point for their respective prophecies, but that Daniel 8 goes on to start its prophecy with a later historical "kingdom." The reason for this may simply be that at the time that the vision of Daniel 8 was given to the prophet (551 BC), Babylon was edging closer to the time when it would be conquered by the second "kingdom" (empire) in the sequence,[157] so it was an anticipatory prediction of that conquest and of further conquests that would happen to each succeeding empire. It may have been God's way of saying what must have already been obvious to Daniel—living, as he was, in the by-that-time sadly declining empire—that Babylon's days were numbered.

But before I go further, I'd like you also to notice (our first detour)—as food for future thought (and, perhaps, even thought for future *food?*)—another significant detail: **the difference in style and theme between these three prophecies covering essentially the same historical time period.** It tells us how God often tailors visions and dreams to various human perspectives for various reasons, and also, to a degree, how God meets us where we live. Recognition of thematic and perspective elements may help a student of prophecy to better understand the significance of a prophecy's symbolism. In Daniel 2, for instance, the theme is related to things that pagans would well understand, such as the idolic statue; however, in Daniel 7, the "kingdoms" are seen as dangerous wild beasts—clearly ***an outsider perspective*** on the oppressive presence of cruel and controlling big-government empires. **And it is from the very midst of this *outsider perspective* that God's great court of judgment upon the empires convenes!** [158] This thought ought to give profound pause to *insider* leaders of nations and organizations alike (as they sit in kingly board and conference rooms) lest they arrogate power to themselves (through vindictively, greedily, or self-righteously conceiving of ideological, controlling, or punitive policies[159]), without so much as a charitable thought about the effects their policies might have on powerless people who are able to do *nothing* to remedy situations under the thumbs of such great Goliaths—except, that is, to call out to their God from embittered hearts for *His* mercy.[160]

In chapter 8 of Daniel, we find a different tone. There we find only domestic animals of the variety the Scriptures call "clean" animals,[161] animals that, according to Yahweh's ancient law, may be *eaten* by His people, or else used for blood sacrifices—a categorical distinction concerning the

---

157 See Daniel 8:1, as compared with Daniel 5.
158 See Daniel 7:9–10.
159 A mouthful, I *know*.
160 See Luke 18:7–8, and verse 9, too, because it is related (in *my* mind), as is the parable it introduces.
161 See Leviticus 11:1–30, 41–43.

animal kingdom that was recognized as far back as the time of Noah's flood (which, by the way, happened *long* before Leviticus).[162] Contrary to popular conception (and to the probably millions of paintings that have been made of the subject matter) the animals did not *all* come into Noah's ark two by two—at least partly for the reason, I am certain, that there would be *more* animals needed of the types that were to be used as an emergency food source and for making sacrifices to God. And the biblical distinction between clean and unclean animals, first found in the flood story, is still recognized in varying degrees today by Jews, Muslims, and a growing minority of Christians as well. As an aside, some of the minority Christians—of which I am one—see a distinction between ancient "health" laws of Yahweh (especially considering the *nature* of many of the "unclean" animals: spiders, vultures, rats, maggots, and roaches, just to name a few), and the *merely* ceremonial laws that they consider no longer binding. The no-brainer question many ask themselves is: did Yahweh just single out certain animal types *arbitrarily,* or *did He know something* about their various categories and about the consumption of their flesh that humans might not easily recognize, or consider, on their own? Could Yahweh's prohibition of certain meats, I wonder, possibly have been a *health* blessing (maybe even an *intelligence* blessing too via brain health) upon the posterity of the Israelites, Jews, and Jewish converts, affected over many centuries because they trusted *His* wisdom on the subject? Just some food for thought (and thought for food).

However, I consider the *ceremonial* aspect of the animals in chapter 8 (the fact that they were *sacrificial* animals) to be of greater symbolic significance.[163] In any case, **the prophecy in chapter 8 was given to Daniel from a very Jewish perspective, and the sacrificial aspect gives it a particularly Jewish sanctuary flavor**. Historically, this perspective would have been profoundly significant since at the very time it was given, God in His ministrations of judgment to the earth was on the verge, not only of punishing Babylon for its excesses of brutality, but also of restoring some of the fortunes of Daniel's long beleaguered people, and of their crushed kingdom.[164] He was also on the verge of initiating the rebuilding of His sacred sanctuary on Mount Zion through the construction of the very same temple that Jesus, the promised Messiah, would eventually come to.[165]

---

162 See Genesis 7:2–3.
163 Perhaps a subject to touch on in more depth in another volume?
164 See Daniel 9:1–2; Jeremiah 25:11–12, 29:10.
165 See Malachi 3:1.

In Pursuit of Prophetic Ground Zero (Part 1)

But back let's go to the main highway of identifying "kingdoms"—though not for long; I see another sightseeing detour up ahead.

Although Daniel 2 only lists the kingdoms represented in its statue by number, we *do* know at least the identity of the head of gold. It is Babylon. And Daniel 7's four numbered kingdoms correlate directly to the four kingdoms of Daniel 2. However, Daniel 7 does not directly tell us the various identities of these kingdoms either, beyond the fact that we already know the first "kingdom" to represent Babylon, of course. So, it is only through the divine insight we are given later, in *chapter 8*—**in the prophecy given from a *Jewish* perspective**—that we are finally able to see *clearly* the identities of further kingdoms! This is a delicious irony to me (as well as another *detour* coming on), since it was also only through a *Jewish* Messiah that the gracious "light of the world" shone down[166] upon the nations (gentiles) who had so abused the ancient Jews!

> ***For they persecute those whom you have struck down, and those whom you have wounded, they attack still more.*** (Ps. 69:26)

They had callously and sacrilegiously gone above and far, *far* beyond the punishment God had intended for His wayward chosen children. It was for these excesses, and for excesses like them,[167] that the empires would be judged and removed forever from power, that they would be, "weighed in the balances, and … found wanting" (Dan. 5:27, KJV).

They say (whoever *they* is) that we should be careful who we step on, on our way up, because we might meet them again on our way down. But *I* say we should be careful who we step on going in *any* direction, and for *any* reason, because *every* soul, without exception, is precious in God's sight! This is a *most* practical application of our spiritual reading about God's judgments in prophecy! There are profoundly fallen and even *degraded* souls, but there is no such thing as a "garbage" soul whom it is OK for us to beat into the ground, no matter *what* they might have done, even if it was to us *personally*. And I can *speak* too because I've had some pretty terrible things done to *me* (God knows).

Unfortunately, our society—**and sadly even the Christian church**—sometimes seems headed in the direction of that disgusting self-righteous perspective that allows us to consider some people "garbage": to *demonize* people whom we imagine (or think we *know*) terrible things about,

---
166 See John 8:12.
167 See Jeremiah 50–51.

or with whom we profoundly disagree. **It is the same perspective, I am convinced, that made God inspire a great fish to swallow up Jonah, the ancient prophet, just so it could adequately express God's true feelings, by vomiting him up again!** [168] Jesus, most uncomfortably (even—or *especially*—to me), tells His followers (in every age and situation!) to love and pray for their enemies! [169] God wishes for even the *worst* among us to be redeemed (if at all possible) by His *amazing* grace. The vindictive prophet Jonah reminds me a lot of many unforgiving hurt activists, and figurative witch-hunters, who are sadly multiplying in our modern contexts—even in the church, and in its ever more worldly-styled organizations. Hurt people *do* hurt people, especially with their *tongues!*[170] Jonah had considered *the Ninevites* to be the worst, because they had so badly hurt his own people, and he actually *feared* that God might show the Ninevites mercy![171]

*Blessed are the merciful, for **they** will receive mercy.* (Matt. 5:7)

But *I* think that some of the former "worst"—those who *know* they have been redeemed as it were from the very pit of *hell*—will cling in gratitude closest to Jesus their Redeemer throughout all eternity, and will have the sweetest song to sing!

> *Then turning toward the woman, [Jesus] said to Simon, "Do you see this woman? I entered your house; you gave me no water for my feet, but she has bathed my feet with her tears and dried them with her hair. You gave me no kiss, but from the time I came in she has not stopped kissing my feet. You did not anoint my head with oil, but she has anointed my feet with ointment. Therefore, I tell you, her sins, which were many, have been forgiven; hence she has shown great love. But the one to whom little is forgiven, loves little." Then [Jesus] said to her, **"Your sins are forgiven."** (Luke 7:44–48)*

So how will we, if we hang onto our *bitter* song of unforgiveness[172] (and our raving hunger for vengeance) ever be able to dwell in paradise with these penitent souls at Jesus' very side? And perhaps God sees as "worst" our *own* arrogant self-righteousness (requiring the *greater* forgive-

---

168 See Jonah 2:10, and see also Revelation 3:16.
169 See Matthew 5:44.
170 See James 3:5–9.
171 See Jonah 4:1–2.
172 See the parable in Matthew 18:21–35.

ness!) that arrogates judgment of others, and their motives, to our own sinful selves, without true pity or understanding.[173] It is an attitude that makes a person *almost* impossible to reach[174] since pride feels no need. No! **God does not consider any one of His children garbage (and God help us if we treat any that way!)** any more than good parents lose their love for a child who has made some terrible mistake—no matter *how* terrible! It will weigh down the great heart of God, our heavenly *Father*, to finally, but reluctantly, give up to destruction *even* His one-time covering cherub,[175] a one-time dear child of His whom He had called the "Day Star"—Lucifer[176]—but who, through unchecked self-love, finally became the devil and the Satan[177]—the great destroyer of *all* of us!

> *Your will be done,* **on earth as it is in heaven.** *(Matt. 6:10)*

We should also be careful who we step on because of the fact that our blessings from God just may end up coming through the most unexpected of sources, even sources we had once despised!

> *The stone that the builders rejected has become the chief cornerstone. This is the LORD's [Yahweh's] doing; it is marvelous in our eyes.* (Ps. 118:22–23)

This psalm was sung, once upon a time, as Yahweh's people proceeded through one of the ancient gates of the temple to worship, in which an odd-shaped stone—one that the builders *had* rejected for construction—ended up becoming used as the perfect peak stone in a probably pointed archway over the gate. The once despised stone (tossed to the garbage heap) had ended up being the most important—the top-most stone—the very one that ended up holding the entire archway together. This story about the gate's construction had, no doubt, helped to inspire the *prophetically* inspired ancient song about how God's salvation marvelously surprises us sometimes! Writing this makes me want to start singing, with deep gratitude, a *modern*

---

173 See Matthew 7:1–3.
174 See Mark 10:27.
175 See Ezekiel 28:16.
176 See Isaiah 14:12 ("Lucifer" in KJV, "Day Star" in NRSV, "shining one" in Young's Literal Translation).
177 See Revelation 12:9.

song that I know called "Cornerstone."[178] Its lyrics refer to the New Testament teaching[179] that Jesus became the true Cornerstone of history when He came to atone for all of us sinners, and how, in spite of being rejected and cast out by His own people—the builders God had Originally ordained to erect His *human* temple—He ended up becoming that temple's very *Cornerstone*. He became for us the most important stone in *all* of God's marvelous edifice that is even now still being constructed out of *living* stones (see 1 Peter 2:4–8). He became the very stone on which everything else is utterly dependent, the one which caps off and holds all of the other stones together! *He* is the one who makes us (the living stones) able to weather the storms of sin's curse. I encourage you to look this—one of my favorite songs—up, if you are able! Yes, Jesus *is* the legendary Cornerstone of Bible prophecy, the One on whom we may rest secure whenever the harsh and unforgiving winds of sin begin to howl around us spiritually.

A great place to merge back onto the highway—be the merger ever so brief.

Just to give you a heads up: some interpreters try to divide up what is actually a *single* prophetic "kingdom" (empire)—the second in my chart, which in chapter 8 is symbolized by *one* single animal— into *two separate* historical "kingdoms" (empires) in the parallel sequence found in Daniel chapter 7. This unusual approach makes the very same political entity that is symbolized by only *one* animal in chapter 8, strangely become split into *two* animals in chapter 7 (an oddity that is only noticeable, to most people, if you place the three parallel prophecies side by side, as I have done)! I believe this division is wholly imaginary even though it has been partly based upon a connection assumed—by books 1 and 2 Maccabees published hundreds of years after the time of Daniel—between these prophecies and one particular episode of history[180] that had loomed large to the Maccabees in their era. The connection is not supported, however, by the parallel passages, nor does it gel with actual history. Many other details do not fit either without wresting the text. This artificial stretching of one kingdom into two is simply an attempt to force one particular historic event to fit a part of the prophetic timeline that it does not actually fit.

---

178 Lari Goss, "Cornerstone," *Ceaseless Praise: More Songs for One or Two* (Kansas City, MO: Lillenas Publishing Co., 1983).
179 Mark 12:10–11, Luke 20:17–18, Acts 4:10–12, Eph. 2:19–22, and 1 Peter 2:4–8.
180 I will briefly touch on a few details of that episode in chapter 18.

Although some who honestly espouse these ideas don't recognize the fact, this kingdom-splitting error (and the theory it is related to) is at least partly based on **the unbelieving assumption that Daniel does not contain *actual* predictive prophecy**. The theory is often founded on a presupposition that any real concurrences between predictions of Daniel and *actual* historic events must be cryptic descriptions of history that had already happened before the book was written, that the concurrences are merely masquerading as true predictive prophecy. In skeptical minds, such a thing as predictive prophecy *cannot* exist. This also means (in their skeptical minds) that Daniel could not have even been written at the time period it claims to be, nor by a real prophet, but hundreds of years later, *after* the events that they assume the "prophecies" refer to. These events are easier for unbelievers to accept than the more natural interpretations of the text since the natural interpretations would make the book into a book of real prophecy (go *figure!*). The skeptical assumptions would, if they were true, also make the writer of Daniel to be a total *fraud,* if the book's predictions are pretend. Similar unbelieving interpreters, who discourage recognition of Jesus in Daniel's prophecies, would gladly date its writing to even long after the fact of the historical Jesus too if they *could* (they would chomp at the bit for a chance), if it wasn't so clear that Daniel not only existed in Jesus' day, but that it had long been accepted as part of the sacred Scriptures, as well! "Someone has an axe to grind," as they say. And many unwitting believers get their faith cut up on that sharpened axe by gullibly buying into faithless unbeliever assumptions without examining them more closely.

This kingdom-splitting is one of the more blatant attempts I think I have seen to force a preconceived interpretation (an assumption) *into* a Scripture passage (to force a square peg into a round hole), rather than letting the text and its surrounding context speak for themselves.

Whenever we read preconceived ideas *into* a passage of Scripture, by the way (and "by the way" here means that we are taking one more bumpy excursion into the countryside), that process of interpretation is called *eisegesis.* The "eis" part means, "into," and it simply means that we carry *into* our reading, notions that may or may not have *actually* been intended by the original author, or (as in the case of visionary prophecy) by God, more directly. Although humans often do this almost instinctively—thus *almost* innocently—without even realizing it, the process still does not result in a faithful interpretation, and it leads us into error. It makes me think of the famous counsel the apostle Paul once gave a young pastor named Timothy about properly interpreting God's Word:

> *Do your best to present yourself to God as one approved by him, a worker who has no need to be ashamed,* **rightly explaining the word of truth**. (2 Tim. 2:15)

The New King James version translates: "rightly *dividing* the word of truth."[181] This refers to being very careful—and *prayerful*—that we are rightly *understanding* God's Word *before* we explain it. The opposite interpretive process (opposite of the sloppy and bad) which we should seek to always approach Scripture with, is called *exegesis* (as opposed to *eis*-egesis). Exegesis is the "good guy" of interpretation approaches. The "ex" part means, "out of," or "out from," and it means that we try our best to take our interpretation *out* of a passage of Scripture that we are reading—regardless of what notions we might have imagined about a topic *before* we began studying—**instead of reading our own or someone else's worldview and preconceived notions *into* the text**.

This is a great ideal that we will all no doubt say "amen" to, in *theory*, but it can be harder to achieve than we imagine because of human psychology. We humans are not as rational as we like to think. We carry around with us deeply-rooted, preconceived notions and emotionally-charged defenses everywhere we go. Wherever you go, there *you* are! Emotionally—and occasionally *financially*—invested biases are one way we cope with life!

Depending on who we are, and how we make a living, true exegesis may even *cost* us something tangible upon occasion! What begins as an innocent Bible study, for instance—in which we prayerfully reevaluate some cherished passage of Scripture—might just turn into a cross for us to bear for Jesus[182] if some new convicting truth or perspective that we discover, suddenly puts us at odds with accepted notions of other Christian brothers and sisters we happen to be closely associated with. In such a case, a counseled act of humility is certainly in order—the injunction of 1 Thessalonians 5:21 to **"test everything."** However, in testing our new insights, and in seeking counsel with others, we need to be careful not to *despise* new light that God may have *truly* given to us, simply because a crowd might oppose it (a crowd opposed Jesus once too). The other half

---

181 Emphasis is mine.
182 See Matthew 16:24.

In Pursuit of Prophetic Ground Zero (Part 1)

of that counsel says, "hold fast to what is good"! In other words, if we become convinced—after humble self-examination, taking counsel, and re-re-examination *(not* a typo)—that we have not interpreted carelessly or incorrectly, then we *must* stubbornly hold onto what we are convinced is Bible truth, and "follow the Lamb" wherever He leads us![183] This is another practical application of learning spiritual truth. We must do this regardless of what other people think,[184] or even if it brings negative consequences to a cherished career (this may apply to pastors and other religious leaders *especially)* if we are convinced it comes from God! You may cringe at the thought of this very real possibility, but if it ever happens to you, keep in mind:

Whatever is good and perfect comes to us from God *above, who created all heaven's [the sky's] lights.* (James 1:17, NLT)

If God *truly* gave you the insight and direction, then it is God who can, and will, take care of your needs during whatever transition or change He might be calling you to.

[Y]our heavenly Father knoweth that ye have need of all these things. But seek ye first the kingdom of God, and his righteousness; and all these things shall be added unto you. (Matt. 6:32–33, KJV[185])

It may just be, in some cases, that a dependence upon an organizationally provided salary might even have become an *idol* of sorts, without our realizing it, in which we subconsciously placed our ultimate trust for survival, instead of in our heavenly Father and His love for us. But as many pastors know all too well (and indeed have probably often told others) this occasional kingdom conflict of interest may apply equally in almost *any* job or career (as we will see clearly in a future volume) when we begin to take Christ's kingship and beneficent commands seriously in our lives.

The process of exegesis (proper biblical interpretation) cannot be *assumed*; it must be done *on purpose.* And if we want to *truly* understand what God wants us to see, we must prayerfully crucify invested biases even

---

183 See Revelation 14:4.
184 See Acts 5:29.
185 I use the King James version here for the emotional connection its traditional flavor makes—similar to the Lord's Prayer—in the hearts of many who first memorized the passage in "the king's English" of old.

before reading Scripture, through a divine humility of the sort that can only be obtained through fervent sincere prayer:

> *He said to them, "This kind can come out **only through prayer**."*
> (Mark 9:29)

And we must be willing to admit when we have been wrong too, if we are *genuinely* wrong! There is really no shame in that—unless the admission is coerced or driven by false motives such as financial worries or peer pressure—because being wrong (very often) is a natural part of the human condition which we all share. *Figurative* "eating of crow" (although *literal* crow is one of the "unclean" meats of Leviticus) is one of the healthiest *mental* dainties fallen human beings can partake of, provided it is consumed in moderation, of course. *Along* with prayer, "eating crow" often helps to produce honest humility—a "be" vitamin we all need: to *"be"* humble.

And the scenic road winds back to the highway.

Chapter 14

In Pursuit of Prophetic Ground Zero (Part 2)

CAUTION! This portion of highway now goes through a rather long stretch of complex historical territory. Please drive slowly (yes, *you* are the driver; I am but a tour guide) through these canyons that we must traverse to reach our high mountain overlook. Try to take in the scenery gradually and carefully, curve by dangerous curve, giving yourself enough time to think each one through. Taking contemplation and prayer breaks along the way might help. You will look back with awe on it all soon enough (if you don't quit or take your eyes off the road and drive off the cliff) in a bigger *Son*-set picture.

One reason I have lined up all three of these parallel prophecies of Daniel side by side is so that we can avoid gross *eisegetical* violations of biblical interpretation (that is, reading our *own* ideas or ideas that other people or books or media gave us into the text) which violations are often borne out of an isolated analysis, and because **Scripture must be allowed to interpret Scripture** (see chart on the following page).

The "kingdom" (which I mentioned earlier), that some interpreters try to split into two, is the historic Medo-Persian Empire (often referred to as the Achaemenid Empire[186]) which conquered the Babylonian Empire under the leadership of Cyrus the Great. They try in Daniel 7 (since Daniel 7 doesn't name any of its kingdoms as does Daniel 8) to say that Daniel 7's bear, which followed Babylon (the lion), represents the Medes, and that its Leopard then represents the Persians, as if the two—the Medes and the Persians—were separate and distinct in the sequence.

---

186 This title refers to Cyrus's *Persian* prince father, Cambyses (married to his *Median* princess mother, Mandana), having been a direct descendant of Achaemenes, the founder of the Achaemenid clan of ancient Persis' Pasargadae tribe, the tribe that furnished Persis' ruling class. Steven Dando-Collins, *Cyrus the Great: Conqueror, Liberator, Anointed One* (Nashville, TN: Turner Publishing Company, 2020), p. 13.

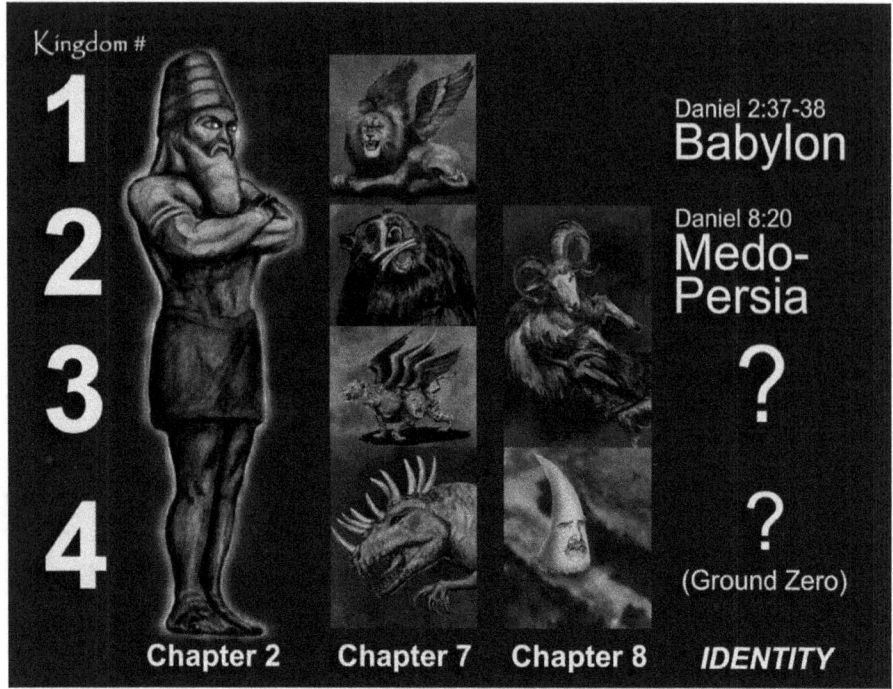

But Daniel, itself, identifies most of the kingdoms by name in at least one of the three prophecies, and I believe this naming clearly debunks such an unfounded theory. I am convinced that God Himself intended these prophecies to be a set of three parallels for us to compare. I also have no doubt whatsoever that Daniel 8 is the intended *key* that God also provided for us to unlock the identities of the later "kingdoms" in all three. It *must* be since only chapter 8 names names beyond Babylon—we have nothing else to go on. Otherwise we are dealing with mere historical guesswork, and that is what some popular interpretations of prophecy actually amount to, unfortunately. At a deep level of my personal interpretive philosophy, I also believe that God gives prophetic symbols and keys to those symbols *consistently*—and that, **as a true prophetic book, Daniel is essentially consistent within itself**—so that for us to turn one animal in one series of kingdoms, into two animals in a parallel series, would be to violently wrest the intent of Scripture. It would be to destroy the purpose and precision of the natural parallels. If you *don't* believe God has some measure of consistency in His revelations—well—then you and I would have trouble talking about *any* spiritual truths together, much less about the more mathematical truths found in prophetic symbolism! **I take**

God's essential consistency—as complex as it may sometimes appear—as *a priori* truth (the philosophical phrase for you to look up today, class, is *a priori*). This means that I consider it to be of the same type and caliber as the truths Thomas Jefferson describes in his opening statement to the Declaration of Independence: truths so basic and instinctive, that they should require no defense (such as: "I think, therefore I am"):

*We hold these truths to be **self-evident**...*[187]

If "the gods" (a tongue-in-cheek allusion to chapter 3)—the one *true* God—are really communicating with mortals, then these communications must have the possibility of making logical sense to mortals. In other words, **there must be a right way and a *wrong* way to interpret them**, which may be discerned from some form of logical *consistency* inherent to that *logos,* that "word," that divine communication. This goes far beyond Daniel to include even our ability to be able to discern *in the prophecies,* the logos—*the "Word"*—that was "made flesh," and that "dwelt among us" (I speak, of course, of *Jesus*[188]).

Notice how Daniel describes the prophetic ram early on in chapter 8, *the key prophecy:*

I looked up and saw a ram standing beside the river. It had two horns. Both horns were long, but one was longer than the other, and the longer one came up second. (Dan. 8:3)

So, there *were* two elements involved in the symbolic ram which may be the self-justification some interpreters try to give themselves for their desire to split up the same kingdom in parallel prophecies. However, in verse 20 we are told, in no uncertain terms, the *identity* of this single animal—which includes its two united elements symbolized by two horns—and we will soon see they are all parallel to the bear in chapter 7 (also only a single animal representing the same two elements).

*As for the ram that you saw with the two horns, **these are the kings of Media and Persia**.* (Dan. 8:20)

---

187 Thomas Jefferson, "The Declaration of Independence" (1776).
188 See John 1:14.

Daniel mentions these kings as a unit and as part of the same symbolic political entity. So although one of the two political people groups represented by the ram's two horns grew stronger over time than the group that had been strongest at first, historians have always recognized these two groups to have been one single unified empire. Indeed, there was *never a time,* even before the conquest of Babylon, when these two entities were *apart* from each other, at least as significant conquering *empires*. We need to also remember (if not realize for the first time) that **the parallel prophecies of Daniel are concerned with the Medo-Persian Empire only at the point in time of its convergence with the Babylonian conquest (its overthrow of the Babylonian power), not with Media as its relatively minor existence coincided with the world dominance of Babylon still in effect**. The prophecy is a sequence of world dominations, not of coinciding minor kingdoms. Media, as it had existed prior to Cyrus the Great, was a *minor* kingdom, and it (in *that* form) did *not* follow Babylon in world dominance—Cyrus's new Medo-Persian alliance *did*. So to say that the relatively minor kingdom of Media followed Babylon, and then that later on Persia followed Media, would be ridiculous to say the least, and would have no concurrence with history.

As if these arguments were not sufficient to demonstrate the understood unity of the Medo-Persian entity in Daniel (and they are), I add yet *another* witness from elsewhere in the book of Daniel that demonstrates (more than conclusively) that the writer, at the very least, and God (if you have faith in the prophecies and stories of Daniel) clearly understood the Medes and the Persians to have been one single unit which conquered Babylon together, *as* a single unit and at the same time. This witness is a verse taken from the famous story in Daniel 5 that describes the last drunken feast of the reckless regent king in Babylon—Belshazzar. Before I share that verse with you, let me first give you the background of the story it comes from.

Belshazzar was the son of Nabonidus, the last king of the Neo-Babylonian Empire, who had years earlier taken his headquarters into Arabia to devote himself to the worship of the Arabian god named Sin, and he had left his son in charge back at Babylon[189] where Belshazzar irresponsibly ran roughshod over the Babylonian population until

---

189 According to the so-called Verse Account of Nabonidus, a cuneiform tablet now located in the British Museum. C. Mervyn Maxwell, *God Cares: The Message of Daniel for You and Your Family,* Vol. 1 (Boise, ID: Pacific Press, 1981), p. 91.

they secretly hated the man (and thus welcomed the later conquest of Cyrus).[190] At the time of Belshazzar's sinfully extravagant last feast—which would have taken place on what we call October 12, in 539 BC—his father Nabonidus had already surrendered Sippar (fifty miles north of Babylon) to Cyrus the Great without a fight and had fled with his army to Borsippa. A military detachment, led by the man many believing Bible scholars think was actually "Darius the Mede,"[191] had then quickly surrounded the walls of Babylon,[192] and, unbeknownst to the city's inhabitants and to its careless king, they were devising an ingenious means to enter the city, though it was beyond the sight of the city's watchmen. They were diverting the Euphrates River, which normally flowed under Babylon's walls directly into the city. But we are told in the story of Daniel 5 that in response to this disastrous turn of events, Belshazzar threw a massive, cocky, drunken feast, feeling so secure, despite his dire circumstances, inside of the mighty walls of Babylon that were once thought to be impregnable. During the feast, as the free-flowing wine began to take its baleful effect, Belshazzar suddenly got the brilliant idea in his befuddled mind to call for the sacred drinking utensils that Nebuchadnezzar had long before taken from the temple of Yahweh in Jerusalem. He then proceeded to blasphemously drink out of golden vessels that had been dedicated to the worship of Yahweh, in honor and praise of the pantheon of ancient pagan gods. It was at that fateful moment that a mysterious "bloodless" hand suddenly appeared out of nowhere, and slowly wrote an obviously menacing cryptic inscription onto the wall of Belshazzar's banquet hall. It was a message of doom

---

190 Steven Dando-Collins, *Cyrus the Great: Conqueror, Liberator, Anointed One* (Nashville, TN: Turner Publishing Company, 2020), pp. 120 and 141.
191 This was probably actually a man known to history as Gubaru (Gobryas) in the Nabonidus Chronicle. The name Darius, referring to the "king" whom the aged Daniel became fast friends with, was probably Gubaru's "throne name" which he used as a temporary regent ruler of Babylon under Cyrus. He would have been designated Darius the Mede in the book of Daniel to prevent confusion with the later Persian king known to history as Darius the Great. See C. Mervyn Maxwell, *God Cares: The Message of Daniel for You and Your Family,* Vol. 1 (Boise, ID: Pacific Press, 1981), pp. 104–105 for an in-depth discussion on who Darius the Mede actually was.
192 "The clay tablet known as the Nabonidus Chronicle says that the military commander who attacked Babylon on October 12, 539 B.C., was called Gubaru. (His attack occurred about two-and-a-half weeks before Cyrus made his triumphal entry, which took place on October 29.) The ancient novelist-historian Xenophon tells about the special help which a person called Gobryas gave to Cyrus in the conquest of Babylon. Gobryas is the Greek-language equivalent of Gubaru." C. Mervyn Maxwell, *God Cares: The Message of Daniel for You and Your Family,* Vol. 1 (Boise, ID: Pacific Press, 1981), p. 104.

which no one present knew how to interpret, even though it was written in Aramaic, a common language of the Babylonians:

> *And this is the writing that was inscribed: MENE, MENE, TEKEL, and PARSIN.* (Dan. 5:25)

When Belshazzar, in his sudden panic, was unable to find anyone who could interpret the mysterious writing, the old queen mother (possibly a still-living wife of Nebuchadnezzar) who had heard of the frenzied discussions regarding the mysterious omen, entered the banquet hall to lend Belshazzar her assistance. She reminded Belshazzar about the history of a famous prophet named Daniel, the Hebrew interpreter of dreams, from Judah, who was now an old man, but who was still living in Babylon. Daniel was called for, and he gave the following interpretation of the cryptic message:

> *This is the interpretation of the matter: MENE, God has numbered the days of your kingdom and brought it to an end; TEKEL, you have been weighed on the scales and found wanting; PERES,* [193] **your kingdom is divided and given to the Medes and Persians.** (Dan. 5:26–28)

And, of course, that very night Belshazzar met his end. The Euphrates is normally somewhat low flowing in October, and two ancient historians—Xenophon and Herodotus—both tell the story of how Darius's[194] men lowered the water even further that fateful fall, by temporarily diverting its flow out of sight of the Babylonian sentinels on the walls. His soldiers then waded through the lowered water, and discovered, to their great joy, that the river gates had been left open. By this devise, they stealthily gained access to the streets of Babylon, killed the unsuspecting guards, and the rest, as they say, is history. There is a lot more that can be said about this fascinating and instructive story, but right here I am especially interested in the interpretation Daniel gave of that last word, PERES—a word, which once meant "divided" in the singular, but was also ancient slang for "Persians" in the plural. But Daniel did not say, "your kingdom is given to the *Persians*," nor did he say "to the *Medes*" only. Daniel clearly recognized and understood the empire that

---

193 This is the NRSV's transliteration of the Aramaic *singular* form of the same word that in its *plural* form is transliterated above (in verse 25) as "PARSIN."
194 *Presumed,* see my earlier comment about "Darius the Mede" in footnote 192.

was that very night conquering Babylon, to be a unified coalition made up of both:

> *... the Medes and Persians.* (Dan. 5:28)

The political entity created by Cyrus came to be known, at least as regards the early period when it conquered Babylon, as the "Medo-Persian Empire," and for a good reason. Cyrus, the conqueror who *formed* the allied empire, *wanted* it that way! Cyrus the Great—most likely at least half Mede by birth (somewhat ironically), but also king of the then Median province called Persia—was believed to be the grandson of King Astyages, the last king of Media, which had in earlier times been a minor independent kingdom.[195] I will let the author C. Mervyn Maxwell describe the diminutive relationship of Persia to Media as it had existed in the years before Cyrus usurped power from his grandfather—thus subjugating Media under his own "Persian" power—and also before he had conquered Babylon at the head of the combined armies of a newly formed Medo-Persian alliance:

> *At its height Media stretched through mountains from the river Halys in the northwest to the Persian Gulf in the southeast. By contrast* **Cyrus at first ruled only the tiny Median province of Persia.** *At that time the Median horn was much taller than the Persian horn.*[196]

But the seemingly tall horn of Media did not remain the greatest since in 553 BC (the same year that Daniel received the judgment-infused vision of chapter 7) Cyrus, the king of the *Persian* province, rebelled against his maternal grandfather, and took control of all Media. In 547 BC Cyrus annexed another kingdom—the kingdom of Lydia—which acquisition then extended his borders far beyond the river Halys, all the way to the Aegean Sea. In 539 BC he finally added Babylon to his rapidly growing realm—**three major conquests for Cyrus in a relatively short span of years.**[197]

The horn that came up second (the Persian one) definitely was outstripping the first horn (the Median one) even though the actual "kingdom"

---

195 C. Mervyn Maxwell, *God Cares: The Message of Daniel for You and Your Family,* Vol. 1 (Boise, ID: Pacific Press, 1981), pp. 155–156.
196 Ibid., p. 155, emphasis mine.
197 Ibid., p. 156.

(empire) did not change. Media was simply swallowed up (almost cannibalistically) by one of its own ambitious provinces, which eventually turned the combined kingdom into a world-class empire. But even though Cyrus had conquered the Median horn (and the remains of its political body were being digested, as it were, in Cyrus's political belly) he chose not to extinguish the Median horn's prestige from his empire. Although the empire was now in his hands, he was—and still considered himself and his empire to be—just as much Median as Persian. This is how, ironically, the "Medo-Persian" Empire could *conquer* the Medes and still be *Median*. Again, I will let Maxwell speak on the growing subject of Cyrus and his Medo-Persian uprising:

> *Broad-minded and generous,* **Cyrus treated the Medes as allies rather than as subjects, giving rise to the term "Medo-Persian Empire."** *In time, however, the Persian horn grew so tall that the empire was known simply as "Persian."* [198]

These descriptions of the Medo-Persian Empire gel perfectly also with the descriptions Daniel gives us of the parallel animal in chapter 7: the bear. Just as the ram was said to have unequal horns, so the bear also had a strange symbolic indication of inequality about it.

> *Another beast appeared, a second one, that looked like a bear.* **It was raised up on one side**, *had three tusks [ribs] in its mouth among its teeth and was told,* **"Arise, devour many bodies!"** (Dan. 7:5)

The language indicates that the animal resembling a bear was somehow higher on one side than it was on its other side, indicating that one-half of the Medo-Persian alliance would be greater than the other. This corresponds exactly with the symbolism of unequal horns in chapter 8. (The three ribs in the bear's mouth, which I will not deal with in this book, symbolize *political* bodies that got consumed by Cyrus the Great's grab for *Persian* world dominance.)

The next "kingdom" in the parallel sequence is identified in Daniel 8:21 as the "king" (kingdom/empire) of Greece:

> **The male goat is the king of Greece, and the great horn between its eyes is the first king.** (Dan. 8:21)

---

198 Ibid., p. 156, emphasis mine.

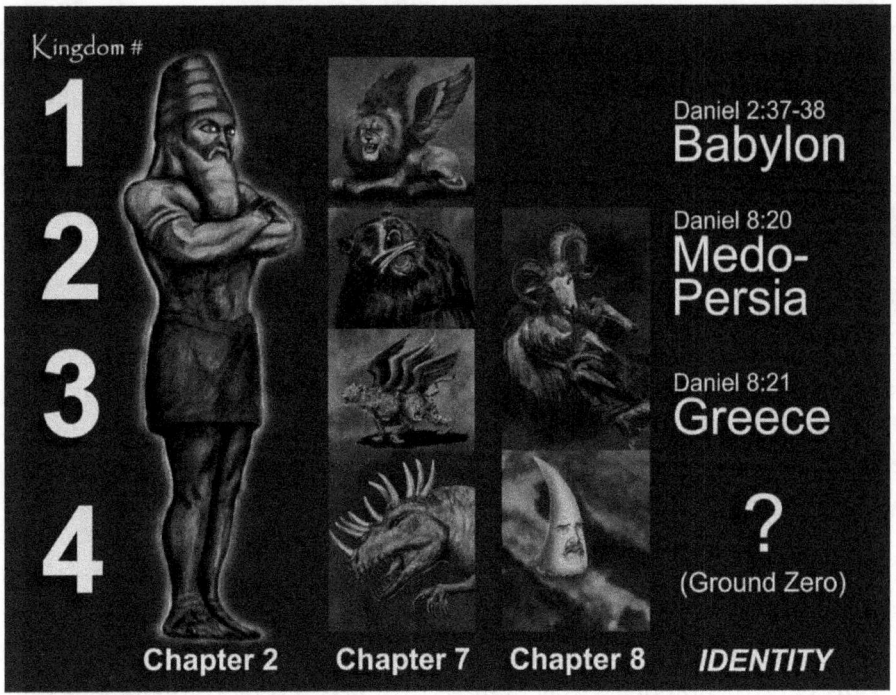

The vivid vision of Daniel 8 portrays the decisiveness and swiftness of the conquest with which the Greek power would overthrow the ancient Persian power, and take control of world dominance for itself:

I saw the ram [Medo-Persia] charging westward and northward and southward. All beasts were powerless to withstand it, and no one could rescue from its power; it did as it pleased and became strong. As I was watching, **a male goat [Greece] appeared from the west, coming across the face of the whole earth without touching the ground.** *The goat had a horn between its eyes. It came toward the ram with the two horns ... it ran ... with savage force. I saw it approaching the ram. It was enraged ... and struck the ram, breaking its two horns. The ram did not have power to withstand it; it threw the ram down to the ground and trampled upon it, and there was no one who could rescue the ram from its power. Then the male goat grew exceedingly great; but at the height of its power,* **the great horn was broken, and in its place there came up four prominent horns toward the four winds of heaven [the sky].** (Dan. 8:4–8)

Anyone who knows anything about ancient world history must recognize in this description of the goat's great horn, a symbol relating to Alexander the Great who smashed the Persian power and conquered the world for the ancient Greeks. It is so recognizable, in fact, that this precise description is one of the reasons many skeptical scholars—who find it hard to believe that anyone, including God, can know the future so *exactly*—try their hardest to date the writing of Daniel very late in history. The problem is that they have not been able to *pretend* a date late enough to prevent other astounding concurrences with real history from the book of Daniel from dumbfounding and amazing my own seeking mind as I came to know the prophetic book through study and prayer. Indeed, one prophecy of Daniel (that we will explore in a later volume) so exactly predicted the time of Jesus' arrival in history that Sir Isaac Newton, one of the fathers of modern math and science, is reported to have called the mathematical prophecy "the foundation stone of the Christian religion."[199]

Something fascinating about the prophecy foretelling Alexander the Great is that Josephus, a famous Jewish historian who lived at the time of the infant Christian church (and who witnessed and participated in the events of Titus's destruction of Jerusalem in AD 70) makes a more-than-interesting claim based on historic sources at his disposal 2,000 years ago. They were, no doubt (directly or indirectly), sources such as very old scrolls from libraries that have long been lost to us today, but that ancient historians like him serve as witnesses to. Josephus tells a fascinating story about Alexander the Great stopping to visit with the Jewish High Priest in Jerusalem[200] as he and his armies went through Judea in hot pursuit of world conquest.[201] It was a story apparently accepted without skeptical comment until the modern era, which people in Josephus' day (including the imperial family of Rome, for whose sake Josephus mostly wrote his history) apparently felt no reason to disbelieve.[202] And they lived a lot closer to the time of Alexander than *we* do.

---

199 "SIR ISAAC NEWTON CALLED IT 'THE FOUNDATION STONE OF THE CHRISTIAN RELIGION,'" Pioneer Memorial Church, December 22, 2009.
200 Almost the equivalent of the Jewish ruler in that period.
201 *The New Complete Works of Josephus*, revised and expanded ed., translation and dissertations by William Whiston (Grand Rapids, MI: Kregel Publications, 1999), pp. 384–386.
202 One reason they may have easily accepted the story is that scholars of the ancient world still had in their possession an intensive compilation about the life of Alexander the Great that has been lost to the modern world. This anecdote may, in fact, have come directly out of that once-famous work, which Josephus no doubt had access to (though the story may just as well have—or also—been written down in still extant Jewish scrolls). Rollin's Ancient History states: "Ptolemy Soter [the founder of the famed library in Alexandria] had been careful to improve himself in polite literature, as was evident by his compiling the life of Alexander, which [work] was greatly esteemed by the ancients, but is now entirely lost." Charles Rollin, *The Ancient History of the*

Indeed, Alexander's well-preserved body could presumably still be viewed in their day where it once lay under transparent glass in Alexandria, Egypt. Alexander's body was later lost to history (as was, no doubt, much incidental knowledge about him) when an earthquake caused a significant portion of ancient Alexandria to sink into the Mediterranean Sea. **Josephus' story tells us how the High Priest sat Alexander down, opened up the scroll of Daniel,[203] and showed him this exact prophecy, which led Alexander to conclude on his own that he, himself, must be the prominent Grecian horn![204]** This would have been to the pagan Alexander just one more welcome evidence, among others he received along his route of conquest, that he was indeed destined by "the gods" to conquer his ancient world. To him, Yahweh—the Jewish God—would have been just one more god among all the others, as easy for him to believe in, nominally, as in any others—perhaps easier, since a very old scroll written by a prophet of Yahweh was predicting his success! At the very least, the story by Josephus demonstrates to us that the Jews in Christ's day clearly understood the scroll of Daniel to be of very ancient origin, even in their day, as did even the Maccabees, who lived very near to the general period modern skeptics try to claim the book was actually written.

Before going any further, however, I would like to clarify one significant principle of prophetic interpretation as it is derived out of the apocryphal visions and dreams found in the Bible, because this interpretive principle may seem to get blurred a bit in this one striking prophecy that foretold Alexander the Great's conquests. However, **the blurring will be seen to be only apparent if we consider the facts carefully**.

The principle I mean is that in Bible prophecy a horn coming out of a symbolic animal does not signify *just* a single person, but rather a political power or "kingdom" (even though it is called, singularly, a "king")— usually a *rising* power—related to the larger animal it came out of. The animal itself (also called a "king" or "kingdom") represents the larger political body, the domination by a particular people group (Babylonians, Persians, Greeks, Romans, etc.), which kind of "king" or "kingdom" today we would call an *empire*. **So, the animal is the empire, and the horns are the kingdoms within or arising out of the larger empire.**

Egyptians, Carthaginians, Assyrians, Babylonians, Medes and Persians, Macedonians and Grecians, vol. 4 (Philadelphia, PA: Lippincott, Grambo & Co., 1855), p. 402.
203 This is the part skeptics most dislike since it is evidence for an ancient dating of Daniel—I would even venture it is the only *actual* prejudiced reason that many scholars reject the story.
204 *The New Complete Works of Josephus*, revised and expanded ed., translation and dissertations by William Whiston (Grand Rapids, MI: Kregel Publications, 1999), pp. 384–386.

I am in general agreement with an observation made by that most logical thinker Sir Isaac Newton (yes, *the* Isaac Newton of falling apple fame who, by the way, I have been told wrote more about Bible prophecy in his lifetime than he ever did about math and science) when he says:

> *A horn of a beast is never taken for a single person: it always signifies a new kingdom.*[205]

My only slight objection to his wording is that a horn may, in fact, be represented as an *old* horn (which, of course, we know once had to have been "new"), and thus may signify an *old* kingdom—as in the case of the already old Median horn at the time of the Medo-Persian conquest of Babylon, which is the focal point of the prophecy when the ram with two horns gets introduced. The horn which Isaac Newton's quote is referring to, however (as I will point out in chapter 18 when I deal with the larger context of his quotation), was clearly a "new" horn arising late within the prophecy he was writing about, and so his statement is not—in this case—affected by my slight objection to his indiscriminate use of the word "always." Indeed, he himself points out, for the purpose of contrast, in the same passage I took the quotation from, that at the time of the new horn *he* refers to, another horn, which is also in play in his argument, was already an *"old"* horn. So maybe my slight objection is merely teasing with semantics, but I like to be clear in anything I state to be categorically true.[206] And I suspect that Isaac Newton himself would have appreciated such an instinct.

The reason that the goat's prominent horn sometimes gets seen as representing only Alexander, and not an actual "kingdom," is simply that the kingdom which Alexander's conquests created, ended ("was broken") when Alexander suddenly died at the very young age of thirty-three, while he and his army were encamped at the city of Babylon, the very city where the fates of Alexander and his kingdom had already been written down more than 200 years earlier in the scroll of Daniel. The fates of Alexander and his kingdom—very much like the fates of some popular mega churches and their rare, *irreplaceable,* brand of popular leaders today—were bound up together. When one died, so did the other.

---

[205] Isaac Newton, *Sir Isaac Newton's Daniel and the Apocalypse,* ed. Sir William Whitla (London: John Murray, 1922), p. 222, emphasis mine.
[206] Though I too make my share of inadvertent erroneous statements from time to time, I'm sure.

Chapter 15

A Deepwater Detour

I feel compelled at this point to let Alexander's kingdom hang on the perilous cliff of history, and to take you on **one more detour**, this time down into the cool canyon depths—to taste of some most refreshing water—the most refreshing you will ever drink, I assure you—which has the ability to more than quench the deepest desert thirst we can work up on these tiresome trails, and to even quench it *forever!* [207] I'll be briefly taking you down to that crystal clear river running below us through these blood red canyon walls of history, which river flows out from "the throne of God and of the Lamb."

> *Then the angel showed me the river of the water of life, as clear as crystal, flowing from the throne of God and of the [slaughtered] Lamb.* (Rev. 22:1, NIV)

It is a river that was elsewhere symbolically shown—in the ancient scroll of Ezekiel—to actually grow deeper, the farther from its source it flows. It is not unlike the most unusual motto that is found in Latin on the official seal of the state of New Mexico which translates to: "It grows as it goes."[208] Perhaps this similar oddity in Ezekiel was at least partially intended to indicate the symbolic river's quenching of a greater and greater *thirst* as its winding waters reached greater and greater multitudes throughout time with a message of hope from God. That message was always intended to go "into all the world," just as the altar stone "kingdom of God" in Daniel 2 was to grow into a mighty mountain that would eventually fill the whole earth.

---

207 See John 4:4–34.
208 This was explained to me at the time that I moved to New Mexico, when I asked a state inspector (inspecting my house) the meaning of the state seal that was printed on the door of his vehicle.

> *[H]e brought me ... to the entrance of the temple ... water was flowing from below ... south of the altar .... Going ... eastward with a cord in his hand, the man [an angel] measured one thousand cubits ... and it was ankle-deep. Again he measured one thousand ... and it was knee-deep. Again he measured ... and it was up to the waist. Again he measured ... and it was ... deep enough to swim in, a river that could not be crossed .... I saw on the bank ... many trees [these correspond to the symbolic tree of life in Revelation[209]]* **on the one side and on the other [perhaps both sides of Christ—BC and AD—before and after the Lamb of God had come]**. *He said to me, "This water flows toward the eastern region ... and when it enters ... the sea of stagnant waters [the Dead Sea], the water will become fresh. Wherever the river goes, every living creature ... will live, and ... everything will live where the river goes.* (Ezek. 47:1, 3–5, 7–9)

I think this odd prophecy, which is obviously about the Savior of the world (a life-giving river coming out from the altar of sacrifice?) also tells us that our experience with Jesus can become richer and deeper as we allow His grace to continue flowing through *our* histories. It brings healing and new life wherever it flows. It brings life into both our past and present experiences. Through its cover of grace, it even allows us to discover meaning in the work His Spirit was doing in our pre-Christian periods as well as in our post-conversion periods—even in the midst of failures and setbacks we may experience along the way.

Jesus once said about Himself:

> ***I have come that they may have life, and that they may have it more abundantly.*** (John 10:10, NKJV)

It is ironic to me that when Alexander the Great died he was around the same age that most scholars calculate Jesus to have been a few centuries later when He also conquered the world—though in a very different manner than Alexander had. Jesus actually re-conquered—in a very real, though almost unrecognizable, sense—all of fallen humanity that ever has been or ever will become willing to accept His kingship in their hearts and minds and souls. However, Jesus did this without a *physical* sword in His hand, and while dying naked, persecuted, and pierced on our own criminal's cross. In the profound words of the pre-Christian prophet Isaiah:

---

209 See Revelation 22:2.

> *[H]e was pierced for our transgressions, he was crushed for our iniquities; the punishment that brought us peace was upon him, and **by his wounds we are healed.** We all, like sheep, have gone astray, each of us has turned to our own way; and the LORD [Yahweh] **has laid on him the iniquity of us all.** He was oppressed and afflicted, yet he did not open his mouth; he was led like a lamb to the slaughter, and as a sheep before its shearers is silent, so he did not open his mouth.* (Isa. 53:5–7, NIV)

Jesus did not want to go to that cross (the equivalent of our own culture's electric chair[210]) at all, but even in inconceivable anguish beyond our ability to comprehend, He humbly submitted His *human* judgment and reasoning up (colored as it was by suffering pain we cannot possibly fathom, because it went far deeper into his soul than merely his human flesh, all the way down to His eternal, divine core) to the will and to the understanding of His passionately loving, and (at the same time) *just*, Heavenly Father.

> *Let us fix our eyes on Jesus, the author and perfecter of our faith, **who for the joy set before him endured the cross, scorning its shame**, and sat down at the right hand of the throne of God.* (Heb. 12:2, NIV)

We were "the joy set before him!" If Jesus had wanted only to go back to His Father's throne room, He could have gone at any time! He told combatant Peter on the night of his betrayal:

> *Don't you realize that I could ask my Father for thousands of angels to protect us, and he would send them instantly?* (Matt. 26:53, NLT)

Jesus could have done just that! He need only to have called out to his Father! He could have disclaimed all guilt for our sins! He could have refused to stay! He could have refused to pay the heart-sickening price of our ransom!

But that isn't what Jesus did! Instead He told His Father ***"not my will"*** (Luke 22:42). Despite His feelings of utter despair, Jesus went right ahead and drank our poison cup down to the very last dregs. He went the full distance, He endured the full agony—the unspeakable shame—of a most dark and mysterious ordeal which deep down He knew He had to

---

210 Except the electric chair is probably a little more merciful—it at least causes a faster death.

pass through to save us. In a very real way we are all therefore to blame! You and I caused all of His pain! Because, as He humbled Himself so profoundly to become our sacrifice, "The Lamb of God," the King of Creation wore *my* crown and *yours* on His bruised and bleeding brow! (If you want to be truly inspired, I recommend that you look up another favorite song of mine that speaks to this theme, entitled "The Day He Wore My Crown"[211]).

I'm just humble enough to admit that I cannot fully understand this whole reality, but it still never fails to move me. When Jesus hung by giant Roman iron nails, physically and spiritually haggard in the midst of our crisis, He could not see through to the other side either. He cried out at about three in the afternoon "with a loud voice" using words that King David had been inspired to write down 1,000 years earlier (Ps. 22:1),[212] and those despairing words still echo, painfully, through the corridors of time:

My God, my God, why have you forsaken me?![213]

And the question Jesus asked finds its mysterious[214] answer only in our ransom from sin. It was *His* hope for us that gave us *our* hope in Him, that made Him *surrender Himself* on our behalf into the utter darkness of oblivion, and into an apparent eternal separation from His Father, beyond which He could not then see, and that made His Father *surrender up* His one and only Son (a humanizing metaphor Jesus used one dark night[215] to try and make us understand, if even just a little bit, the truly unfathomable love of God—our *original* Father—for us).

---

211 Phil Johnson, "The Day He Wore My Crown," *Favorites Number 9: A Collection of Gospel Songs* (Brentwood, TN: Singspiration Music, 1981).
212 See Mark 15:34.
213 The words are nearly identical in any translation.
214 It is mysterious because even the most brilliant human minds have difficulty understanding how the exchange of Jesus for us actually works. Some theologians call this reality that the prophets predicted, and that Jesus endured, a "substitutionary atonement" while others reject the long-prophesied exchange between the Messiah and us altogether because they cannot wrap their intellects around it, or because of punitive perversions that got attached to the doctrine in the Middle Ages. Some simply attempt to reduce the biblical teaching to the status of a *mere* metaphor in order to take the sting of its divine mystery away. But I say believers should tread this ground with utmost reverent caution, just as Moses was told at the burning bush: "'[T]he place on which you are standing is holy ground'" (Exod. 3:5).
215 See the story of Nicodemus coming to Jesus by night in John 3.

And just as Moses lifted up the serpent in the wilderness,[216] *so must the Son of Man*[217] *be lifted up, that whoever believes in him may have eternal life.* **"For God so loved the world that he gave his only Son, so that everyone who believes in him may not perish but may have eternal life."** (John 3:14–16)

In the Garden of Gethsemane, not long before His arrest, mock trials, torture, humiliation, and crucifixion, Jesus had pleaded with His Father:

"Father, if you are willing, remove this cup from me; yet, not my will but yours be done." *Then an angel from heaven appeared to him and gave him strength. In his anguish he prayed more earnestly, and his sweat became like great drops of blood falling down on the ground.* (Luke 22:42–44)

But for *our* sakes His Father gave Jesus up, even though His heart was crushed by that surrendering act, as it will be again someday, when He finally *surrenders up* any of His blood-bought children who *will not* be redeemed (who stubbornly and persistently *choose* not to accept His marvelous offers of salvation) to the inevitable end that sin naturally leads to—*death.*[218] In response to the Son of Man's anguished prayer in an ancient olive grove, His Father said no! He said "no" to His Son, so that He could say "yes" to us! He had determined in His profoundly loving (yet also legal) heart that this gruesome painful ordeal, so long symbolized in the sacrifices of unnumbered innocent animals, was the *only* way—whether we can yet fully comprehend that fact (lovingly, legally, fairly, morally, justly, ethically, influentially, substitutionally) or not—to do true heavenly justice to the depths of the demands created by "iniquity and transgression and sin" (Exod. 34:7). Sin, in all its ugly degrees and variations, if left undealt with—and only the divinely predestined and appointed ordeal that Christ went through could properly deal with it—would inevitably unravel the very fabric of God's moral universe based on love. **If the Father, in His infinite wisdom and love, had seen any other possible way** to properly deal with sin's profound stain—and cancer—on the universe, without giving all of us up to its inevitable destruction [219] in the process, **Jesus would not have had to die.**

---

216 See Numbers 21:8–9.
217 A term borrowed directly from the book of Daniel.
218 See Romans 6:23.
219 "[M]ay not perish": see the above quote of John 3:16.

Fortunately, we don't have to fully *understand* this amazing gift of grace (which God the Father has given us through Jesus' life, death, and resurrection) before we may partake of its benefits and blessing, and before we may revel in its hope restored! If we did, I fear we would all be *without* hope. It is not *understanding* that saves us, but Jesus *Himself!* The gift—thank God for it—is not an it! *It* is a *Person* whom we may go to right now, just the way we are, and throw ourselves upon His mercy and love. We may freely enjoy the warmth of His friendship and parental embrace right now, and we may freely unload our heavy burdens at the foot of His cross and be refreshed and revived at His healing stream of living water, even before we understand just how it is that His plan of salvation saves us.

> **We may freely enjoy the warmth of His friendship and parental embrace right now, and we may freely unload our heavy burdens at the foot of His cross and be refreshed and revived at His healing stream of living water, even before we understand just how it is that His plan of salvation saves us.**

I encourage you now (if you haven't yet) to go to Jesus just as you are in prayer, and to do it right now! Don't wait until you are a better person because you cannot ever be made a truly better person without Him! Throw your unworthy records of sin and selfishness onto His perfect merits—you don't have to understand how His forgiveness works; you only have to trust Him. Ask Him to take a firm hold of your own weak hands, and heart, and life, and then ask Him—in faith[220]—to lead you into the saving relationship with Him that you were destined[221] to enter by God's love in eternity past. Trust in His power to make a real change in your life as you choose to cooperate with His Holy Spirit. He will answer your prayer, no matter who you are, if it is prayed sincerely from the heart, and if you keep coming to Him, and never stop, no matter what.[222] You will not regret your decision to turn your life completely over to Jesus, and to enter into the saving

---

220 See Hebrews 11:6.
221 See Ephesians 1:5.
222 See Matthew 24:13.

relationship—an eternal friendship with, and spiritual adoption[223] by, none other than Yahweh *Himself!*[224]

Whoever has the Son has life; whoever does not have the Son of God does not have life. (1 John 5:12)

As we get ready to hike back up to the main road, I'd like to leave you with three quotations for you to meditate upon, to ponder over before we return, if you will. The first two are inspirational passages taken from the Old Testament (one a continuation of that powerful passage I already quoted from—Isaiah 53) which speak to this unspeakable truth I have been trying to share with you "down by the riverside."[225] The last quotation was written by a brilliant former atheist, whose unbelieving heart and mind Christ finally captured one day by His Spirit, and then turned that once skeptical man into one of the greatest Christian apologists of the twentieth century.

By oppression and judgment he was taken away. And who can speak of his descendants? For he was cut off from the land of the living; for the transgression of my people he was stricken... though he had done no violence, nor was any deceit in his mouth. **Yet it was the LORD's [Yahweh's] will to crush him and cause him to suffer, and though the LORD [Yahweh] makes his life a guilt offering, he will see his offspring** *and prolong his days, and the will of the LORD [Yahweh] will prosper in his hand. After the suffering of his soul, he will see the light of life and be satisfied;* **by his knowledge my righteous servant will justify [forgive] many, and he will bear their iniquities**. (Isa. 53:8–11, NIV)

The LORD [Yahweh] passed before [Moses], and proclaimed, "The LORD [Yahweh], the LORD [Yahweh], **a God merciful and gracious**, *slow to anger, and abounding in steadfast love and faithfulness, keeping steadfast love for the thousandth generation,* **forgiving iniquity and transgression and sin**, *yet by no means clearing the guilty" [those who choose not to accept His inexplicable means of forgiveness, or who refuse to respond to the persistent gentle proddings of the Holy Spirit, which come to all human hearts in their lifetimes].* (Exod. 34:6–7)

---

223 See Romans 8:15.
224 "Jesus said to them, 'Very truly, I tell you, before Abraham was, I am' *(John 8:58).*
225 Referring to a phrase from the famous negro spiritual "Down By The Riverside."

> **Won't you too surrender to the Holy Spirit now, drink deeply of His healing stream, and accept the priceless gift of Christ (which cost an unfathomable price to your merciful Maker) as your own?**

Theories about Christ's death are not Christianity, they are explanations about how it works. Christians would not all agree as to how important these theories are. But I think they will all agree that **the thing itself is infinitely more important than any explanations that theologians have produced** .... We believe that the death of Christ is just that point in history at which something absolutely unimaginable from outside shows through into our own world .... if we found that we could fully understand it, that very fact would show it was not what it professes to be—the inconceivable, the uncreated, the thing from beyond nature, striking down into nature like lightning. You may ask what good it will be to us if we do not understand it. But that is easily answered. A man can eat his dinner without understanding exactly how food nourishes him.[226] A man can accept what Christ has done without knowing how it works; indeed, he certainly would not know how it works until he has accepted it.[227]

Won't you *too* surrender to the Holy Spirit now, drink deeply of His healing stream,[228] and accept the priceless gift of Christ (which cost an unfathomable price to your merciful Maker) as your own?

John 19:33–34:

[W]hen they ... saw that [Jesus] was ... dead ....

one of the soldiers pierced his side ...

and ... blood and water came out.

---

226 And I might add, he can also drink refreshing water without understanding exactly how it quenches his thirst!
227 C.S. Lewis, *Mere Christianity*, Revised and Enlarged ed. (New York, NY: Macmillan, 1952), p. 43, emphasis mine.
228 "O taste and see that the LORD [Yahweh] is good; happy are those who take refuge in him" *(Ps. 34:8).*

Chapter 16

In Pursuit of Prophetic Ground Zero (Part 3)

And now let's return to where we were on that dusty trail of history, before we took our deepwater detour, to briefly finish our necessary discussion of Alexander the Great's kingdom, and of the Greek world domination symbolized by that goat in Daniel 8.

True to the prophecy of Daniel 8, Alexander the Great's short-lived, but powerful, kingdom was, at the time of his death, broken up into four *new* Greek kingdoms—represented by the four prominent horns that came up in the great horn's place:

> *Then the male goat grew exceedingly great; but at the height of its power,* **the great horn was broken, and in its place there came up four prominent horns toward the four winds of heaven [the sky].** (Dan. 8:8)

These four horns correspond directly with the four heads of the leopard from the prophecy in Daniel 7.

> *After this, as I watched, another appeared, like a leopard.* **The beast had four wings of a bird on its back and four heads;** *and dominion was given to it.* (Dan. 7:6)

The heads, of course, represent controlling powers—the four Hellenistic Greek kingdoms that followed Alexander's conquests—and the wings represent the same super swiftness of conquest that the goat never touching the ground symbolizes in chapter 8.

> *As I was watching, a male goat [Greece] appeared from the west,* **coming across the face of the whole earth without touching the ground.** (Dan. 8:5)

In other words, the goat figuratively "flew" across the earth (just as a leopard with a double set of wings would fly swiftly), the conquest of the Greek power would be lightning swift.

Not all of the new horns arising from the Greek goat had the same strength, or lasting power, however, as is evidenced by the history that followed, and by the fact that at least one—the kingdom of Lysimachus—is hardly known to most casual students of history today, and it rarely gets mentioned. One could almost not be blamed for thinking it didn't exist. But each kingdom *did* very much exist, during Hellenism's first generation, at least, in the shifting political landscape that followed the breaking off of the goat's great horn (which, despite its greatness, had been shorter-lived than even the shortest-lived of the four horns that followed it since Alexander's kingdom broke up almost immediately after its establishment, following his untimely death).

After the death of Alexander in 323 BC, his generals immediately began to quarrel over who should fill the power vacuum his sudden absence had created. The quarrels began even before Alexander's interment, and the bloody infighting that ensued continued for twenty-two long years, until the battle of Ipsus in 301 BC finally crushed a determined last attempt by a general named Antigonus to reunite the fractured Hellenistic Empire into one single unit under his rule, and with this decisive battle (and Antigonus's death) any future hope for Greek unity was also crushed as well.[229] What had emerged when the dust finally settled, was exactly what the text of Daniel 8 had indicated: four kingdoms, all Greek, yet going their own directions toward the four "winds" of the sky ("heaven"). Four of Alexander's generals carved up Alexander's kingdom into four distinct Hellenistic Greek kingdoms. Some names, geography, and other circumstances of the various kingdoms shifted significantly over time in a never-ending struggle for control. However, here are the names of the four generals, and of general territories they held as the kingdoms emerged:

1. *Cassander* originally held Macedonia and Greece.
2. *Lysimachus* held Thrace, and a great deal of Asia Minor.
3. *Ptolemy* held on to Egypt, Cyrenaica, and the land that would later be known as Palestine.

---

229 Charles Rollin, The Ancient History of the *Egyptians, Carthaginians, Assyrians, Babylonians, Medes and Persians, Macedonians and Grecians,* Vol. 3 (Philadelphia, PA: Lippincott, Grambo & Co., 1855), pp. 384–386 and C. Mervyn Maxwell, *God Cares: The Message of Daniel for You and Your Family,* Vol. 1 (Boise, ID: Pacific Press, 1981), pp. 109, 111.

4. *Seleucus* held the rest of Asia, including Syria and the eastern lands that Alexander had conquered.[230]

This four-way division remained distinct until the last days of Lysimachus when a revolting populous in his kingdom led to a series of overturning events, including the invasion of Lysimachus' kingdom by Seleucus, and finally to Lysimachus' death, as well as the vanishing of his kingdom as a distinct entity, in 281 BC.[231] There remained for some time afterward three major, but always shifting, Hellenistic Greek kingdoms—Ptolemaic Egypt, Seleucid Syria, and Macedonia—as well as a few minor ones.

---

[230] Charles Rollin, *The Ancient History of the Egyptians, Carthaginians, Assyrians, Babylonians, Medes and Persians, Macedonians and Grecians,* Vol. 3 (Philadelphia, PA: Lippincott, Grambo & Co., 1855), pp. 386–387 and C. Mervyn Maxwell, *God Cares: The Message of Daniel for You and Your Family,* Vol. 1 (Boise, ID: Pacific Press, 1981), pp. 109, 111.

[231] Charles Rollin, *The Ancient History of the Egyptians, Carthaginians, Assyrians, Babylonians, Medes and Persians, Macedonians and Grecians,* Vol. 3 (Philadelphia, PA: Lippincott, Grambo & Co., 1855), pp. 414–417.

Chapter 17

A Primer Lesson in Christianity 101 (or 201)

I could take a sloppy shortcut right here and now, if I wanted to, since almost anyone with even a tiny taste of ancient history could now jump in at this proven point and shout out exactly what earth-crushing empire actually followed the Greek world dominance, and thus say: we've hit prophetic ground zero! We know now where in history the Davidic slingstone was supposed to collide with the prophetic Goliath according to Daniel 2! Let's move on to the finishing conclusions of the book! But no! As tempting as such a shortcut may be (and I have taken it before in public speaking where clocks are despotic kings), if I were to cut off the purposeful pursuit at just this point, there might still remain nagging questions in some minds, as to whether or not I had reached my conclusions honestly.

It is not unlike God's conundrum when sin first entered His once perfect universe (and yes, you recognized it; I am once again taking one of my detours—this, a most important one, to explain a related bit of **Christianity 101**). At that time God could also have taken a sloppy shortcut in the great controversy over His character of love, that sin and rebellion had brought into sudden existence. He might have seemingly saved the universe—and humans in particular—a horrifying ordeal. He could have cut short the career of that once angelic being who had so recently turned himself into a devil— *the* devil[232]—who was now spreading questions about God's goodness far and wide among heavenly beings. God could have stepped back at once and removed His ever-present shielding—and sustenance—of life. This would have instantly allowed the inevitable consequences of sin to freely run their final course, and with justification He could have long ago

---

232 I plan to get to that in more depth in another volume.

finally said, *"Enough!"* He could have permitted His unshielded, sin-devouring presence to then do its "strange" natural work of cleansing, which would have wiped out Lucifer—the "Day Star"—and his growing following, then and there.[233]

> *How you are fallen from heaven, O Day Star [Lucifer], son of Dawn!* (Isa. 14:12)

But if He had done that, there would have forever existed in the minds of God's untold multitudes of children—created thinking beings wherever they exist throughout the universe—a certain nagging fear of Him, under the surface of their love. Then the subtle seed of sin would always remain, in the form of nagging questions simmering in the back of billions of minds, as to whether or not Lucifer's deceptive questions about God's goodness might possibly have had merit.

Instead, the Father permitted the tragic seed to grow where it had found a soul soil to sprout in, in our unfortunate world. But into the fallen planet a promise of hope would be instantly sent,[234] and His deep and abiding love for the fallen world would finally be demonstrated by a profound action—by the sending of His one and only Son to grace us, among all of the other unfallen worlds, with the sole privilege of our becoming related *directly* to God, who through the miraculous (from *our* perspective) birth of Jesus was to become also human. And *as* a human being, God would somehow (I don't think any can fully understand or explain it) take upon Himself our *own* sin, *our* shame, *our* deserved "punishment"—the natural consequences of sin before a sin-consuming presence—upon His *human* self, until in the bleakness of the despair that should have been *ours*, He would finally say, not *"Enough!"* but, *"It is finished!"* (John 19:30).

WARNING! This is complex "food for thought" I'm throwing in right here. Perhaps there's also a bit of Christianity 201 in it, as well as 101? But don't worry, class, you won't be tested on it (by *me*, at least). It might be a good idea to chew this food slowly, and to digest it one element at a time, if anything I'm saying is new and unfamiliar to you.

We may derive some very precious information about an ancient great controversy in our universe, which explains a lot about the pain in our

---

[233] See chapter 10 regarding God's sin-devouring presence.
[234] Genesis 3:15, a prophecy of hope given to the disobedient Adam and Eve, constitutes the very first Messianic prophecy in all of Scripture. Although the serpent (Satan) would strike the heel (cause a great injury and excruciating pain) of the woman's Offspring (the Messiah), the woman's Offspring would actually crush the serpent's head (a *fatal* injury).

present existence, from revelations that have been granted to humanity by God over time. These scriptural revelations tell us that God, in His infinite love and wisdom, knew that He could not take a shortcut to wipe out sin and rebellion. He knew that the noxious seed of sin, once planted by the freewill choice of Lucifer (possibly one of the first, if not *the* first, *created beings*)[235]—and transplanted into the human soil of our earth through our first parents' freewill choice—must be allowed to grow and fully mature in our world. The onlooking universe must be allowed to watch the poisonous plant bloom, in order to see what pestilential fruits it would finally produce, so that its existence might ever after be honestly abhorred.

> *These scriptural revelations tell us that God, in His infinite love and wisdom, knew that He could not take a shortcut to wipe out sin and rebellion.*

But in the middle of this bitter universal experiment with rebellion (which has made our world the ground zero of its devastation) God would also unveil, for the very first time,[236] a precious plan that God had devised within His mysterious triune existence far back in the misty eternity of time past which is beyond our ability to comprehend.

> *You know that **you were ransomed** from the futile ways inherited from your ancestors, not with perishable things like silver or gold, but **with the precious blood of Christ**, like that of a lamb without defect or blemish. **He was destined before the foundation of the world**, but was revealed at the end of the ages for your sake.* (1 Peter 1:18–20)
>
> *... **things into which angels long to look!*** (1 Peter 1:12)

That "triune"[237] existence I speak of is a profound three-in-one unity—and community—that must reside in God's *single* existence. It has always been a perpetual conundrum to believers in Christ, but it is based on many scriptural revelations, and especially on the very claims of Jesus Christ to deity (see, for instance, John 8:58). It is a doctrine that Christians have named the "Trinity," and which has been argued over, debated, described,

---

235 as is evidenced by his secondary description, "son of Dawn" (see Isaiah 14:12).
236 (it had apparently been a deep secret, kept even from the heavenly angels to some degree—see 1 Peter 1:12 above)
237 Meaning "three in one."

and often attacked (even literal wars have been fought based upon it)[238] over the last 2,000 years (in at least 1,000 ways), but **which is still ultimately inconceivable to our limited mortal perspectives, though I believe it is absolutely true** (again, I may deal further with that deep subject in another volume, God willing and providing).

From the eternity of Yahweh's mysterious existence in *His* form of deep time[239] (also inconceivable to us in our limited existence[240]) within that inconceivable triune Family of One, a deep plan was devised to deal with sin in the previously witnessed event that it would arise out of the mental faculty of freedom to choose, a faculty which God had purposely built into all His thinking, sentient beings. From God's deep love, a way of gracious escape was to be made available to all who would fall victim to sin's deadly poison. Through the descent (the coming down to earth)—and the *human* descent (a divine conception and human birth, which put the Godhead into direct family relation with us)—of One who was part of that triune unity, an also inexplicable ransom would be achieved for those who might choose to accept it. A profoundly dreadful price would be paid as that member of the Godhead would become our Sin-bearer. He, being both fully divine *but* also fully human, would (inexplicably) become sin *for* us, so that we might live in and through Him, and so that we might be made righteous again *for* Him who so loved us, "that he gave his only Son" (see John 3:16)! In the immortal words of the inspired apostle Paul:

> *For our sake he made him to be sin who knew no sin, so that in him we might become the righteousness of God.* (2 Cor. 5:21)

When God looked down upon us in our degraded state, He did not (and *does* not) gaze upon our nakedness in disgust, as people might (and certainly *do*), but He looked with eyes of pitying compassion and longing, that saw in each degraded sinner the hopeful promise of what we might become again in Him! Despite our despicable dirt, He demonstrated His

---

238 Prokopios, *The Wars of Justinian*, translated by H. B. Dewing, revised and modernized by Anthony Kaldellis (Indianapolis, IN: Hackett Publishing Company, Inc., 2014), pp. 167–168 and Prokopios, *The Secret History with Related Texts*, edited and translated by Anthony Kaldellis (Indianapolis, IN: Hackett Publishing Company, Inc., 2010), pp. 52, 60, 62, 82, 88.
239 A phrase I am commandeering from the *errors* of Darwinism but am using in a very *different* way to speak of the inexplicable eternal past belonging to *God* rather than to blind chance.
240 See Psalm 90:2.

unfathomable love by sending us His only Son to die in our place *while we were yet degraded sinners.*

> *But God demonstrates his own love for us in this: While we were still sinners, Christ died for us.* (Rom. 5:8, NIV)

And though God may (and does) sometimes use fear to awaken us to our condition, to our imminent (and *immanent*[241]) danger, it is not fear (an emergency measure) that He uses to finally win our hearts and minds back to Himself, because true love cannot be coerced! To win our misguided minds, He uses reason, and to win our wounded hearts He uses the tender attractions of His kindness and love, which has been demonstrated most clearly in the sacrifice of His Son. He pleads—even at this moment—with us:

> **" *To win our misguided minds, He uses reason, and to win our wounded hearts He uses the tender attractions of His kindness and love, which has been demonstrated most clearly in the sacrifice of His Son.* "**

> *"Come now, and let us reason together," says the LORD [Yahweh]. "Though your sins are like scarlet, they shall be as white as snow; though they are red like crimson, they shall be as wool."* (Isa. 1:18, NKJV)

He offers to pardon us freely, so long as we are willing, at the very least, to be *made* willing, to pardon *others.*

> *[A]nd forgive us our sins,* **as we have forgiven** *those who sin against us.* (Matt. 6:12, NLT)

> *The LORD [Yahweh] has appeared of old to me, saying: "Yes,* **I have loved you with an everlasting [eternal] love; Therefore with lovingkindness I have drawn you.** *Again I will build you, and you shall be rebuilt."* (Jer. 31:3–4, NKJV)

---

241 As I often say to my "literary" daughter: look it up!

We love God, not because we now naturally love Him. Sin is enmity against God,[242] and our natural condition of being outlaws to His law of love can produce only terror of Him in our hearts all by itself, and true love is never developed through terror! Nor do we love God because we can understand His mysterious existence; we simply cannot, fully. Rather, we love God because (though we can't quite understand it all, and though we know we don't deserve it) we have discovered in our experience, first, that He is *real,* and second, that in spite of our outlaw position, He *first* loved us.

> *There is no fear in love, but perfect love casts out fear; for fear has to do with punishment, and* **whoever fears has not reached perfection in love. We love [only] because he first loved us.** (1 John 4:18–19)

On the cross Jesus took our "punishment"—the Father surrendered Him up to sin's inevitable consequences[243]—in order to take that dread terror and outlaw prospect of destruction away from us.

However, even our punishment being taken away isn't enough (on its own) to turn us away from sin and to make us safe to save. It has to get *personal.* We have to own it, in our hearts and minds and lives. There are many people who have a cheap theoretical belief in Christ's sacrifice for sin, but who are not moved by it in the least, and who certainly don't despise their own sin any more for possessing that knowledge. Just as a lamp must get plugged into a power source to give off its light, so we must connect our amazing guilt and God's amazing grace together in order to experience deep conversion.

> **Just as a lamp must get plugged into a power source to give off its light, so we must connect our amazing guilt and God's amazing grace together in order to experience deep conversion.**

Conversion—compared by Jesus Himself to being born all over again[244]—is a powerful change of heart and mind that sometimes appears to have come on suddenly to a newly born Christian, although it is actually

---

242 See Romans 8:7.
243 *Another* subject I hope to deal with in another volume.
244 See John 3:3–8.

a final result of an often quite-prolonged work of the Holy Spirit, which has been going on without our having even been aware of it, deep down inside the recesses of our souls. This transformation of our insides (that Christians call conversion) will eventually transform our entire lives if we don't abort it or stifle its growth, and if, after first conversion, we keep ourselves, and the new life that has just sprouted in our hearts, connected to the life-giving vine of Jesus.[245] But conversion, though always somewhat of an internal surprise when it happens to anyone (sometimes even to sworn atheists—the author C.S. Lewis's story is one of my very favorites on that line), is not just a momentary event. We may continue to be converted again and *again* throughout our lifetimes on different planes of divine perspective, even long after the time when we had first surrendered to the voice of God's insistent calling out to us. Even then, our conversion(s) may also grow deeper (if not different) and even deeper yet, as we come to know God more and even *more* intimately. That is *God's* deep desire for us! This can happen by our often calling out to Him along the bumpy road of our journey, as well as by taking purposeful time to intensely search His Word, and to patiently and wistfully listen (like Elijah once did)[246] for Yahweh's **"still small voice."** [247] This kind of voice can only usually be heard in **the sound of sheer silence** (the literal translation of the "sound" Elijah actually heard at that mountain cave's mouth):

> *[The voice of Yahweh] said, "Go out and stand on the mountain before the LORD [Yahweh], for the LORD [Yahweh] is about to pass by." Now there was a great wind, so strong that it was splitting mountains and breaking rocks in pieces before the LORD [Yahweh], but the LORD [Yahweh] was not in the wind; and after the wind an earthquake, but the LORD [Yahweh] was not in the earthquake; and after the earthquake a fire, but the LORD [Yahweh] was not in the fire; and after the fire **a sound of sheer silence**.* (1 Kings 19:11–12)

Conversion is the root that grows downward on the plant of our upward redemption. The plant is only able to grow as big in our lives as its root is allowed to go deep into the soil of God's goodness. But in order to plug into that power, we must *first* experience a painful sense of the true

---

245 See John 15:5.
246 See 1 Kings 19:9–13.
247 From the King James Version of 1 Kings 19:12.

greatness of our spiritual hunger, [248] and of our profound need, as well as the blackness of our sin and shame in the light of His law that is based on love! We must view ourselves—more than momentarily—in His mercilessly honest mirror[249]—His perfect law of liberty—which alone can drive us to the suddenly-desperate desire for the mercy that His grace alone can give us, His unmerited favor.[250] And we can only find this grace, as Christians of long experience like to say, "at the foot of His cross," where they also like to point out that "the ground is level" (at the foot of His cross)! *No one* is worth more than anyone else, and no one has an advantage over any other at just that one spot in the entire world.

> **Conversion is the root that grows downward on the plant of our upward redemption. The plant is only able to grow as big in our lives as its root is allowed to go deep into the soil of God's goodness.**

> For **by grace [favor] you have been saved** through faith, and this is not your own doing; it is the gift of God—**not the result of works**, so that no one may boast. (Eph. 2:8–9)

Let me give you the full *resurrection* context of this powerful passage as it is found in the New Living Translation (first edition). *Grace* is such an important concept for us to grasp, and I believe this translation has beautifully grasped the big picture of it, and pleasingly paints it for modern minds in an easy-to-understand language:

> [E]ven while we were dead because of our sins, he gave us life when he raised Christ from the dead. (It is only by God's special favor [grace] that you have been saved!) For he raised us from the dead along with Christ, and we are seated with him in the heavenly realms—all because we are one with Christ Jesus. And so God can always point to us as examples of the incredible wealth of his favor [grace] and kindness toward us, as shown in all he has done for us through Christ Jesus.

---

248 See Matthew 5:6.
249 See James 1:23–26.
250 See Luke 18:13–14.

> *God saved you by his special favor [grace] when you believed. And you can't take credit for this;* ***it is a gift from God.*** *Salvation is not a reward for the good things we have done, so* ***none of us can boast about it.*** *For we are God's masterpiece.* *He has created us anew in Christ Jesus,* ***so that we can do*** *the good things [truly good works, sprouting up from a truly good heart] he planned for us long ago.* (Eph. 2:5–10, NLT, first edition)

But to be raised with Christ, we first must *die* with Christ. **We first must confess and acknowledge the painful perversity that we are also a part of, just as much as any other sinners we have ever proudly despised**! Even on that note, there is a thought we ought to seriously consider, which could help to humble our hearts since the God who sees all (as we cannot see) *does* consider it. He knows every heart, and He understands what each has had to contend with from the moment of conception. It is the thought that if *we* had been born in exactly the same circumstances that *they* were born into (whoever it is we are despising), or *we* had experienced the particular temptations, the harrowing traumas, the warping formative educations, or whatever stunting circumstances might have influenced their lives, it is entirely possible (God knows) that **we might have ended up even worse than they did**. We might not have been able to bear up even half as well as they! So our sin of pride, falsely estimating and harboring evil imaginations *about* others, each for whom Jesus died, may, in fact, be our ugliest sin in God's eyes. It may be the very sin that we most need to be forgiven and that we most need our hearts to be cleansed from! But He says to us, just as He says to the vilest sinner:

> *But if we confess our sins to him, he is faithful and just to forgive us and to cleanse us from every wrong. If we claim we have not sinned, we are calling God a liar and showing that his word has no place in our hearts.* (1 John 1:9–10, NLT, first edition)

The honest assessment we must allow God and His Word to make of our sinful natures—and motives—is the *bad* news of the "good news" (the gospel). But we must go through this painful acknowledgment in private prayer, before God's grace will mean anything profoundly beautiful to us! We cannot go on thinking that people (including ourselves) are, by themselves, "pretty good, generally."

> *The [fallen human] heart is devious above all else; it is perverse—who can understand it?* (Jer. 17:9)

> *[S]ince all have sinned and [continue to] fall short of the glory of God.* (Rom. 3:23)

This is why people who are publicly despised for their sin—those who are callously called out and mistreated by so-called "good" people[251]—and who have a painful realization of just how rotten they have been, will go into "the kingdom" before people who feel pretty good about themselves[252] and who have no sense of criminality or guilt, and who self-righteously despise others![253]

When Jesus first started His ministry on earth, His first message echoed the repentance message that John the baptizer had already been preaching:

> *Now after John was arrested, Jesus came to Galilee, proclaiming the good news [gospel] of God, and saying, "The time is fulfilled, and the kingdom of God has come near;* **repent [turn back from sin], and believe in the good news [gospel].**" (Mark 1:14–15)

Repentance implies an internal recognition of the heinousness of *our* sin. But self-righteous people (often the "law and order" types such as the Pharisees of old) simply cannot see that fallen reality (despite its undeniable reality) in *themselves*. They say, "I'm not at fault." Therefore, they cannot repent unless they either fall infamously from their pedestals of pride, or else a **miracle of mercy** humbles their proud hearts, *somehow*, leading them to plead with God for a true view of themselves! A plea like that is one prayer I believe God *will* answer "yes" to. This answered prayer can finally lead *even them* to fall at the crucified feet of Jesus, **with the rest of us**,[254] pleading for His mercy. And Jesus has promised that *"anyone who comes to me I will never drive away" (John 6:37).*

Only when we have gotten a glimpse of our guilt, and of the enormity of *all* human guilt—especially the guilt of our self-righteous pride (an

---

251 Just like the Pharisee in Luke 18:11–12.
252 See Matthew 21:31–32.
253 See Luke 18:9.
254 Though I was once very self-righteous too—as hard as it is for me now sometimes to believe—I now count my unworthy self with the pleading penitents who pray: "'God, be merciful to me, a sinner!'" (Luke 18:13).

unloving self-deception)—can we *really* begin to understand the enormity of God's love for us and for those whom we had once despised.

It is not a fear of "punishment" (though that might wake many up to their great need of help) but a heart-viewing of God's own *goodness* that leads our hearts to *truly* turn away from sin (permanently, rather than temporarily) and forever toward God! Thus, **it is only a revelation of God's goodness**—which gets graphically demonstrated in the gift, the sacrifice, the resurrection, and the revelations of Jesus[255]—**that can make us safe to save**, that can make us *want* to be truly good like Him, that can eradicate the seed of sin and selfishness, finally, from our synapses and souls as we develop an eternal *friendship*[256] with our good Savior and King.

> *Or do you despise the riches of His goodness, forbearance, and longsuffering, not knowing that* **the goodness of God leads you to repentance?** *(Rom. 2:4, NKJV)*

This is one more area where words fail me and seem to fall flat in my effort to describe the wonder of it all—a wonder which I have caught true glimpses of, and that I long to share. Once you witness it in your *own* heart, I know that you'll then agree that there is something undeniably miraculous about the draw of God's love, about the sacrifice of His Son, and about the resulting change of heart by which even the hardiest infidel,[257] and the vilest sinner, have been (and may be) transformed into true children of God! It is one of the few things in this life that I can, without exaggeration, call *wonderful*. It is a priceless thing of fadeless—of actually *growing*—beauty.

But just where in our world, and in its long dark corridors of history, did the ancient prophecy of Daniel 2 predict that God would demonstrate this miraculous love—symbolized by that altar stone cut from Mount Zion without human hands—the Stone *who* draws us with His cords of kindness?

---

255 The Lamb of God as well as the Lion of the tribe of Judah. See Revelation 5:5.
256 See John 15:15.
257 Unbeliever.

Chapter 18

Ground Zero and the Great Controversy

Then the male goat [the Greek political domination] grew exceedingly great; but at the height of its power, the great horn was broken, and in its place there came up four prominent horns **toward the four winds of heaven** *[the sky]. Out of one of them* **[that is, grammatically, out of one of the four winds, or directions]** *came another horn, a little one, which grew exceedingly great toward the south, toward the east [obviously the horn arose somewhere in the northwest relative to the Greek territories and/or Judah], and toward the beautiful land [always a designation, in Daniel, for the land of Judah].* (Dan. 8:8–9)

Here we have arrived at the symbolism in Daniel chapter 8, which corresponds directly with the parallel feet and toes of that mighty colossus Nebuchadnezzar saw in his famous dream of Daniel 2—the dream that contains the symbolism of the very prophetic ground zero we have now so long been in pursuit of on the dusty desert road of history. It is the very spot on the statue where that altar stone cut out from Mount Zion was prophesied to strike. But before I go on to pronounce our imminent arrival at our destination, I need, first, to inform you that there is one more precipitous pitfall we must sidestep together if we are going to arrive safely.

The pitfall is a common misunderstanding about even this particular passage I have just quoted—which I have already hinted at in the brackets I placed inside the quotation. It seems to me that I have spent far too much time in this book giving explanations about common misunderstandings of Bible prophecies! However, I do not do it to speak down to anybody; rather, I do it for clarity and because I believe it is absolutely necessary in the intellectual environment we find ourselves living in today—especially in the age of the Internet, the oftentimes misinformation superhighway. Personally, I am convinced that the main reason I *need* to do this is that we *do* have an invisible enemy in that great invisible controversy I have several times spoken about. This enemy affects our lives and our opinions if we don't stay awake to God's Spirit[258] constantly, and if we don't purposefully seek His guidance continually. You might say we are living on the enemy's own ground, and walking daily through thick, overgrown vegetation that conceals his cleverly camouflaged traplines. And this enemy especially likes to encourage wide distributions, and unquestioning adoptions, of fundamental misunderstandings about any Bible prophecies having anything (in reality) to do with Jesus the Christ, the ancient promised Messiah! **He likes to blind human eyes to the real point of all Bible prophecy** because he knows that anything which lifts up the Christ, and that centers our focus on *Him,* will also end up drawing the world unto Him through our missionary messages.

> *And I, if I am lifted up … will draw all peoples to Myself.* (John 12:32, NKJV)

The above passage from Daniel 8 pronounces by prophetic symbolism the kind of dominating power that would arise next on the scene of ancient world history in those most important regions surrounding Judah following the Greek political dominance and its four divisions that arose after the death of Alexander the Great. I speak again of those divisions which were portrayed by four horns that grew up in his prominent horn's place—that is, four *kingdoms* that would arise *out of* his broken kingdom, and thus would have a direct relationship to it. The misconception I speak of is that this new horn (a new *kingdom* or *empire*) would also arise *out of* one of the four Greek horns, or *kingdoms* (similar to how the four horns arose out of Alexander's horn), that it would thereby also be an extension of Alexander's original kingdom via one of the four horns. This misunderstanding suggests that the new power would be purely Greek! But the relationship of the new horn to the previous four is not so portrayed when the ancient Hebrew this passage was written in gets correctly translated. There is actually **a distinct break in continuity** between the four horns and the new horn. Let me demonstrate.

---

258 See Matthew 26:41.

Ground Zero and the Great Controversy

The illustrative example I am about to describe to you should stand as a warning to all serious Bible students to not lean too heavily on the renderings of any one Bible translation (or on any *so-called* translation) when they seek to precisely investigate the true meanings of any important Bible passage—especially one of symbolic prophecy.

We must know that translator biases can slip into even the most careful of true translations, and that with the much, *much* lesser works that average people often *mistake* for true translations (I speak of paraphrases such as *The Clear Word, The Message,* or *The Living Bible),* translator bias is *everywhere* present. **Such literary works are not actual translations of the ancient languages but simply re-renderings (of other Bible translations) in the author's own words (and own biases).** These usually well-meaning works (which I think have a definite useful place in a Christian's library so long as they are used properly and their limitations are clearly understood) are meant to simplify, to clarify, and to breathe life into the language of Scripture for modern people. They make Scripture more accessible. Unfortunately, such re-renderings, which often gloss over difficult passages and seek to clarify ambiguous wordings, can (in these processes) unintentionally obscure, and actually *kill,* the original intentions of the biblical authors in many important passages. They can also obscure important symbolic details when it comes to complex prophecy.

Now we even have a form of literary crossover that falls somewhere in between a translation and a paraphrase, which brings the biased tendencies of a paraphrase into what is now being erroneously called a true translation. Though the results often produce beautiful and easy-to-read language, the title "translation" still amounts to a slight fudging tendency on the part of the book publishers involved. We need to be seriously aware of this fudging when it comes to serious Bible study. The most famous example of what I am referring to is a so-called "translation" that I *myself* even appreciate. It is called the *New Living Translation.*[259] I hope you don't get the idea here, however, that I am attacking it wholesale because that is not my intention. I have quoted from the *New Living Translation (first edition)* in this book, and one time quite extensively, because I appreciated its beautiful rendering of a passage. It is an increasingly popular literary rendering of Scripture, written in language that most grade schoolers might understand. It has commendably sought to do away with many errors and biases of the old *Living Bible* paraphrase by seeking to anchor its wording

---

[259] This translation has been updated several times since its original edition, which is the edition I happen to still be using.

more firmly to the ancient biblical languages and texts, while still holding onto the simple and easy-reading language style that the old *Living Bible* became famous—and prized—for, in its day. I just want to give you a heads-up warning that such works—as beautiful and useful as they may be for devotional purposes—should not be leaned upon too heavily in any careful Bible study. They still contain misleading biases similar to the less-sophisticated paraphrases.

Even this so-called "translation" shows itself, at least in this particular passage, to not always follow the rules of a true translation. I say this because a true translation must necessarily bind itself to the rules of ancient grammar for any language it is translating (unless, of course, it is abundantly obvious that an ancient writer was not a native speaker of a particular language himself). The *New Living Translation* most obviously ignored the rules of ancient Hebrew, or else *missed them somehow,* at least in this particular spot. Here is how the *New Living Translation (first edition)* renders the first part of Daniel 8:9:

> [F]rom one of the prominent horns came a small horn whose power grew very great. (Dan. 8:9, NLT)

If this particular verse had been *carefully* translated, **it could *not* have attributed the origin of the new horn to the previous horns since that attribution is simply impossible in the ancient Hebrew text**. Obviously, whoever came up with this wording was treating the passage as if it had been written in English rather than in Hebrew. This detail *may* have been overlooked unintentionally (almost unconsciously even) by an average native English speaker, but it should not have been by a Hebrew scholar working on a serious Bible translation. In the grammar of ancient Hebrew, nouns have gender, just as they do in many other languages still commonly spoken today. In all such gender specific languages, it is a hard and fast rule that **pronouns must necessarily agree with their antecedent nouns in gender. They must be similarly masculine, feminine, or neuter**. In the Hebrew of this passage, "horns" is, *and can only be,* feminine, while "winds" can be either masculine or feminine. But in the phrase that is usually translated "out of one of them," the pronoun "them" is actually masculine. This means that **the antecedent noun for "them" cannot possibly be "horns" but must be "winds."** What the passage is really saying, then, is that the new horn must arise out of one of the four *winds,* or rather from one of the four directions of the compass. *That* direction can even be teased out of the passage by simply paying attention to the directions that the little horn was predicted to grow, or to conquer. It must come from a northwesterly direction in relation to ancient Judah (remember, Daniel is an ethnocentric book) and/or the Hellenistic Greek kingdoms, since it would grow great toward the south and toward the east.

Let's return now, briefly—by way of explaining this powerful bias, a bias that even tempts professional translators to ignore ancient grammar rules—to a quotation I shared with you earlier by Sir Isaac Newton (one that I analyzed and critiqued back in chapter 14). At that time I only gave you a mere portion of one sentence, which was cut out from a much larger passage, since I was not yet ready to deal directly with the subject matter the whole passage is about (to see the slight objection I have to his quotation's wording, in case you forgot, please refer back to chapter 14). Here is the small portion I gave you earlier:

> *A horn of a beast is never taken for a single person: it always signifies a new kingdom.*[260]

But now, let's look at the rest of that quotation's story. It is a story about just what subject matter (or common prophetic error) had prompted the world-famous mathematical genius, the discoverer and describer of gravitational laws, and a father of modern science, to make his unequivocal statement about horns in Bible prophecy.

The common prophetic error he was actually speaking against is related to a brief ancient episode of Hellenistic Greek history which I've referred to several times (without naming it or elaborating on it). So many interpreters have erroneously tried to squeeze several of Daniel's prophecies into being about that one episode of history, when they are not, and *cannot* be, even though some Bible study helps confusingly state that the connection is "obvious." Trying to make Daniel to be about this relatively minor episode in history is the erroneous reasoning behind that "kingdom splitting" error I have talked about extensively. Isaac Newton's quotation clearly demonstrates to me that the error is a very old one. His full quotation (below) about the subject also demonstrates that the error had to be squarely dealt with by any author who wanted to carefully interpret Daniel to the public in his day, just as it must at least be *mentioned* in any careful analysis of Daniel made in our day. This frustrates me because

---

[260] Isaac Newton, *Sir Isaac Newton's Daniel and the Apocalypse*, ed. Sir William Whitla (London: John Murray, 1922), p. 222.

it intrudes (as an unnecessary distraction) from the real *Christ-centered* issues of the prophecies we are studying. I suspect that stooping to deal with this Scripture-twisting error gave logical Isaac Newton a similar frustrating feeling, too, since he somewhat tersely (or so it seems to me) wrote the following rather large passage to rebut it. It is a passage that my giving to you in full at this point, without a real introduction to the subject matter and to its many details, is somewhat akin to suddenly shoving a dry and unexpecting person into deep water. But, alas, sometimes the best way to enter a body of cold water is to just jump in! So here we go! *Splash!*

> *This last horn is by some taken for ANTIOCHUS EPIPHANES, but not very judiciously. A horn of a Beast is never taken for a single person: it always signifies a new kingdom, and the kingdom of ANTIOCHUS was an old one. ANTIOCHUS reigned over one of the four horns, and the little horn was a fifth under its proper kings. This horn was at first a little one, and waxed exceeding great, but so did not ANTIOCHUS. It is described great above all the former horns, and so was not ANTIOCHUS. His kingdom on the contrary was weak, and tributary to the ROMANS, and he did not enlarge it. The horn was a King of fierce countenance, and destroyed wonderfully, and prospered and practised; that is, he prospered in his practices against the holy people: but ANTIOCHUS was frightened out of EGYPT by a mere message of the ROMANS, and afterwards routed and baffled by the JEWS. The horn was mighty by another's power, ANTIOCHUS acted by his own. The horn stood up against the Prince of the Host of heaven, the Prince of Princes; and this is the character not of ANTIOCHUS but of ANTICHRIST. The horn cast down the Sanctuary to the ground, and so did not ANTIOCHUS; he left it standing. The Sanctuary and Host were trampled under foot 2300 days; and in DANIEL'S Prophecies days are put for years: but the profanation of the Temple in the reign of ANTIOCHUS did not last for so many natural days. These were to last till the time of the end, till the last end of the indignation against the JEWS; and this indignation is not yet at an end. They were to last till the Sanctuary which had been cast down should be cleansed, and the Sanctuary is not yet cleansed.*[261]

---

261 C. Mervyn Maxwell, *God Cares: The Message of Daniel for You and Your Family,* Vol. 1 (Boise, ID: Pacific Press, 1981), p. 192.

Now, although I won't go into details in this volume, I don't agree with every perspective Isaac Newton expressed in this quotation first printed in 1733—almost 300 years ago. However, I *do* believe he presented a withering argument against the "not very judicious" assumption some people have made, that this latter horn in Daniel 8 (as well as a somewhat similar horn in Daniel 7) stands for a minor king of the Greeks who at one time harassed the ancient Jews.

Unfortunately, a few of the minute details that this quote may have piqued your interest in, and which I may see a slightly different perspective on, are beyond what I plan to deal with in this volume. This mysterious "2300 days," for instance, and the cleansing of the sanctuary, which Isaac Newton mentions (and that I have a slight difference of perspective on) are both subject matters I have slated for a future volume since they go far beyond the foundational purpose of this volume. However, I *will* briefly tell you, here and now, who this Antiochus Epiphanes was.

Antiochus Epiphanes (Antiochus IV) was a rather strange, though relatively insignificant, king who came approximately in the middle of the line of the Seleucid kings. The Seleucid dynasty was one of those four Hellenistic Greek kingdoms represented by the four horns of the prophetic goat; it was the kingdom started by Alexander's general Seleucus. "Epiphanes" refers to Antiochus's claim to be a manifestation, or epiphany, of a god. There were, to be sure, certain shadowy similarities to the little horn power in the character of Antiochus, but on a profoundly smaller scale than the prophecy would indicate for the new horn, which is clearly presented as a new *growing* world domination of profound proportions. Of the new little horn power, for instance, it was said that "in his own mind he shall be great" (Dan. 8:25), indicating that the new horn power, though indeed profoundly great and successful from a *human* perspective (it would "grow strong in power,"[262] something Antiochus never did), would not be viewed that way at all from *God's* perspective.[263] For Antiochus, the saying that "in his own mind he shall be great" could be said just as well, but with the exception that in *his* case he was **a king who was big only in his own mind even from a *human* perspective**. He was never considered to be great by people in actual history, nor did he ever succeed in his attempts at conquest. In fact, some of his contemporaries

---

262 Daniel 8:24.
263 The perspective of Bible prophecy.

contemptuously referred to him during his lifetime as "Epimanes," the mad man.[264]

Antiochus Epiphanes did persecute the conservative Jews. Partly due to the support of liberal Hellenizing Jews, he was enabled to desecrate and suspend the Jewish temple services for a brief time sometime between either 168 and 165 BC, or 167 and 164 BC, depending on whose calculations you follow.[265] It is abundantly understandable how his desecrations of the temple in ancient times loomed large in the eyes of conservative Jews of the time. The desecrations loomed so large, in fact, that 1 and 2 Maccabees (two non-canonical books contained in the Apocrypha) quote phrases from Daniel 8 and 9 when they discuss Antiochus' activities.[266] Also, the erection of a new altar of sacrifice following the persecution (to replace the one Antiochus, at the instigation of liberal Hellenizing Jews, had sacrificed "unclean" animals on),[267] led directly to the famous Jewish celebration of the rededication of the temple, which we know as Hanukkah. However, Daniel nowhere states such a connection to that brief episode in history.[268] Every attempt to fit the events of Antiochus's persecution into elements of these prophecies in Daniel fails miserably upon a closer, Sherlock Holmes inspection, just as Sir Isaac Newton (a Holmes in his own right) so astutely outlined in the above quotation. I also believe the lion share of Bible scholars today recognize this on some level (even though many of them still promote the idea of these prophecies being about Antiochus for reasons of prejudice). Those who recognize them, often choose to ignore the obvious discrepancies because their acknowledging would not suit certain pet theories and conclusions they have already jumped to. It is not unlike (I think) the fictional Scotland Yard detectives of the famous Sherlock Holmes detective stories, who so often misinterpreted *their* clues for the same sorts of reasons.

---

264 Charles Rollin, *The Ancient History of the Egyptians, Carthaginians, Assyrians, Babylonians, Medes and Persians, Macedonians and Grecians,* Vol. 4 (Philadelphia, PA: Lippincott, Grambo & Co., 1855), p. 151.
265 C. Mervyn Maxwell, *God Cares: The Message of Daniel for You and Your Family,* Vol. 1 (Boise, ID: Pacific Press, 1981), p. 159.
266 Ibid.
267 And on which a statue of Zeus had also been erected during the persecution.
268 One would think that if Daniel really *had* been written after the fact of Antiochus's persecution, as skeptics contend, that a much clearer connection would have been made by its author between these prophecies and Antiochus, and that the time prophecies, which numberless scholars have struggled in vain to match up with the events, would *actually* fit.

Just to summarize a few significant ways Antiochus does *not* fit the prophecy, let me give you a brief list:[269]

1. Horns represent kingdoms, but *he was only a single king* who was actually part of one of the *four* horns.
2. And Antiochus did *not* appear "[a]t the end of their rule" (Dan. 8:23), but approximately in the middle of the line of Seleucid kings.
3. He did *not* keep "prospering" (verse 12) in what he did.
4. He did *not* grow "**exceedingly great** toward the south, toward the east, and toward the beautiful land" (verse 9).
5. Although he temporarily suspended sanctuary services, Antiochus did *not* overthrow "the place of [the] sanctuary" (verse 11), regardless of how you interpret that phrase.
6. All attempts to fit his desecration of the temple into "two thousand three hundred evenings and mornings" (verse 14) fail uniformly because the time span of the events (if not the exact years) is a matter of well-known record.
7. Furthermore, even though 1 Maccabees 1:54 applies the phrase "desolating sacrilege"[270] to the temple desecrations done by Antiochus Epiphanes, Jesus, in His Olivet discourse said that Daniel's "desolating sacrilege" (Matt. 24:15) was still in the *future* as of His day. I think I'd rather go with *Jesus!*

And I especially like the way C. Mervyn Maxwell concludes his discussion of the problems with trying to connect Antiochus to the new horn of Daniel 8:

> *[Jesus] added, "Let the reader understand."*[271] *So, if we really want to understand the meaning of the little horn of Daniel 8, we shall have to conclude, with Jesus, that it cannot have been Antiochus Epiphanes, who died in 164 B.C., almost two hundred years prior to the Olivet Discourse.*[272]

---

269 Though this is not an exhaustive list by any means.
270 Greek: βδέλυγμα ἐρημώσεως, —a phrase which is almost certainly borrowed from the related prophecy in Daniel 9:27, and which proponents of Antiochus being the new horn like to say he brought about. C. Mervyn Maxwell, *God Cares: The Message of Daniel for You and Your Family,* Vol. 1 (Boise, ID: Pacific Press, 1981), p. 160.
271 Matthew 24:15.
272 C. Mervyn Maxwell, *God Cares: The Message of Daniel for You and Your Family,* Vol. 1 (Boise, ID: Pacific Press, 1981), p. 160, emphasis mine.

The odd episode of Antiochus in Egypt, which Sir Isaac Newton referred to, is actually a very pertinent illustration of the *real* dominating power that was actually coming next onto the world scene, and which matches the prophecy of the little horn in its *every* detail (unlike Antiochus' reign),[273] and that was already growing in dominance even at the time of Antiochus. It was a power that would eventually expand from the northwest, just as did the little horn in the prophecy, and it would eventually take over all of the former realm once belonging to the four horns and *more!* The curious story of Antiochus' encounter with this very power while in Egypt demonstrates how this little king (who was *not* so great after all) became actually paralyzed with fear from a mere message sent by the ambassador from the still-small, but unquestionably growing power that would far, *far* outstrip anything ever done by Antiochus in time (though we won't go fully into the details in this book).

Antiochus Epiphanes did enjoy a very short-lived conquest of Ptolemaic Egypt. However, that was soon turned into total and humiliating defeat without so much as a battle. The defeat came by mere words from a man's mouth, when the Roman ambassador, C. Popilius Laena, arrived to inform Antiochus that the Roman senate wished for him to leave Egypt. The ambassador grimly drew a circle around Antiochus with his cane, and then demanded a decision from him before he should step out of the circle.[274]

The reason he was so intimidated and humiliated by the presence of a mere ambassador from Rome is, in itself, a most fascinating and revealing story about Antiochus's *own* connection with this rising power. This power really *was* the fulfillment of the little horn prophecy, and it just happened to also be the very power that allowed Antiochus to be a king in the first place. You see, Antiochus had been partly raised by the Romans, in *Rome!*[275]

Antiochus Epiphanes was the son of the *truly* great (from a human perspective) Antiochus III, who had restored the original Seleucid dominations, pushing his kingdom's borders back to their original extent. That

---

273 Though we won't analyze *all* of those details in *this* book since some relate to an element of history I will be coming to in another volume.

274 C. Mervyn Maxwell, *God Cares: The Message of Daniel for You and Your Family,* Vol. 1 (Boise, ID: Pacific Press, 1981), p. 159 and Livy, *Rome's Mediterranean Empire: Books 41–45 and the Periochae,* translated with an introduction and notes by Jane D. Chaplin (Oxford, England: Oxford University Press, 2007).

275 C. Mervyn Maxwell, *God Cares: The Message of Daniel for You and Your Family,* Vol. 1 (Boise, ID: Pacific Press, 1981), p. 190.

is, until the Romans took from him the greater portion of that reconquered land at the battle of Magnesia in 190 BC (they took the whole of Asia Minor, in fact) and then "liberated" the region, giving it some degree of autonomy. In order to assure that Antiochus III would honor the treaty they had then imposed upon him, the Romans took hostage one of his youthful sons, also named *Antiochus*, the same who would later call himself "Epiphanes."[276]

While captive in Rome, and especially during one particular visit he made to Greece, the young Antiochus became fanatically enthused with the form of Hellenism (Greek thought and culture) which was all the rage among even the Romans by that time period in history. Even before their conquest of the Greek world, the Romans themselves were already well on their way to becoming *Greco*-Romans. So there is surely still a connection between the little horn and the prophetic goat in this prophecy. Even though the little horn did not come directly out of Alexander's replacement horns, it did arise out of the milieu of the dominating Greek culture[277] which the goat's conquests had spread. Suffice it to say that Antiochus soon made it his main mission in life to make the wide acceptance of Hellenism universal. He saw himself as the Hellenistic ambassador to the world. It was partly through this mission he pursued with religious zeal that he sought to make a name for himself, after the Romans finally allowed him to take the throne of his father's Seleucid kingdom following his father's death. He determined at that time to spread Hellenism at *any* cost, even as he sought to enlarge his domain, just as his father had once done.

Antiochus failed pretty miserably at his military dreams, but he did succeed somewhat in his cultural dreams, helping to spread Hellenism into enclaves that it had not yet fully permeated. But that cultural success—which involved granting money to various cities (including Jerusalem) so that they could build Greek temples and gymnasiums—reduced his nation

---

276 Charles Rollin, *The Ancient History of the Egyptians, Carthaginians, Assyrians, Babylonians, Medes and Persians, Macedonians and Grecians,* Vol. 4 (Philadelphia, PA: Lippincott, Grambo & Co., 1855); C. Mervyn Maxwell, *God Cares: The Message of Daniel for You and Your Family,* Vol. 1 (Boise, ID: Pacific Press, 1981); Livy, *Rome's Mediterranean Empire: Books 41–45 and the Periochae,* translated with an introduction and notes by Jane D. Chaplin (Oxford, England: Oxford University Press, 2007); Harold W. Attridge et al., eds., *The HarperCollins Study Bible: New Revised Standard Version, with the Apocryphal/Deuterocanonical Books* (San Francisco, CA: HarperSanFrancisco, 2006).

277 It is interesting to me as a student of history that the Roman Empire, in the end, even lost much of its Latin character and language in favor of Greek, at least in its later Eastern division that was ruled from Byzantium (or Constantinople—modern-day Istanbul, Turkey).

finally to bankruptcy. It ultimately led to his downfall, as well, since he died while on a military campaign to recoup finances by robbing the treasure of an Eastern *pagan* temple, just as he had once done to the temple in Jerusalem.[278]

According to the book of 2 Maccabees (5:11–21),[279] it was after his humiliating experience in Egypt that Antiochus had, at the instigation of liberal Hellenizing Jews, gone on all of his rampages in Jerusalem, desecrating the Jewish temple and suspending its services for a time, as well as taking away the citizens' religious freedom in the process. No doubt, like many other defeated bullies, he was simply taking his frustrations out on a power he thought to be smaller than himself and which he imagined would remain easily under his control. He then robbed the temple as a means of recovering the costs of his Egyptian campaign, also with the guidance of Hellenizing Jews. In his final initial attack, Antiochus fully plundered and destroyed the city, carrying off any wealth that was moveable while burning most of the city's great buildings and houses and tearing down its walls. He gave callous orders to butcher all the men and to take the women and children captive to sell as slaves.

Eventually, Antiochus was once again sent packing when conservative Jews rallied around the military leadership of Judas Maccabaeus, who won an important series of victories over the armies of Antiochus (see 1 and 2 Maccabees). But I am loathe to go into more details about Antiochus Epiphanes, or the Maccabean wars, since that is not what this book is about. If I have piqued your interest, however, I encourage you to check out a library book about the events, or better yet, look up some of the original ancient sources that tell about Antiochus and his persecutions, such

---

278 C. Mervyn Maxwell, *God Cares: The Message of Daniel for You and Your Family,* Vol. 1 (Boise, ID: Pacific Press, 1981), pp. 190–191.

279 Although the book of 1 Maccabees suggests there had already been an attack two years earlier on Jerusalem (see 1:20-29), and that book attributes Antiochus's robbing of the temple's furnishings and gold to that supposed earlier attack; however, it is quite likely that the writer of 1 Maccabees—which some commentators suspect was written later than 2 Maccabees—may have been motivated to slightly adapt the story (according to 2 Maccabees, there had been some prior looting of the temple (see 4:31-34) but not by Antiochus) to make it fit better to his own biased understanding of a prophecy in Daniel (see 11:28) as being all about the experience with Antiochus. 1 Maccabees is the only one of 1 and 2 Maccabees that connected Antiochus's profanation of the temple with the so-called "desolating sacrilege" (see 1 Maccabees 1:54) predicted in Daniel 9:27 and 11:31, an assumption which Jesus Himself contradicts by saying it was still future in His own day, almost 200 years after Antiochus's death (see Matthew 24:15).

as the Roman historian, Livy,[280] the Greek historian, Polybius,[281] or the anonymous historians who wrote 1 and 2 Maccabees in the Apocrypha.

What Daniel 8 actually says about the new power that would arise goes far beyond the actions of that strange little King Antiochus (though he too was certainly a puppet of similar unseen evil forces in heavenly realms, whose sinister strings had been actuated by the very same behind-the-scenes spiritual beings who later also actuated many earthly movements of the much more powerful, and lasting, new horn). The language is a cryptic unveiling (a pulling back of the concealing curtain) of the great behind-the-scenes cosmic controversy in heavenly realms, which the new earthly power would end up playing a pivotal puppet role in, due to its propinquitous[282] placement within the timeline of history relating to that mysterious "kingdom of God," which the stone in Daniel 2 stood for! The language in the following passage clearly betrays the fact that the cosmic conflict it portrays must go far beyond mere *human* elements in history, even into the hidden spiritual realms obscured from our view behind a veiling curtain, the very backdrop of the theatrical stage on which the visible scenes of our world history are being played out.

> *Out of one of [the four winds] came another horn, a little one, which grew exceedingly great toward the south, toward the east, and toward the beautiful land [Judah]. It grew* **as high as the host of heaven [the sky]**. *It threw down to the earth some of the host and some of the stars, and trampled on them.* **Even against the prince of the host** *it acted arrogantly; it took the regular burnt offering away ... and overthrew the place of his sanctuary. Because of wickedness, the host was given over to it together with the regular burnt offering;* **it cast truth to the ground, and kept prospering** *in what it did. Then I heard a holy one [an angel] speaking, and another holy one [angel] said to the one that spoke, "For how long is this vision concerning the regular burnt offering, the transgression that makes desolate, and the giving over of the sanctuary and host to be trampled?" And he answered him, "For two thousand three hundred evenings and mornings; then the sanctuary shall be restored to its rightful state [cleansed]."* (Dan. 8:9–14)

---

280 *History of Rome*, books 44 and 45.
281 *The Histories,* books 27 and 27.
282 Look it up, class!

But to understand these things better from a human perspective, we have to come back down to earth, somewhat, by reading the slightly more earthy elements of an interpretation of these cryptic words, which the angel Gabriel[283] gave to Daniel at (what I believe was) Christ's command.

> *As for the horn that was broken, in place of which four others arose, four kingdoms shall arise from his [Alexander's] nation,[284] but not with his power. At the end of their rule, when the transgressions have reached their full measure, a king [kingdom/empire] of bold countenance shall arise, skilled in intrigue. He shall grow strong in power, shall cause fearful destruction, and shall succeed in what he does. He shall destroy the powerful and the people of the holy ones. By his cunning he shall make deceit prosper under his hand, and in his own mind [a human perspective] he shall be great. Without warning he shall destroy many and shall even rise up against the Prince of princes.[285] But he shall be broken, and not by human hands.* (Dan. 8:22–25)

Let's look at this pretty plain description, without the distorting Antiochus assumption clouding our interpretive lenses, and see what it would say to us on its own merits placed beside the story of world empires in the history books. Antiochus' pathetic story was anything *but* about a new empire. It says that "at the end" of the rule of the four kingdoms that came directly from Alexander the Great's original nation, a new world power would arise. It would be "bold," "skilled in intrigue," it would "grow strong in power," cause "fearful destruction," actually "succeed" in what it did (unlike Antiochus), and "destroy the powerful" (not just the *weak,* as the bully Antiochus did).

And now, let's compare *that* description with other descriptions of the fourth empire in the parallel series of empires from our list of parallel prophecies to see how well the descriptions match up! Let's begin with the description of the fourth empire in the colossal statue of Daniel 2.

> *And there shall be a fourth kingdom, strong as iron; just as iron crushes and smashes everything, it shall crush and shatter all these.* (Dan. 2:40)

---

283 See Daniel 8:15–16.
284 The horn represented Alexander's "nation."
285 This corresponds directly with the earlier Prince of the host (army) of heaven. A clear portrayal of *Jesus,* I believe.

That's a pretty significant match between "fearful destruction," destroying "the powerful," and "it shall crush and shatter all" the previous prophesied empires! Now, let's see what the prophecy in *Daniel 7*[286] had to say about *its* fourth wild animal, **which should be a direct parallel to the new horn** in chapter 8, **and which**, if we're correct in interpretation on chapter 8, **should also stand for Rome**, rather than the erroneous connection some have made between it and Greece for the purpose of forcing part of *its* prophecy to stand in for Antiochus Epiphanes (the same way the same interpreters want to make the prophecy of chapter 8 to stand for Antiochus). We already determined, earlier, that the leopard-like animal in chapter 7, with the four wings and four heads, stands for Greece.[287] The next animal that follows the Greek animal in chapter 7 is described as follows:

After this I saw in the visions by night a fourth beast, terrifying and dreadful and exceedingly strong. **It had great iron teeth** *and was devouring, breaking in pieces, and stamping what was left with its feet. It was different from all the beasts that preceded it,* **and it had ten horns.** (Dan. 7:7)

Dreadful, terrifying, exceedingly strong, iron teeth, devouring, breaking in pieces, stamping with its feet! What better match up could we expect between all three parallel prophecies? Even the element of iron found in the legs and feet of the statue of Daniel 2 is included in the teeth of the beast in chapter 7! And, interestingly, just as the statue in Daniel 2 had ten toes (and they *were* mentioned in the text as being significant), so this fourth beast of Daniel 7 also later developed ten appendages; it had *ten* horns. Accident? I think *not*. And it almost seems like we're seeing some bizarre Hollywood portrayal of a raving dinosaur here! It certainly is some beast unfamiliar to Daniel, whatever it is supposed to have looked like, because Daniel doesn't liken it to any animal he or his ancient readers happened to be familiar with! But, of course, Yahweh (God), the Creator, would have known all about dinosaurs. Their bones had not yet been rediscovered by humans in those days, where they (the dinosaur bones, that is) still lay mostly buried in layers of the earth.[288] I like to imagine

---
286 A prophecy I plan to go into even *more* detail about in another volume.
287 See chapter 16 of this book.
288 Many of which were probably rapidly deposited during the global catastrophe we call Noah's flood. See Genesis 7.

maybe a T-Rex with horns (with its vicious-looking teeth) in this description,[289] though I could be wrong, and of course such a thing doesn't really matter anyway (except as a bit of fun trivia). What really matters about all of these prophecies is not whether their symbols came from *pre*-history, but what their symbols actually stand for in *His*-story! Because according to what we've learned already about the prophecy in Daniel 2, **the long-promised Messiah was to strike this world during the period of the fourth kingdom (world empire) in our parallel series of prophecies!** I think we can now confidently say that we know what empire constitutes that prophetic ground zero!

Almost everyone in the world knows the answer to what great world empire followed the empire of the Greeks. **It was the *Roman* Empire!** It really *is* a no-brainer! Or it *should* be.

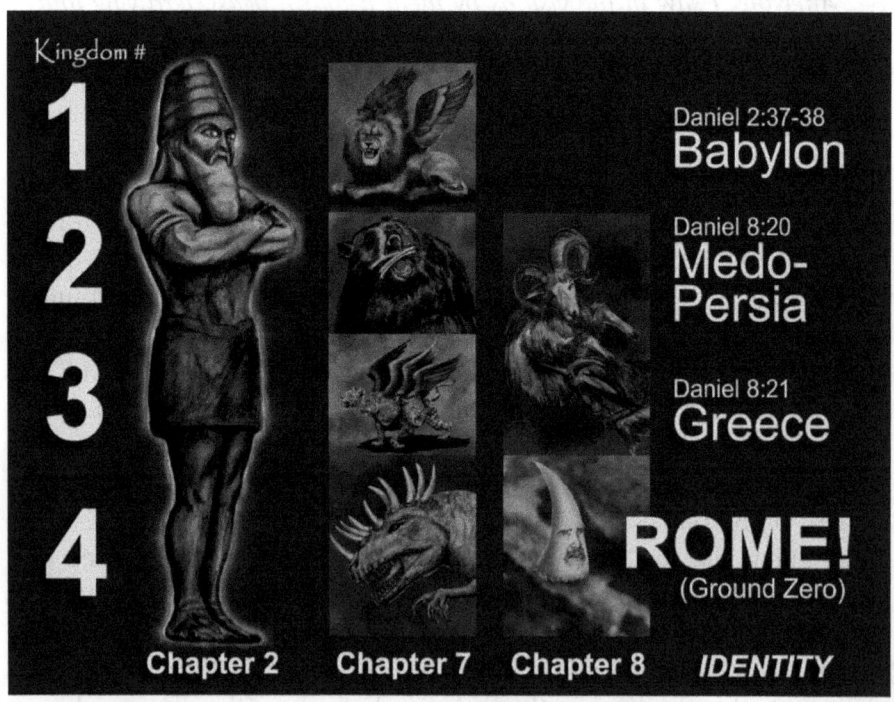

---

289 On another note of trivia, I also like to imagine that in a dreadful prophetic description found in the book of Habakkuk (Hab. 3:3–16), God may have also pulled the veiling curtain back a bit, showing His prophet a vision of catastrophes that took place on the earth in prehistory. Possibly even cosmic events related to a comet strike (verse 4) on our planet, that may have caused the catastrophic earth changes we see evidence of all over our planet, during Noah's flood.

Of course, there are a few descriptions in Daniel 8:24–25 that go into further elements of Rome's later relationship with the cosmic behind-the-scenes great controversy, which are beyond the scope of this book, and which will have to wait the writing of other book volumes for me to fully deal with.

But I find *most* interesting what Daniel 8 tantalizingly says at the end of its description of the new little horn power, which we now know to be the Roman domination. It would …

… be broken, and *not by human hands.* (Dan. 8:25)

What does that mean? I think it is a direct tie to Daniel 2, and that it clearly means it would be "broken" by "the kingdom of God" (the same kingdom Jesus later talked so much about),[290] which "kingdom" was represented by a divine altar stone in Daniel 2 that the ancient Messianic prophecy said would be cut out from Mount Zion, "**not by human hands**" (Dan. 2:34)! And that brief statement in Daniel 8 about the new horn getting "broken" becomes all the more intriguing to me when it gets placed beside the following statement from Daniel 2 about the statue's fourth kingdom [empire].

> ***And in the days of those kings** [those involved in the later history of the fourth kingdom which we now know to be **the Roman domination**] the God of heaven will set up a kingdom that shall never be destroyed, nor shall this kingdom be left to another people [i.e., it will never get overturned like the other kingdoms]. It shall crush all these kingdoms and bring them to an end, and it shall stand forever; just as you saw that **a stone was cut from the mountain not by hands**, and that **it crushed the iron, the bronze, the clay, the silver, and the gold**. The great God has informed the king what shall be hereafter. The dream is certain, and its interpretation trustworthy.* (Dan. 2:44–45)

---

290 See, again, chapter 11 of this book.

Chapter 19

The Fracturing Birth

Now, let me ask you a simple, no-brainer thought question.[291] Under which of these four great empires was Jesus *actually living*, when He declared "the kingdom of God" to be at hand? Of course, it was **Rome!** Do you remember how I told you that I used to assume the image from the dream in Daniel 2 described all of the great ancient empires in the world of the ancient Jews from the time of Babylon until Rome? And then that everything else in all of history following Rome I imagined just had to be lumped into the statue's toes all the way down to the end of time? Let's review a few main problems that exist with this theory upon careful consideration (I will number these in parentheses). These are problems I have shared already (in pretty great detail) in this book, but I did it before I had clearly identified for you this fourth "kingdom" as the Roman domination.

For starters (#1), let's reconsider the elements of the fourth kingdom in Daniel 2. Even though in the statue of Daniel 2 there are divisions between the legs, the feet, and the toes, **all three elements are all still part of the fourth kingdom, both logically and grammatically**, as I have already demonstrated.[292] So what is actually going on within the fourth kingdom (empire) of Nebuchadnezzar's statue is that there are some distinct changes prophesied to take place throughout three different phases of the fourth kingdom's history (at least the history of it that is covered in the symbolism of the statue), or as we *now* can think of it, the history of ancient Rome. Also, I shared how the toes on the feet were a clear division of this fourth kingdom[293] which we have now identified definitely with Rome. Some interpreters occasionally *miss* that fact, but **Daniel distinctly mentions the toes as being one of the divisions of Rome** (where a distinct change would take place within the Roman Empire according to the

---
291 If this was a test, my whole class would get 100%.
292 See chapter 7.
293 See, *again*, chapter 7.

ancient prophecy). It is another instance in Daniel where (like the mountain) this element is only mentioned in a *second* telling of the dream's contents, so it gets easily overlooked by those who are casually reading the text.

In the three divisions that were prophesied for the Roman domination, there should be a purely Roman period (symbolized by the purely iron legs), which should then be followed by two periods in which other *non-Roman* elements (symbolized by the clay, or earthenware material, contained in the feet and toes) would gradually, but increasingly, over time, get mixed into the political reality of this great empire of history. This non-Roman element would then seem to even come close to tipping the scales in its favor by the time period that the toes stand for, since the emphasis of the prophecy by that point becomes only division. There are two iron and clay periods, but something significant related to this division finally begins to happen at the time period of the toes, a disintegration of some kind. But what do you think the toes stand for?

Let me ask you another no-brainer thought question.

How many toes do you have? *Most* of you probably have ten. I have ten, at least at this point in my life, because I have never had a toe cut off—*yet*. I've never slipped on a hillside and gotten my foot caught under a running lawn mower (as a relative of mine once did). Nor was I born with the genetic mutation that occasionally causes a few people to be born with six toes on each foot, and six fingers on each hand, such as the genetic defect chronicled in the Bible as having existed among the ancient Philistines[294] (who, incidentally, may also have carried in their gene pool the defect known today as giantism, which may have been responsible for the infamous Goliath having been such a giant). So, we can safely assume there were also ten toes on the statue of Daniel 2, which toes I believe clearly stand for ten divisions the Roman Empire would get broken up into at some point in its history. But I don't believe that even the toes of Nebuchadnezzar's statue were meant to portray all of history down to the end of time.

Some interpreters *do* try to say that those later divisions of the ancient Roman Empire (of which there were originally ten) are still in full effect today as part of the prophecy of Daniel 2 (and just as surely part of the ancient Roman dominion), and that they will remain part of what was

---

[294] There has even been archaeological evidence possibly backing up this ancient report, as certain sarcophagi belonging to the ancient Philistines have been found containing relief depictions of the deceased showing six fingers on each hand. See 2 Samuel 21:20 and 1 Chronicles 20:6.

symbolized in Daniel 2 even until the end of time (imagining, as they do, that the stone, which they see as symbolizing *only* Christ's *second* coming, would strike the image on its *toes*). However, even though ancient Rome's memory and *influence* do most definitely continue even today, it seems to me that we strain Daniel 2 to the extreme when we try to call all of history that would follow after the ancient world still a part of the Roman Empire as it was prophesied in Daniel 2. I am *not* saying that modern history doesn't have *any* relationship to the ancient Roman world. **I am simply saying that I don't believe the colossus of Daniel 2 was meant to portray all of that extended history in its toes.**

Which thought brings me to another significant objection (#2) to the theory that I at one time just assumed[295] had to be. There are, significantly, striking differences between the parallel prophecies when it comes to these ten later divisions of Rome, most notably between the prophecies found in Daniel 2 and in Daniel 7, since both of these prophecies signify, by the same number, that ten appendages would divide up the later Roman Empire. But the latter of the two prophecies (Daniel 7) seems to take the very same history further down the corridors of time than does the prophecy found in Daniel 2. Although I won't be discussing this later *new* "Roman" history in *this* book, it is important to note because it helps us to distinguish what particular characteristic of Roman history Daniel 2 is specifically focusing itself on, as opposed to Daniel 7, which takes on a more sweeping picture of the eventualities that would arise *out of* the ruins of ancient Rome. Daniel 7 contains a beast representing the very same Roman domination, but having how many horns upon its head, do you suppose? It had *ten* horns to symbolize the same ten later divisions that the toes in Daniel 2 stand for! ***But!***—But, whereas the great statue of Daniel 2 ends its timeline narrative *at* the ten toes, Daniel 7 symbolically extends its prophecy onward into further history, to a time when three of its horns (symbolizing the same reality as the toes of Daniel 2) get uprooted,[296] and another horn—another great power that would slowly grow to greatness, but of a very different character than the four empires—then arises *in their* place (though not *from them*). This *new* "Roman" power then goes on to do some pretty astonishing things, which I plan to talk about in a later volume. We don't find that historical parallel in Daniel chapter 2 at all, though, which leads me to believe that **far too many interpreters have missed the big picture of Daniel 2, and have also assumed much more**

---

295 See the first paragraph of this chapter.
296 See Daniel 7:7–8, 20, and 24.

about the prophecy in Daniel 2, historically, than it was meant to portray. Its particular timeline (as contained in the statue) actually stops at an earlier period than the timelines of both Daniel 7 and Daniel 8. I think if we look again, and try to think of the whole matter from a slightly different angle, we might start to understand what is *actually* going on here.

The question we need to ask first, though, is: Did ancient Rome really have ten appendages added onto its later history? The answer to that question is a resounding **Yes!** If you are genetically of European stock, then you are most likely a direct descendant of one or more of these ten appendages which got added onto the ancient Roman Empire in its later period. I myself am of almost exclusively European stock, which means that I, too, come from (my very existence, itself, is *tied* to) the history of these ten appendages to Rome! What am I speaking about? I'm speaking about the ten historical "tribes"—or rather *political confederacies*—that inherited the ancient Roman Empire in its latter days, and which eventually became the roots out of which modern European nations sprouted and then later developed. The actual history is quite complex and nuanced, but a generally agreed upon list of these ten so-called "tribes" goes something like this, (with approximate correlations to modern nations put in parentheses):

1. Alamanni	(German)
2. Burgundians	(Swiss)
3. Franks	(French)
4. Lombards	(Italians)
5. Saxons	(English)
6. Suevi	(Portuguese)
7. Visigoths	(Spanish)
8. Heruli	(Extinct as a political unit—uprooted in fulfilment of the prophecy)
9. Vandals	(Extinct as a political unit—uprooted in fulfilment of the prophecy)
10. Ostrogoths	(Extinct as a political unit—uprooted in fulfilment of the prophecy)

One cool thing about this particular element of the prophecies is that once we *do* realize this prophecy has to relate to the Roman domination, it is then impossible for anyone to still suggest that the prophecy only fits history since Daniel must have been written after the fact! It is the element which predicted the ten "tribes" of eventual Europe and also the uprooting of three of them. No one can downplay that fulfillment by simply claiming that Daniel got written down after that period in history[297] and yet get away with such a deception (like far too many *do* far too often on other false claims regarding an imagined late dating of Daniel).

> *I was considering the [ten] horns, when another horn appeared, a little one coming up among them;* **to make room for it, three of the earlier horns were plucked up by the roots.** (Dan. 7:8)

God actually *knew* what was going to happen before it happened! Here is this fact that three of the horns on the Roman beast (the same as the toes in Daniel 2) would be uprooted, and that another power would then arise sometime quite a while *after* the time of Christ on earth.

Yet, as we've seen before, the prophecy in Daniel 2 says:

> **[T]he stone that struck the statue became a great mountain and filled the whole earth.** (Dan. 2:35)

So, finally (#3), if we read carefully, we must notice that the stone starts out as a *little* stone which strikes the Roman domination at some point in its history but then becomes, or *grows* into, a great mountain. Please remember[298] that it doesn't strike **as a mountain!** Like all things that grow, it begins small. This often-overlooked detail of the Daniel 2 prophecy specifically implies a process *within* history, not *after* history.

But can we identify when *exactly* in Roman history the stone should have struck, small as it *would* be,[299] in order to fulfill the prophecy?

It is interesting that Daniel says,

> *And* **in the days of those kings** *[the iron and clay periods of the Roman Empire] the God of heaven [the sky] will set up a kingdom that shall never be destroyed.* (Dan. 2:44)

Also take note of the fact that it doesn't say God will *finish the growth* of this kingdom during those time periods, but simply that during these two time periods He would *set up* His everlasting kingdom—that is, He

---

297 The scroll was indisputably in existence long, *long* before the history it points to happened.
298 Refer back to chapter 7 of this book.
299 It may be of interest to you that a prophetic word attached to the coming Messiah in Isaiah, Jeremiah, and Zechariah, which usually gets translated "branch," actually means "sprout," or "growth," as in something that starts out tiny and then grows. See Isaiah 4:2, 11:1; Jeremiah 23:5, 33:15; Zechariah 3:8–9 (notice the stone symbol), and 6:12.

would *establish* it upon its divine Foundation Stone! I speak of the *mere*[300] Foundation Stone, as in the title of this book volume, which stone I believe is (and was) none other than *Jesus!* Jesus, and His full reality, *is* the foundation altar[301] Stone of Daniel 2, which was prophesied to smash into the timeline of the Roman Empire. But at what exact point was this fracturing[302] strike prophesied to take place?

The above verse definitely suggests to us that the Davidic[303] slingstone was to strike Rome sometime during the *later* periods of its ancient history, as that history is symbolized in the legs, feet, and toes of the ancient Goliath statue: **it was to strike on either the statue's feet, or its toes (we still must determine** *which*). Again, remember that the feet became mixed up (unlike the iron legs) with a foreign element (the clay). When laying the prophecy down beside books of Roman history, this earthenware mix-up clearly indicates to me a well-documented period when Rome *did,* in fact, start to become profoundly mingled with a foreign element. This element was the element of *people* making up its new exploding subjugated population centers. Over time, they were starting to partake of Rome's anciently cherished citizenship rights, as well as gradually beginning to take over some of its positions of military and political power. This foreign element symbolized more and more *people* who were no longer purely Roman, and who did not partake of the historic Roman nature, mentality, and culture, nor of Rome's early genetic makeup.

Remember, in the description of the legs of Rome, that:

> ... *as iron crushes and smashes everything,* **it shall crush and shatter.** (Dan. 2:40)

In the purely *iron* period of ancient Rome, we see the legs doing just that: crushing, crushing, *crushing!* If any of you have spent much time studying ancient Rome you already realize that Rome spent literally hundreds of years rising up out of its ancient obscurity, and then in decisive battle after decisive battle, in war upon war leading up to the time of Christ, it was, *indeed,* crushing out all opposition from other kingdoms (even by so-called "barbarians," as it expanded its territory into even as yet uncivilized regions) with victory after glorious Roman victory. This

---

300 I borrowed the idea of using this word from the famous apologetic book *Mere Christianity,* written by C.S. Lewis.
301 A symbolism of Christ's cross.
302 Refer back, again, to chapter 7 of this book.
303 Cut out from the monarchical lineage of King David as Jesus *Himself* was. See Luke 18:38.

reality happened during the *expansion* of Rome, or what historians call the "Republic" period of ancient Rome. It was indeed an *iron* power that once rocked the ancient pagan world to its foundations, just before *another* event I will speak of shortly, began to rock its *very* foundation. But it was this massive expansion during the time of the Republic, which, *itself,* led directly to the *next* period in Roman history.

The iron power of Rome, having conquered, then reformed what had become the *Hellenistic* world (the *Greek* world), into a truly Greco-Roman world. Rome did this, *I* am convinced, in unwitting preparation for the message of Christianity to easily spread far and wide. You see, Alexander the Great had *first* been an unwitting tool of Yahweh when his earlier, sudden, and lightning-swift conquests had led to the unification of his before-that-time-diverse-and-divided ancient world by creating one common international language[304] and culture. He did this in preparation (it turns out) for the spread of the "good news of the kingdom of God" into "all the world." Then the Romans became the next unwitting tool of Yahweh (and of His coming eternal kingdom). They added to Alexander's new linguistic and cultural unity, a before-then still-lacking *political* unity (what became known as the *Pax Romana,* the Roman peace) all across their ancient world. They didn't realize the real purpose, of course, was to enable the easier spread of that same "good news," which Jesus not only announced, but also brought into being! Yet after their task anticipating Christianity had been fully completed, and the whole world had become "Roman" (so to speak), that same whole world—which was not *truly* Roman—began, little by little at first, to dilute the Roman strength, characteristics, and identity. This reality was foreshadowed by the clay earthenware mixing into the iron in the Daniel 2 statue. The evidence of this reality can be found even in the New Testament, as even Paul (Saul) the apostle, though Jewish, was counted as a Roman citizen,[305] possibly because the citizens of the city he was born in had been granted the widely coveted prize of *Roman* citizenship, a bauble many paid a precious high price in those days to obtain.[306]

The very character of the one-time Roman Republic changed dramatically at that decisive mixing point in history. And there was a great tipping point in Roman politics, as well, that came about through consequences of

---

304 Greek, the very language the message of Jesus went out to the world in and which the New Testament is written in.
305 See Acts 22:25–28.
306 See verse 28.

the same conquests which had brought on the gradual change in Roman character. This tipping point has been recognized by historians as one of the great dividing walls in Roman history, dividing everything that came before it from everything that came after it, in significant ways.[307]

This was the period when the Caesars took control, and they changed the ancient Roman Republic into a virtual dictatorship, a worrisome eventuality which ancient Roman laws had tried to guard against. These laws Julius Caesar highhandedly violated the moment he crossed the anciently forbidden line of the Rubicon River, with his army in tow, in order to usurp power by force of arms. He thus ended the endless arguments that are endemic to any free form of government, and he thus ended[308] the ancient notion of a Roman *Republic* forever—although the Caesars for a time pretended homage to the ancient republican forms in many ways. This pretense was a political necessity during the first several generations of what historians call the *Imperial* period of Roman history. The Caesars called themselves emperors, a title which at the time carried connotations less tyrannical than other sorts of totalitarian labels, but in actual point of fact the Republic was turned by them (over several generations) into something very much like autocracy: the rule of one. The ancient Roman liberties had been suppressed.

But it was also the Caesars who helped bring about a fulfillment of the prediction found in Daniel 2:41 which says of their time period:

[I]t shall be ... divided ... but some of the strength of iron shall be in it [some of the true Roman-ness], as you saw the iron mixed with the clay.

If we logically follow the symbol of iron, then we see that this must refer to a mixing of Roman and non-Roman people in the same "kingdom," which is an experimental phenomenon that actually was exploding

---

307 Some would consider this to be not entirely unlike the dividing effect 9/11 has had so recently on historic American liberties and on American law. In some ways everything *we* once took for granted as fundamental also suddenly changed (as it had for the ancient Romans) after 9/11. Just as in *our* recent change, many believe the change has been definitely for the worse (a profound understatement since civil liberties and protections they believe have now been undermined, are so fundamental to what "America" stands for that they were even enumerated in our Bill of Rights), so also in the ancient world, the opinion prevailed among champions of ancient Roman liberties, that the change taking place was nothing short of an abomination. But as Julius Caesar so infamously said (after *he* had cast it for ancient Rome), "the die is cast."
308 Though not without opposition, to be sure: we all probably know the famous story of how Julius Caesar's life ended.

onto the stage of history at the beginning of the Caesars. Notice what one historian had to say about a program of international integration begun by the very *first* Caesar:

> [Julius Caesar] had ... plans ... to blend the races and peoples ... he admitted to the senate sons of freedmen, and ... the Gauls, and conferred [rights] upon individual[s]... and ... classes ... in the provinces.[309]

This did not sit well with *many* Romans in his day, who sometimes felt threatened by this liberality (some of whom were already quite upset over the fact that Caesar was turning the ancient Republic into an autocratic rulership).

Julius Caesar, like Alexander the Great long before him, desired to make all the world one.

> *His action ... [the historian continues] marks an epoch in the history of Rome.*[310]

It was when the Caesars took control that Rome *then* truly ruled its world, but they ruled it at a terrible price:

> [T]he major ... conquest had been ... during the centuries preceding this. Following the consolidation of gains, the major concern was holding the vast empire together and putting down revolts and intrusions all over the world.[311]

The thought comes to my mind that just as the prophecy predicted:

> **[T]hey will not hold together**, *just as iron does not mix with clay.* (Dan. 2:43)

Trying (sometimes desperately) to hold their vast empire together is what the Romans did for the rest of their long history. They weren't generally conquering *new* territory; they were most often trying to hold onto the territory that they already possessed. In their latter days they were

---

309 Philip Van Ness Myers, L.H.D., *Rome: Its Rise and Fall* (Boston, MA: Ginn & Co., 1900), pp. 298–299.
310 Ibid.
311 Author currently unknown. (The reference got accidentally left out of a previous reworking of this subject matter many years ago and is presently unlocatable.)

even forced to begin withdrawals of Roman legions from some of their far-flung outposts which eventually became too much to manage.

Do you see a picture developing?

There were three distinct periods of ancient Roman history: **The Republic**, **The Empire**, and **The Decline** of Rome. The Decline is that time period when the invading "barbarian" "tribes" were gradually taking over the functions, the authority, and the territory that had once been controlled by Rome's central government. These three periods perfectly correspond to three of the segments found in Nebuchadnezzar's colossus: **the legs**, **the feet**, and **the toes**. And even the number of toes perfectly matches up with divisions taking place during Rome's decline, because how many tribes did we learn there were at the end? There were *ten* (although three were later uprooted).

But on which of these three segments does the text say the stone *actually* struck?

> *[I]t struck the statue **on its feet**.* (Dan. 2:34)

When that statement first struck home in my mind—as meaning something distinct, a distinct period within Roman history—I said: *Wow!* A new realization was suddenly sinking in. What is fascinating to me (and this is the beautiful part) is that many historians actually put the official beginning[312] of the empire (the second stage in ancient Roman history) and the full end of the Republic at the very point in history that:

> *[A] decree went out from Emperor Augustus that all the world should be registered.* (Luke 2:1)[313]

When I first made this connection, chills ran up and down my Christian spine! I have never been so moved by a mere three words of Bible prophecy ("on its feet")!

The world conquest of Rome by that time was pretty much complete. The image of the smashing legs no longer fit the new epoch which had fully dawned in Roman history. The great concern was now holding things together. That is why at that very time, Emperor Augustus undertook to consolidate the monumental gains Rome had already achieved,

---

312 The final culmination of a change that had been already taking place.
313 *Verse 2 adds:* "This was the first registration and was taken while Quirinius was governor of Syria."

by conducting an unprecedented registration of his entire ancient world. He did this for the purpose of raising revenue (through taxation) to help the empire in its unimaginably difficult task of holding itself together in a brand-new context. That context was the attempt to intermingle clay with iron: to seamlessly incorporate all of the conquered nations and peoples into the now politically unified world government, which had been brought into being by the Roman Empire.

Now permit me the artistic license, if you will, to do something that may seem odd to some readers: to quote *myself*, from an earlier passage in this very book. The quotation is taken from the last paragraph of chapter 12, where I then gave you a teaser of content which would not be dealt with until this chapter:

> *But there is another shining event that strikingly stirs (I almost said <u>stars</u>) my soul as well .... It is the enlightening astronomical event around which a Davidic slingstone struck a Goliath statue in the midnight of human history. In <u>this</u> version of David and Goliath, however, the slingstone got aimed, not at Goliath's forehead, but at another specific location on his gigantic body, because the Goliath in this version—the idol in Nebuchadnezzar's dream—represented a particular chunk cut out from a timeline of human history .... [W]hen I had a sudden flashing realization of **the significance of that spot in history where the slingstone <u>actually</u> hit**, it blew me away!*[314]

The reason I was blown away is that the specific event historians point to as marking the culmination of Rome's change from Republic to empire (or from legs to *feet,* in the Daniel 2 statue), is the very context of those internationally famous words introducing a tenderly told story of Christ's birth in the book of Luke. Caesar Augustus' first registration was the occasion that brought Joseph and Mary to Bethlehem where the Messiah had been prophesied to be born![315] The story was well placed in the context of an astronomical event too. A bright star[316] of hope came shining in the midst of our darkness! Even a classic PEANUTS cartoon movie[317] once centered itself almost entirely around the reverent reading of a portion of this timeless inspired passage from Luke that (when read in full) actually

---

314 From chapter 12 of this book.
315 See Matthew 2:6; Micah 5:2, and 2 Samuel 5:2.
316 See Matthew 2:1–11.
317 Charles Schulz, *A Charlie Brown Christmas*, PEANUTS, (United Feature Syndicate, 1965).

> *"And suddenly there was with the angel a multitude of the heavenly host praising God, and saying, Glory to God in the highest, and on earth peace, good will toward men."*

starts out with a reference to Caesar Augustus and to his registration of the Roman world! It is a passage which has warmed untold millions of hearts with its message of hope that was borne down into our dark world when the Christ-child was born. I even heard a preacher once share how listening to those words recited in that PEANUTS Christmas special as a boy was the very first experience he ever remembers of his heart being powerfully drawn to Jesus! Many English speakers are more familiar with the King James version of it:

> *And it came to pass in those days, that there went out a decree from Caesar Augustus that all the world should be taxed …. And all went … every one into his own city. And Joseph also went up from Galilee, out of the city of Nazareth, into Judaea, unto the city of David, which is called Bethlehem; (because he was of the house and lineage of David:) …. [W]ith Mary his espoused wife, being great with child. And so it was, that, while they were there, the days were accomplished that she should be delivered. And she brought forth her firstborn son, and wrapped him in swaddling clothes, and laid him in a manger; because there was no room for them in the inn. And there were in the same country shepherds abiding in the field, keeping watch over their flock by night. And, lo, the angel of the Lord came upon them, and the glory of the Lord shone round about them: and they were sore afraid. And the angel said unto them, **Fear not: for, behold, I bring you good tidings of great joy, which shall be to all people. For unto you is born this day in the city of David a Saviour, which is Christ the Lord.** And this shall be a sign unto you; Ye shall find the babe wrapped in swaddling clothes, lying in a manger. And suddenly there was with the angel a multitude of the heavenly host praising God, and saying, **Glory to God in the highest, and on earth peace, good will toward men.** And it came to pass, as the angels were gone away from them into heaven, the shepherds said one to another, Let us now go even unto Bethlehem, and see this thing which is come to pass, which the Lord hath made known unto us. And they came with haste, and found Mary, and Joseph, and the*

babe lying in a manger. And when they had seen it, they made known abroad the saying which was told them concerning this child. **And all they that heard it wondered at those things which were told them by the shepherds.** *But Mary kept all these things, and pondered them in her heart. And the shepherds returned, glorifying and praising God for all the things that they had heard and seen.* (Luke 2:1, 3–20, KJV)

Historians affirm that the circumstance which occasioned the prophesied *location* for this tender story was a major turning point in history, and they could not be *more* right about the *timing*. They are right in more ways than one, of course, since this turning point in Roman history was the very occasion of Christ's birth! The time of that event became the point in history that forever *split* history in two! BC turned into AD (the years of "our Lord"). It is a point in time that even unbelievers today, around the globe (and even the few who may still be totally ignorant of Christ), unwittingly recognize every single day of their lives. They recognize the birth of Jesus[318] every time they write down, think about, or speak about the date on the calendar, which date (whenever the year is included) daily points the whole world backward to the birth of its Savior! That profoundly significant point in time is where the *feet* of Nebuchadnezzar's image fully began! And *that* ("on its feet") is where the prophecy foretold that the stone, which symbolized the coming Christ, would strike!

> **The birth of Christ was to the mighty Romans such an apparently insignificant event they could not have then possibly known that this tiny babe would eventually undermine everything spiritual that they (and the mighty colossus of Nebuchadnezzar's dream) then stood for.**

Roman conquest was solidified at the *exact* time of Christ's birth! Doesn't that send a chill up your *own* spine? I think this is such a beautiful connection: the consummation of Roman conquest happened when Christ hit our world! It happened at that very *moment* in time! But there is also a great irony involved in this connection. At the very pinnacle of Rome's ancient glory (which is what this culmination represented), also at the very point of the full shameful

---
318 Although the date was later calculated slightly wrong.

subjugation of God's people under Roman rule, a then-still-tiny stone struck the intimidating graven image upon its *feet* in one of the far-flung outposts of the Roman Empire. When it struck, it sent out what were at first only tiny fracture lines into history, but the fracture lines grew and *grew* with time, as did the reality of this tiny babe in Bethlehem. The birth of Christ was to the mighty Romans such an apparently *insignificant* event they could not have then possibly known that this *tiny babe* would eventually undermine everything *spiritual* that they (and the mighty colossus of Nebuchadnezzar's dream) then stood for. They could not have known that it would eventually bring the ancient pagan glory, which the Romans were the final inheritors of, cascading to the ground in a pile of proverbial dust and rubble! (Jesus can do the same with *our* Goliaths too!)

Even though baby Jesus was little, His reality was *colossal,* and the fractures of His impact with our world ran deep, even from the manger. The demons and angels[319] (if not the people) were all astir! Satan recognized the significance of this tiny babe wrapped up in swaddling clothes, and the one-time "Day Star"[320] set up a desperate demonic attempt to destroy the promised Messiah-King before He ever had a chance to grow up. Satan made this sadistic attempt through subjects who had (through the stubborn selfishness of their hearts and the persistent rejection of God's Spirit) long before opened themselves up to his mesmerizing[321] influence and sinister suggestions. The heart-sickening methods Satan deployed through his human instruments in pursuit of the innocent babe[322] demonstrate the depravity of Lucifer's character. They are reminiscent today of atrocities carried out through the more modern medium of Nazi Germany, which were also surely carried out under his demonic spell.

But heavenly agencies protected the promised Messiah-King through warnings and directions given in dreams[323] to those near to the babe. His significant birth did not go unnoticed by even pagan "wise men" from the East, who were actually magi (the word from which we get "magician"): astrologers, who in their innocent *ignorance* were most probably dabblers in many of the ancient occultic arts (the lesson here is: Please don't sell

---

319 The *fallen,* and the *unfallen* angels.
320 "Day Star" in the New Revised Standard Version, "Lucifer" in the King James and New King James versions, "morning star" in the New International Version, and "shining one" in Young's Literal Translation (see Isaiah 14:12).
321 Hypnotic.
322 See Matthew 2:16.
323 See Matthew 2:12–13.

short whom you believe God is able to work through!). But they were also true, unselfish seekers after truth, and as such their hearts were susceptible to the influence of Yahweh's Holy Spirit. When these superstitious students of the stars saw a brilliant new star hanging stationary[324] in the direction of Judea, they searched their probably extensive archive of ancient prophecies with spiritually open hearts and minds to make their divinely inspired connection between that star and an anciently prophesied Israelite Savior.[325] Anyone could have looked up and seen that unusual new star, but the wise men were the unlikely (in our minds) candidates who happened to be spiritually open to its profound significance, and to the profoundly significant time in which they were living. "God moves in a mysterious way, His wonders to perform."[326]

> [A]fter Jesus was born in Bethlehem of Judea, wise men [magi] from the East came to Jerusalem, asking, "Where is the child who has been born king of the Jews? For we observed his star at its rising, and have come to pay him homage." When King Herod heard this, he was frightened, and all Jerusalem with him .... [When Herod] sent them to Bethlehem .... there, ahead of them, went the star ... until it stopped over the place where the child was. (Matt. 2:1–3, 8–9)

Jesus became, as it were, the "Night Star": a true royal star shining brightly in the midst of our darkest human night, which heralded a new dawn of hope, of freedom from sin and from its dark consequences for all humanity! The rest, as *I* say, is **His**-story: the story of His self-sacrificing life in a Roman world, His sacrificial death on a Roman cross, His life-assuring resurrection, His ascension to His Father and then of the establishment of His church, which in its pure forms constitutes the expanding

---

324 I deduce it was stationary because when the wise men reached Jerusalem, this "star" moved around, even leading them to a specific house; therefore, it could not have been a *literal* star circulating with the heavens in the far reaches of space.
325 Many believe one prophecy the magi got a hold of was that pronounced by Balaam when he intended to curse Israel, but instead found himself blessing and prophesying extensively of a coming Messiah-King: *"I see him, but not now; I behold him, but not near—a star shall come out of Jacob, and a scepter shall rise out of Israel"* (Num. 24:17).
326 Jonathan Aitken, *John Newton: From Disgrace to Amazing Grace* (Wheaton, IL: Crossway, 2007), p. 217. This is the first line of the classic hymn "God Moves in a Mysterious Way" by William Cowper, a bosom friend of John Newton. He wrote these verses on Friday, January 1, 1773, about an hour or two after he heard John Newton introduce, for the first time, his famous hymn now known as "Amazing Grace." Cowper wrote this expression of faith in spite of severe trial, right after he experienced a sudden premonition that his mentally ill brain was about to descend again into madness, which it did that very night.

mountain of His good news about the "kingdom of God." Today it is still expanding into all the world as a witness to all the nations—an expansion which must be completed before Jesus finally returns the second time to receive the fullness of His long-growing kingdom of liberated souls unto Himself!

When I finally got this beautiful connection between the birth of Christ and the ancient idol's[327] feet, I wondered how I had missed it for so long with it staring me in the face every time I read the text! It means for us that Christ, the "Rock of Ages, cleft for me,"[328] struck the Roman world on its feet, and *not* on its toenails, as I had once imagined. This simply means that the rock was to strike Rome *within* its flow of ancient history *not* merely at history's end! The promised Messiah was not simply to rescue us from a distance; He was first to walk in our moccasins (so to speak), to tread our streets, to get dirty with our dirt, to experience our daily pain and heartaches, to live the life *we* have to live, to touch our untouchables, to unbind our entangled, to set at liberty our entrapped, to heal our diseases, to open our spiritual eyes, to demonstrate God's love right where we happen to live, to become "Emmanuel, God with us"!

> *When [Jesus] came to Nazareth, where he had been brought up, he went to the synagogue on the sabbath day, as was his custom. He stood up to read, and the scroll of the prophet Isaiah was given to him. He unrolled the scroll and found the place where it was written: "The Spirit of the Lord is upon me, because* **he has anointed me to bring good news to the poor. He has sent me to proclaim release to the captives and recovery of sight to the blind, to let the oppressed go free, to proclaim the year of the Lord's favor."** *And he rolled up the scroll, gave it back to the attendant, and sat down. The eyes of all in the synagogue were fixed on him. Then he began to say to them,* **"Today this scripture has been fulfilled in your hearing."**
> (Luke 4:16–21)

After that symbolic altar stone of blood sacrifice[329] (which made all these beautiful purposes possible for unworthy souls) struck the Goliath

---

[327] This word is a hint of the statue's historical meaning.
[328] The first line of another classic Christian hymn: Augustus M. Toplady, "Rock of Ages," *Hymns of Faith* (Wheaton, IL: Tabernacle Publishing Company, 1980).
[329] See chapters 9 and 10 of this book.

on its feet, then the setting up of Christ's kingdom of *grace* continued on into the early period of the toes! It continues growing even to this day into a mighty mountain of hope! We call that hope, that *mountain,* Christianity. Although Rome didn't know it at the time, a humble baby had *struck* its eventual doom! This is something to meditate upon.

That time period in history represented at the same time both the pinnacle of Roman power, and also an abysmal era of Roman moral depravity which helped bring about Rome's eventual decline. Rome had at this time also reached the pinnacle of *paganism's* fruits, and this is why it now approached an utter demise of its pagan glory, because, you see, **Nebuchadnezzar's image was nothing short of a symbolic** *idol.* It was a *false god!* It was frightening in *appearance,* but it was *still* a false god! That's what I believe is the *key* to understanding what Nebuchadnezzar's frightening image stands for. It stands for the earth's great *pagan* powers with which God's ancient people had to deal—powers which had their origins in gods which are *not* gods. They were gods which do not *forgive!* How many of us ever need real forgiveness? They were gods which (as Nebuchadnezzar's wise men attested) do not *dwell* with human *flesh!* They were gods which *couldn't* care less, gods which do not offer *hope* of eternal *life!* (I'm planning to give readers some *astounding* evidence for our hope in a coming promised resurrection of the dead, in a future volume.) These were gods which could not satisfy the *needs* of the human *soul!* Such gods *look* like they're with us but they just don't *satisfy* as if they are. They sometimes *look* like escape; they sometimes *look* like salvation, but no matter how hard we work for them, they just don't meet our needs brought on by guilt. They, at times, *seem* to give us meaning, but it's a hopeless, it's an *empty,* meaning. It will not satisfy in a time when it really counts!

When the world was reaping the degradation of Roman decadence— the gladiators, the unending games of violence, the royal extravagance, debauchery, endless intrigue,[330] and even royal insanity (that I believe was often brought on at least partly by demonic possession), the empire had one unexpected *royal* event to reckon with. It was the coming of a long-promised Christ-child who would be a true "shepherd" king: a king who would tenderly and unselfishly *shepherd* His people[331] in the ancient

---
330 See Daniel 8:23–25.
331 As opposed to the "kings of the gentiles" who Jesus said, "lord it over" their subjects. See Luke 22:25–26.

tradition of a *good* king.³³² Because of that first coming of Jesus, the final great empire of ancient paganism (symbolized by the *idol*) would never be the same! Into the seeming triumph of paganism (the frightening, imposing idol)—while even Yahweh's small nation of people languished under persecutions and under unjust taxation—came a Savior, Emmanuel, which means:

"God with us!"

> *He would be a helper who didn't need to help us run away from reality because He faced our dark reality for us! He came into that little manger during earth's darkest night. He came to live among us, to share our genetics, to involve Himself in our humanity! I love Him for all of these things!*

He would be a *helper* who didn't need to help us run *away* from reality because He *faced* our dark reality *for* us! He *came* into that little manger during earth's darkest night. He came to live among us, to share our genetics, to *involve* Himself in our humanity! I *love* Him for all of these things! He came to reunite us with our Creator, to be God in *human* flesh! Have you ever meditated over what it means that *we*, fallen humans, are now related to *God?!* He embraced our *cross!* He drank *our* bitter cup to its depths! (And some of us have tasted a *lot* of bitter.)

Here was a poor baby in a manger, bedded down in a habitation of animals, and from the most unlikely of Roman outposts (a mere swampy backwater in the minds of proud Romans) whose inhabitants even denied the Roman gods. But this baby became the undoing of the vast pagan system that Rome was the final inheritor of. A rock, cut out of the God-ordained religious system of ancient Israel, had struck the great and terrifying idol upon its base, and then the rock began to grow. And the growth was rapid! Did you know that historians are still proverbially spinning, and *wondering,* at the amazing feats of conquest caused not by the sword, but

---

332 Even ancient Egyptian Pharaohs had a symbolic shepherd's crook placed over their chests on their sarcophagi.

by the Living Word of God who dwells with human flesh? Here is what one historian says on the subject:

> *Perhaps the most spectacular triumph of Christianity in history [was] its conquest of the Roman Empire in roughly twenty decades .... **the growth of Christianity sounds impossible, almost unbelievable.***[333]

And yet it happened!

You say that I am a king. For this I was born, and for this I came into the world. (John 18:37)

This is the "kingdom of God" that Jesus said comes not with observation,[334] and yet I ask you: Are its effects obvious? They cannot be *missed!* It is now the kingdom of *grace*, but soon we'll enter that kingdom of *glory* (as prophecies I intend to share in coming volumes will demonstrate). Right now we are still living in that in-between time period. Two massive worlds have collided, and they are still *colliding!* That's what's happening right now. If you want to understand all the *crazy* stuff in our world, *this* explains it! Two worlds have collided, and they are still colliding, and the spiritual conflict involved is profound. The invisible battles being fought over our souls are often vicious! Christ's expanding kingdom is now somewhere in the in-between time. It is already (Jesus long ago said the kingdom is at hand[335]) but it's not fully *yet*. It's a kingdom that has been growing now for 2,000 years! It is a rival kingdom, intruding upon another kingdom that still tries to make its diabolical claim upon your soul! The kingdom of God is a rival *authority,* which purchased its right to redeem your life from the enemy kingdom when Jesus died on a Roman cross in *your* place. And when He died for you, Jesus became the rightful

> **The kingdom of God is a rival authority, which purchased its right to redeem your life from the enemy kingdom when Jesus died on a Roman cross in your place.**

---

333 "The Kingdom Strikes Back: Ten Epochs of Redemptive History," *Perspectives on the World Christian Movement: A Reader,* Revised Edition, ed. by Ralph D. Winter and Steven C. Hawthorne, (Pasadena, CA: William Carey Library, 1981, 1992), p. B-7, emphasis mine.
334 See Luke 17:20.
335 See Mark 1:15.

rival *Master* of any who would accept the free gift of *Himself* that He now offers.

Satan knew, and recognized, this rival reality! *Herod* (inspired by his master, *Satan*) recognized it, too, on his *own* level! That's why they both tried to destroy baby Jesus! Was that act in history a mere whim of a madman? No! It was of purely *satanic* origin! I really like this classic quotation which speaks of the continued satanic attack on Christ even *after* He had ascended to His Father. It is taken from a book I highly recommend called *The Great Controversy*:

> *The powers of earth and hell arrayed themselves against Christ in the person of His followers.* **Paganism foresaw that should the gospel triumph, her temples and altars would be swept away; therefore she summoned her forces to destroy Christianity.**[336]

The gospel (the "good news of the *kingdom*") *did* triumph in those early centuries. When Christianity first conquered, paganism's temples and altars *were* swept away, as the mighty Goliath of ages—the shimmering idol of Nebuchadnezzar's dream, symbolic of ancient *paganism*—came cascading to the ground in a proverbial pile of dust and rubble, to be blown away by the winds of history.

But, as we will see in further volumes (and as we must instinctively know in our own experiences), the larger invisible battle is still not over. However, we have a "blessed hope"[337] that very soon the "kingdoms of this world," as Revelation says, will truly "become the kingdoms of our Lord, and of his Christ; and he shall reign for ever and ever" (Rev. 11:15, KJV). And there is but one sign of the times predicted by Jesus that is still remaining to be fully completed, before He has promised to come again to this earth—the second time in *glory*—to receive His fully grown kingdom unto Himself. What is that last sign before Jesus comes back again? It is:

> **[T]his good news of the kingdom** will be proclaimed throughout the world, as a testimony to all the nations; and **then** the end will come. (Matt. 24:14)

---

336 E. G. White, *The Great Controversy* (Mountain View, CA: Pacific Press, 1911), p. 39, emphasis mine.
337 See Titus 2:13.

The good news of *what?* Of "the kingdom of God," which the expanding mountain represents! That's the last sign before Jesus comes back! The everlasting good news ("of the kingdom") was prophesied to go to "every nation and tribe and language and people" (Rev. 14:6). It is a massive worldwide expansion of good news about the *true* God. It is the incredible expansion of the stone mountain of hope found in Daniel 2. And we will see in the coming volumes that not everyone is happy about this expansion, or wants you to receive the *blessing* of this mountain that through baby Jesus was first brought into our world.

Jesus *Himself* embodies the stone of Daniel 2. *Jesus* is the expanding mountain, the expanding *kingdom*. *Jesus* is the "kingdom of God," the *foundation* stone beneath *all* solid foundations;[338] and *all* of Bible prophecy, and *all* of sacred Scripture, centers ultimately around J-E-S-U-S and His expanding kingdom of love.

> *Jesus Himself embodies the stone of Daniel 2. Jesus is the expanding mountain, the expanding kingdom. Jesus is the "kingdom of God," the foundation stone beneath all solid foundations; and all of Bible prophecy, and all of sacred Scripture, centers ultimately around J-E-S-U-S and His expanding kingdom of love.*

ADDENDUM (Christmas Day, 2019)

After this book was ostensibly already complete, and I had already shared it with a good many good people, a thought suddenly struck me while I was working on the preface[339] for volume 2 (perhaps ironically on Christmas day). I felt I should add it to the ending of *this* volume, which ends as it does with thoughts about the story of Christ's birth and its profound meaning in human history.

---

338 See Matthew 7:24–25.
339 Which later turned into chapter 1.

That story we commonly call the *Christmas*[340] story, although it originally had nothing at all to do with the much later established holiday *(holy day)* that became designated *Christmas,* or even (I might point out) with the particular date that Christmas was eventually tied to in our calendars. The holiday itself may have been of human origin, but the inspired and inspirational story of Christ's birth most certainly was *not!* It was a heaven-inspired and heaven-originated story. The profound event it heralds to all who will listen with spiritual ears, led even heavenly hosts to sing out with joy unspeakable at the arrival of our Hope, the Desire of the Ages, in the birth of a baby! And that same joy is echoed in many a "Christmas" song that has been written by some inspired songwriter in deep contemplation of the joyous reality that the priceless gift of the Christ-child brought into our darkened world. On whatever day it is *(even on Christmas)* that we gratefully contemplate this most sacred story of God's condescension to save sinners such as us, I'm convinced it will inevitably lift our souls to a higher spiritual plane. It is also my firm conviction that despite the fact that the holiday we call Christmas contains numerous elements and associations of a purely human origin,[341] Christmas *songs themselves* have truly felt a special touch from the Holy Spirit down through the ages Christmas has been celebrated. I believe this is true not because of the *holiday,* but because of the inspired scriptural *story* their creation was intended to herald.

The so-called Christmas story is a *divine* story, one that "Angels From the Realms of Glory"[342] themselves were (and I believe still *are*) heralds of. We would do well to join them in that mighty chorus celebrating that same sacred story, and in heralding that same blessed event, no matter *what* day of the year we do it on[343] (including on the day which now causes the whole world's thoughts to turn toward the ancient story!). We who have been rescued from a very great fall may proclaim with the *unfallen* angels:

---

340 Meaning the *Christ "mass,"* or rather *"communion,"* or *"Eucharist"* (giving of thanks), or celebration of the *"Lord's [last] supper,"* depending upon the terminology you use. It was a designation for the holiday *(holy* day) on which the Medieval church gathered for a special celebration of the Eucharist in honor of the birth of Jesus (we clearly know it is not the actual date of Christ's birth, of course), and on which it was customary to read the story of Christ's birth.
341 And some that are even of *pagan* origin.
342 Title of a famous Christmas carol by James Montgomery (words, 1816) and Henry Smart (tune, 1867). James Montgomery, "Angels From the Realms of Glory," *Hymns of Faith* (Wheaton, IL: Tabernacle Publishing Company, 1980), emphasis mine.
343 I personally like to sing "Christmas" carols in the summer (when I'm not sick of non-stop Christmas music)!

"Joy to the world, the Lord is come! Let earth receive her king! Let every heart prepare him [or her] room, and heaven and nature sing!"[344]

It is because of my conviction that God *Himself* directly inspired many Christmas carols, that I was deeply touched when I heard a new *Christian* version of a famous secular Christmas song a number of years ago, an alternate set of lyrics to the tune traditionally sung as **"Have Yourself a Merry Little Christmas."**[345] I watched a televised interview with the famous song's author, Hugh Martin, which had been filmed in 2002, about nine years before his death.[346] In the interview, Hugh recalled the sometimes humorous circumstances surrounding his original writing of the magical tune which he first wrote for Judy Garland to sing in the musical *Meet Me in St. Louis*.[347] For instance, the original lyrics started out:

> Have yourself a merry little Christmas
> It may be your last
> Next year we may all be living in the past.[348]

Judy Garland, of course, objected to such fatalistic lyrics (Hugh himself used the big word "lugubrious"[349] to describe his originally dismal lyrics), but she still loved the "magical little tune" and persuaded Hugh to come up with more uplifting words. But even the words Judy finally used in the movie *Meet Me in St. Louis* still left something to be desired in the *joy* department with such lines as: *"Until then, we'll have to muddle through somehow."*

According to Hugh, he altered a few more phrases later on for Frank Sinatra's Christmas album *A Jolly Christmas* (released in 1957) to include more positive (and wishful) lines like:

> Hang a shining star upon the highest bough.
> *and*
> From now on[350] our troubles will be out of sight.

---

344 "Joy to the World," by Isaac Watts (words, 1719), now sung to a tune taken from Handel's *Messiah*, as arranged by Lowell Mason (1830). Isaac Watts, "Joy to the World," *Hymns of Faith* (Wheaton, IL: Tabernacle Publishing Company, 1980), emphasis mine.
345 "Have Yourself A Merry Little Christmas" was first published in 1944 (for the production of *Meet Me In St. Louis*) by the publisher Leo Feist, Inc.
346 "Del and Friends," 2002 (video tape), produced by the Voice of Prophecy, Newbury Park, CA.
347 *Meet Me in St. Louis*, starring Judy Garland, was an MGM (Metro-Goldwyn-Mayer) musical movie, released in the US in January of 1945.
348 Words and music by Hugh Martin and Ralph Blane.
349 Meaning "exaggeratedly or affectedly mournful."
350 *As opposed to* "*Next year* all our troubles will be out of sight."

Hugh claimed Frank Sinatra had asked him if he could please "jolly up the lyrics a bit" for his *"Jolly" Christmas* album and that it was this alteration which resulted in the song version nearly everyone in the world is now familiar with. The *highest* level of joy, however, the joy of the actual *Christmas story* (the polar opposite of the song's original tone), would still have to wait about four decades before it was finally wed to the magical melody.

In that same interview Hugh described his *new* version of the same song—a specifically *Christian* version—that he had written (with some help) in his declining years. I later learned that his decision to write the new lyrics was prompted by a friend named John Fricke (who also just happened to be Judy Garland's biographer). John Fricke sent Hugh a letter containing some Christianized lyric changes he had made in order to sing "Have Yourself A Merry Little Christmas" at his church. As soon as Hugh got the letter, he immediately fell in love with the idea of creating Christian lyrics. He set out at once to write a complete new *Christian* version, incorporating John Fricke's effort into the new lyrics. The pleased publishers then added their own touch to the ostensibly finished product by suggesting changing the word "merry" to the word "blessed," and a new carol was born ("Have Yourself A Blessed Little Christmas").[351]

The effort seems to have meant a great deal to Hugh because of his newfound devotion to Jesus Christ in later life, and his deep-seated conversion to the message—the "good news"—of Christianity. While he had never been an entire unbeliever even in his younger years,[352] Hugh had found Jesus—or rather had been found *by* Jesus (whom he referred to in his autobiography as the "Hound of Heaven,"[353] an allusion, of course, to the famous poem by that name)—in a profoundly personal sense in his later life. The Hugh I witnessed in that interview had impressed me as being a devout *gentle* man with a burning love for Jesus in his heart. That burning love, and his desire to lift up the name of Jesus using his internationally famous tune, is what touched my heart. And now that new song, every time I sing it or hear it, touches my heart deeply because of

---

351 Special thanks to Fredrick Harrison (in whose home Hugh was living at the time he worked on the new lyrics) for clarifying for me the writing process which took place, and the credit due to all involved. According to Hugh's book (Hugh Martin, *Hugh Martin: The Boy Next Door* [Encinitas, CA: Trolley Press, 2010], pp. 359–360.), the idea for the new alternate lyrics first came up in 1997, and when Dave Olsen of Warner Brothers Publishing heard it, he said, "Why don't we publish the alternate lyrics directly under the traditional lyrics when we re-publish the song?"

352 Hugh once told a singer who changed out the phrase *"if the fates allow"* with *"if the Lord allows,"* "That's the way I *wrote* it!"

353 Francis Thompson, The Hound of Heaven (New York, NY: Dodd, Mead and Company, 1930).

the songwriter's longing desire to lift up the name of Jesus to the world. Though certainly not *flawless* even in his old age, Hugh Martin became a man whom I deeply respected for this desire, a man who (after reading his autobiography[354]) I felt sure I could even have become true friends with if I had ever met him before he passed away.

Remember that Jesus once told a seeking man:

"And I, if I am lifted up from the earth, will draw all peoples to Myself." (John 12:32, NKJV)

Jesus *was* lifted up from the earth on *our* cross of consequences to pay the profound penalty due for the sins of all peoples. He was treated as *we* deserve so that we might be treated as *He* deserves! No matter *how* that reality takes place, it is a thing of unutterable beauty "in my book" (and I guess that expression now applies to me both figuratively *and* literally). And now, whenever that mysterious but astounding reality is lifted up as the "good news" that it is, with the name (the reputation) of Jesus, that beautiful message (rightly understood) still draws all peoples toward *Him!*

Since Hugh Martin's deep desire for his song's new *Christian* lyrics so perfectly gels with my own deep desire for this book—that it might lift up JESUS to the world so that *He* might draw all peoples unto Himself—I have decided to end this final chapter (once again) by sharing Hugh's *new* lyrics to "Have Yourself a *Blessed*[355] Little Christmas":

> Have yourself a bless-ed little Christmas
> Christ the King is born
> Let your voices ring upon this happy morn

> Have yourself a bless-ed little Christmas
> Serenade the earth
> Tell the world we celebrate the Savior's birth

> Let us gather to sing to Him
> And to bring to Him our praise
> Son of God and a Friend of all
> To the end of all our days

> Let us all proclaim the joyous tidings
> Voices raised on high

---

354 Hugh Martin, *Hugh Martin: The Boy Next Door* (Encinitas, CA: Trolley Press, 2010).
355 Pronounced with two syllables as *"bless-ed."*

Send this carol soaring up into the sky
This very merry bless-ed Christmas lullaby

Let us gather to sing to Him
And to bring to Him our praise
Son of God and a Friend of all
To the end of all our days

Sing hosannas, hymns, and hallelujahs
As to Him we bow
Make the music mighty as the heav'ns allow
And have yourself a bless-ed little Christmas now.[356]

---

356 "Have Yourself a Blessed Little Christmas," by Hugh Martin, Ralph Blane, and John Fricke.

I don't know who you are,

what wrong you might have done,

or what tangles might surround your life,

but I do know Jesus

is able to bring healing and hope,

in every situation,[357]

and that He is worthy of your worship,

even if your experience on earth now seems bleak.

If you have never asked Jesus into your heart before,

I wonder:

Won't you do it right now,

before you close the covers of this book?

It is one decision in life

you will not regret.

---

[357] *"Cast all your anxiety on him, because he cares for you" (1 Peter 5:7).*

Afterword

A few times in this book I have resorted to sharing words to songs or titles that I recommend you look up, in my feeble efforts to try and express certain precious thoughts about God. Although these thoughts are bound up inside a grateful heart, I sometimes find it difficult to express them nonetheless, since they occasionally go far beyond mere words. I suppose this inadequacy of words is one of the reasons God may have also given us the emotionally packed vibrations of music: in order to help us express, and to release, certain almost inexpressible godly elements (including beautiful thoughts about Him) that we occasionally find bound up somewhere deep inside the cores of our shared human nature. These are elements which we were *designed* to discover there and then to rapturously revel in whenever we *did* find them (what unusual godlike animals we humans *can* be!). Music somehow has that inexplicable quality which gives it an ability (in people, at least) to bypass all of our merely *logical* circuits, and our merely *physical survival instinct* circuits, in the supercomputers we call our brains. And using only shifts in frequencies and rhythms of sound waves (mere vibrations of energy), it communicates mysteriously powerful messages of otherworldly rapture to our spiritually hungry souls. It accomplishes this with complex cognitions, the likes of which no human-made computer has ever even *begun* to reproduce, since we ourselves cannot even fully understand them, much less reproduce them in an artificial brain.

Through music, we, as sentient, living, loving, hating, laughing, crying, hurting, healing, higher beings are able to be transported, upon occasion, in our nebulous spirits to fantastical realms of thought and feeling that are just a little bit closer, I think, to the spiritual realm which the mysterious Godhead cohabits. Have any of your brain cells blown just yet as you try to compute logically what I'm attempting to describe? As much as I myself hate to admit it, the sometimes ethereal phenomenon of music is not exactly *logical*, at least on *our* limited plane of reasoning.

The main reason I have shared songs is to try and convey certain feelings that I felt sure at least *some* readers must have also associated with one song or another at one time or another. I felt by doing so I might have a better chance of truly conveying some priceless shared spiritual experiences I was hoping to communicate through mere words. Music can almost magically evoke feelings in most people[358] (a thing unknown to human-made machines) whereas words alone are able only to *describe* those feelings. So the actual evocation of feelings must be imagined into existence by every reader of words, somehow (if not actually prompted by God's unseen Spirit, who may truly attend our reading if we are in tune with Him). The mental shifts and rhythms provided by the profound thought-nibbles of some types of poetry—partaking, as poetry may, of the mesmeric nature of music—may help a great deal toward the reattaching of feelings to dead words on a page. But simply attach a well-worded work of poetry to the vibrations of an emotionally associated tune, and all of a sudden the words, for some people at least, will rise up with their attached emotions, like Lazarus miraculously coming out of his tomb,[359] and will take on new lives all their own!

The mere words of a national anthem, for example, read by just the right patriotic person, coming from just the right region of this earth, might suddenly evoke a world of *patriotic* emotion in that one person, as well as in people with a similar devotion to that particular homeland. That particular shared emotion would be mostly *unknown* to all outsiders, as well as to uninitiated readers even from the same land, who might not share the same level of patriotic feeling. It is the knowing of associations between any particular song, and the experientially-attached emotions that it evokes, which gives the words to a tune their special power. But I think this spiritual power of music can be even greater, by far, for those who are spiritually attuned, in the spirit realm of *God's* Spirit! As much more profound as the love of God for us is, over and above the love a patriot might feel for his or her merely human homeland (beset, as all human things presently are, by human fallibility), so the words belonging to a song about God's love for us (which song has formed some deep emotional connection in the heart of a sinner saved by grace) may evoke a spiritual experience that is far and away above that prompted by any merely *human* form of love.

And my wish to end on a note about this love of God that so transcends mere human loves, is the reason I have decided to leave you, at the end of this book about Jesus, with the words to one more song. I hope it

---

[358] Both good *and* bad feelings, just as music can be put to both good *and* bad uses.
[359] See John 11:1–45.

will touch similar emotional chords in your own heart as it has touched in mine.

Even though a great deal academic has been dealt with in this book about Jesus, and about one of the great misunderstood Messianic prophecies which predicted the coming of Jesus,[360] I hope you have also gathered that my heartfelt love for Jesus is about much, *much* more than merely academic notions or ideas about an academically-known being! It is about profound, inexpressible, transforming encounters I've had directly with Jesus *Himself!* Encounters I have just as surely had with the *real* Jesus, as if I had been allowed to be transported back in time[361] to when Jesus physically walked this earth 2,000 years ago, and to have been allowed the sheer pleasure and privilege of being ushered into His physical *human* presence. I've just as surely had those precious encounters with the *real* Jesus, as if I had been able to go, *physically*, and bury my unworthy face in His welcoming breast,[362] sobbing, like Peter once did,[363] in bitter remorse over every single failure of my life, pleading with Him to make me permanently better on the inside, and telling him—though He already knows—about all of my deepest needs, my deepest hurts, my deepest regrets, my deepest wounds, my deepest fears, my deepest hopes and longings. Telling Him even things that I might never, *never* trust to another human soul, who would not understand as *He* understands, with *perfect* sight, and who would not view me as *He* views me, looking at me, as He does, through the rose-colored glasses[364] of His perfect *love.*

That perfect love sees in me, *already*, the promise of His fully fulfilled ransom, viewing only my value *separate* from my sin, which He has by His mysterious sacrifice somehow[365] separated from the still-cherished kernel of me. All so that *I* might someday live without harm, fear, or shame in the sin-consuming presence, and might even one day become *like* Him, when I see Him face to face!

---

[360] I refer you back to chapter 11 (and to the several chapters leading up to it, of course, if you have not read them).

[361] As I've often daydreamed about and have often spoken to God about wishing I could do.

[362] Chest.

[363] See Matthew 26:75.

[364] The scarlet-colored glasses that He paid an unknowable, profound price for at Calvary because He loved me *personally*.

[365] I am convinced there will *always* remain some elements of Christ's atonement which go beyond our human ability to comprehend. Therefore, we ought to always approach the subject with intellectual humility and reverent caution, making sure we aren't denying things revelations affirm about it just because we can't wrap our human notions around them.

For now we see in a mirror [glass], dimly, **but then we will see face to face.** *Now I know only in part; then I will know fully, even as I have been fully known.* (1 Cor. 13:12)

Beloved, we are God's children now; what we will be has not yet been revealed. What we do know is this: when he is revealed, **we will be like him, for we will see him as he is.** (1 John 3:2)

And Jesus *Himself* has just as surely responded to me as if He had *physically* embraced me warmly, uncondemning, assuring, comfortingly, and as if He, in person *physically,* had answered my barrage of blubbering blurtings by saying to me, as He once said to His distressed disciples of old: "**Peace be with you**" (Luke 24:36). And perhaps, if I had been physically present with Him, Jesus would have even taken my clutching fingers, like Thomas of old, and would have thrust them into the scars on His body.[366] He would not have done this for me to know that He is physically real and alive (as was the purpose in Thomas's case after His resurrection[367]), but to remind me, rather, of His precious cross that purchased my pardon on Calvary's tree (and that also enabled the never-ending power of His personal presence to abide with me). This blood-stained tree was the source of the peace He has provided, "on earth as it is in heaven" (Matt. 6:10).

Oh! Words will *always* fail me whenever I try to do justice to this subject. However, words of deep meaning attached to music of great beauty (partly derived from its emotional association with the meaning) do help me along in my effort. So this is why I decided that, to help express why I so love Jesus, I would leave you with the simple, but profound, words of a well-known and long-beloved Christian hymn, a song.

On the evening I began writing this afterword, I had asked my oldest daughter to put some music she had ripped from CDs onto a music device, so that I might listen while riding an exercise bike. It just so happened that the song I'm sharing now ended up being the first song in the list on my device: the first that played as I turned it on. As the old familiar words and melody of this very old Christian classic began playing in my ears, I suddenly realized I was at that moment hungry and thirsty for the exact message the song was expressing, as well as for the emotional realizations the words suddenly reawakened within my heart at that moment. I felt the sudden need to listen to the same song several times, and to sing along with it

---

366 See John 20:27.
367 I have had abundant assurance on that account, as I hope to be able to write about in the future.

out loud. I realized, then and there, with this book in the back of my mind, that the words to that song had captured better than any words I might write, the real reasons why I learned to love Jesus. Chiefly among those reasons is the fact that I have found true solace in my life *only* at the foot of Christ's cross, and nowhere else in all of my life experiences, regardless of how many times I have foolishly tried! It was there, at that one spot, at the foot of the cross,[368] that I first found hope, that I first saw any real light. It was there, in the warmth of His forgiving and healing embrace, purchased at such a dreadful price that I cannot fully, or even more than slightly, comprehend it, that I first learned how very deeply He loved me in spite of my everything bad! When I realized how well this song had put my own story into emotion-packed words, as well as the stories of unnumbered others I am certain, that's when I knew that I needed to leave you with *these* words.

If you don't know the song, I hope you might learn it (with the melody attached) someday. But more importantly I hope that, if you haven't already, you will learn the meaning of the *experience* with Jesus that these words are trying so hard to express, so that one day such words may nourish your *own* spirit in the same magical way they do mine, through the invisible touch of the Holy Spirit, through whom Jesus *Himself* still abides with and speaks to us![369]

The words go like this:

Alas! and did my Savior bleed?
And did my Sov'reign die?
Would He devote that sacred head
For [such a worm][370] as I?
At the cross, at the cross where I first saw the light,
And the burden of my heart rolled away, [it rolled away!]
It was there by faith I received my sight,
And now I am happy[371] all the day!

---

368 As 1 Corinthians 1:23 points out, a stumbling block to the self-righteous ("the Jews"), and foolishness to the secular mind, and to the philosophically worldly wise ("the Greeks"), but to me, I can testify with 1 Corinthians 1:18 that it has been the wonderful "power of God" to awaken my heart to the love of God, as well as to longings for His true goodness.
369 See Matthew 28:20.
370 Many modern versions change this to "sinners such as I," or "someone such as I," but "worm" was Isaac Watts' original word.
371 The refrain is a later addition to the original words by Isaac Watts, and it uses the word "happy" where I think the word "joyful" would have been more appropriate, since I don't believe that accepting Jesus means we are guaranteed to be "happy" all of the time. We can, however, always have a deep, abiding joy regarding our confidence in Jesus, even when happiness—which is dependent upon happenstance—may elude us.

Was it for crimes that I have done
He groaned upon the tree?
Amazing pity! grace unknown!
And love beyond degree!
At the cross, at the cross where I first saw the light,
And the burden of my heart rolled away,
It was there by faith I received my sight,
And now I am happy all the day!

But drops of grief can ne'er repay
The debt of love I owe:
Here, Lord, I give myself away,
'Tis all that I can do!
At the cross, at the cross where I first saw the light,
And the burden of my heart rolled away,
It was there by faith I received my sight,
And now I am happy all the day![372]

---

[372] Stanzas to "At the Cross" were written by Isaac Watts (1674–1748), and the refrain, as well as the presently used tune, were written by Ralph E. Hudson (1843–1901). Isaac Watts, "At the Cross," *Hymns of Faith* (Wheaton, IL: Tabernacle Publishing Company, 1980).

Endnote A

In the year prior to my beginning a nebulous writing on this book, I had one day a most indelible spiritual experience while I was praying that is really beyond my ability to fully describe. That profound personal encounter with God, which surprisingly came to me during a time when I was still struggling with a significant clinical depression accompanied by anxiety attacks, made me suddenly see how great a debt of gratitude I actually owed to God for all the very precious things He had done for me. These things included salvation from sin, to be sure, but also much in addition that He was seeming to bring before my spiritual gaze like a mighty parade. I sensed a most holy and royal presence in the humble place I was praying. In my own realization of my unquestionable human unworthiness, this procession of blessings parading before my spiritual eyesight created a sudden (and lasting) overwhelming need in my spirit to say thank you to God (see Luke 17:12–18) in some tangible way. A song went through my mind (as you will see is usual with me). It was the Andrae Crouch song called "My Tribute" (1972). My unusual desire to sing that particular song publicly, in order to express my profound gratitude in front of other people, lasted for more than half of a year, until I finally did sing it for a church service, during which I felt the Spirit of God take possession of my expression to a degree I don't usually experience while singing.

The beginning of writing down my deep-seated gratitude (along with scriptural insights God had given to me in the past) in the form of a book only a few months after that performance, seems to me now, in hindsight, to have been part of the Holy Spirit's answer to the question which that song begins with. It was also a question that my spirit was sincerely asking God while I was singing it. In the lyrics of the song I was asking God how I could ever possibly thank Him for all the good He had done for me. At least part of the answer to that question seems now to have been to me: You can say thanks by writing it down.

Bibliography

Aitken, Jonathan. *John Newton: From Disgrace to Amazing Grace.* Wheaton, IL: Crossway, 2007.

Attridge, Harold W. et al. Eds. *The HarperCollins Study Bible: New Revised Standard Version, with the Apocryphal/Deuterocanonical Books.* San Francisco, CA: HarperSanFrancisco, 2006.

Eusebius, Bishop of Caesarea and Christian Frederic Crusé. *The Ecclesiastical History of Eusebius Pamphilus: Bishop of Caesarea, in Palestine.* Translated by C. F. Cruse. Watchmaker Publishing, 2011.

Dando-Collins, Steven. *Cyrus the Great: Conqueror, Liberator, Anointed One.* Nashville, TN: Turner Publishing Company, 2020.

"Del and Friends." 2002 (video tape). Produced by the Voice of Prophecy. Newbury Park, CA.

Finley, Mark. *Solid Ground.* Hagerstown, MD: Review and Herald, 2003.

Goss, Lari. "Cornerstone." Bridge Building Music: Heartwarming Music, 1977.

"Have Yourself A Merry Little Christmas" was first published in 1944 (for the production of *Meet Me In St. Louis*) by the publisher Leo Feist, Inc.

Jefferson, Thomas. "The Declaration of Independence."

Johnson, Phil. "The Day He Wore My Crown." *Favorites Number 9: A Collection of Gospel Songs.* Brentwood, TN: Singspiration Music, 1981.

Lewis, C.S. *Mere Christianity.* Revised and Enlarged ed. New York, NY: Macmillan, 1952.

Livy. *Rome's Mediterranean Empire: Books 41–45 and the Periochae.* Translated with an introduction and notes by Jane D. Chaplin. Oxford, England: Oxford University Press, 2007.

Martin, Hugh. *Hugh Martin: The Boy Next Door.* Encinitas, CA: Trolley Press, 2010.

Maxwell, C. Mervyn. *God Cares: The Message of Daniel for You and Your Family.* Vol. 1. Boise, ID: Pacific Press Publishing Association, 1981.

Meet Me in St. Louis, starring Judy Garland, was an MGM (Metro-Goldwyn-Mayer) musical movie, released in the US in January of 1945.

Montgomery, James. "Angels From the Realms of Glory." *Hymns of Faith.* Wheaton, IL: Tabernacle Publishing Company, 1980.

Myers, Philip Van Ness. L.H.D., *Rome: Its Rise and Fall.* Boston, MA: Ginn & Co., 1900.

Newton, Isaac. *Sir Isaac Newton's Daniel and the Apocalypse.* Edited by Sir William Whitla. London: John Murray, 1922.

Prokopios. *The Secret History with Related Texts.* Edited and translated by Anthony Kaldellis. Indianapolis, IN: Hackett Publishing Company, Inc., 2010.

———. *The Wars of Justinian.* Translated by H. B. Dewing. Revised and modernized by Anthony Kaldellis. Indianapolis, IN: Hackett Publishing Company, Inc., 2014.

"The Kingdom Strikes Back: Ten Epochs of Redemptive History." *Perspectives on the World Christian Movement: A Reader, Revised Edition.* Edited by Ralph D. Winter and Steven C. Hawthorne. Pasadena, CA: William Carey Library, 1981, 1992.

The New Complete Works of Josephus. Revised and expanded ed. Translation and dissertations by William Whiston. Grand Rapids, MI: Kregel Publications, 1999.

Toplady, Augustus M. "Rock of Ages." *Hymns of Faith.* Wheaton, IL: Tabernacle Publishing Company, 1980.

Rollin, Charles. *The Ancient History of the Egyptians, Carthaginians, Assyrians, Babylonians, Medes and Persians, Macedonians and Grecians.* Vol. 3. Philadelphia, PA: Lippincott, Grambo & Co., 1855.

Rollin, Charles. *The Ancient History of the Egyptians, Carthaginians, Assyrians, Babylonians, Medes and Persians, Macedonians and Grecians.* Vol. 4. Philadelphia, PA: Lippincott, Grambo & Co., 1855.

Schama, Simon. *Citizens: A Chronicle of the French Revolution.* New York, NY: Alfred A. Knopf, 1989.

Schulz, Charles. *A Charlie Brown Christmas.* 1965 (cartoon movie). PEANUTS (United Feature Syndicate).

"SIR ISAAC NEWTON CALLED IT "THE FOUNDATION STONE OF THE CHRISTIAN RELIGION." Pioneer Memorial Church. December 22, 2009.

Stockton, John H. "Only Trust Him." *Hymns of Faith.* Wheaton, IL: Tabernacle Publishing Company, 1980.

Watts, Isaac. "At the Cross." *Hymns of Faith.* Wheaton, IL: Tabernacle Publishing Company, 1980.

———. "Joy to the World." *Hymns of Faith*. Wheaton, IL: Tabernacle Publishing Company, 1980.

Webster's Deluxe Dictionary. 10th Collegiate ed. Pleasantville, NY: Reader's Digest, 1998.

White, E.G. *The Great Controversy*. Mountain View, CA: Pacific Press Publishing Association, 1911.

———. *Life Sketches*. Mountain View, CA: Pacific Press Publishing Association, 1915.

———. *Thoughts From the Mount of Blessing*. Mountain View, CA: Pacific Press Publishing Association, 1896.

TEACH Services, Inc.
P U B L I S H I N G

We invite you to view the complete
selection of titles we publish at:
www.TEACHServices.com

We encourage you to write us
with your thoughts about this,
or any other book we publish at:
info@TEACHServices.com

TEACH Services' titles may be purchased in
bulk quantities for educational, fund-raising,
business, or promotional use.
bulksales@TEACHServices.com

Finally, if you are interested in seeing
your own book in print, please contact us at:
publishing@TEACHServices.com
We are happy to review your manuscript at no charge.

www.ingramcontent.com/pod-product-compliance
Lightning Source LLC
Chambersburg PA
CBHW070551160426
43199CB00014B/2456